LUGBARA RELIGION

ABOUT THE AUTHOR

John Middleton is professor of anthropology and director of the African Studies Program at Yale University. He has taught at Northwestern and New York universities in the United States, and at University College and the School of Oriental and African Studies in the University of London. At the latter, he was professor of African ethnography. His research has spanned the African continent, inluding Kenya, Zanzibar, Ghana, and Uganda, where he worked with the Lugbara. In addition to *Lugbara Religion,* John Middleton has written numerous books and articles on such diverse topics as African political systems, social change, modes of thought, ritual and symbolism, and dance. Professor Middleton has served as director of the International African Institute and is a life member of its council.

Ivan Karp is curator of African ethnology at the National Museum of Natural History, Smithsonian Institution. He has done extensive field research in Africa, and writes on African systems of thought, social theory, and social organization and change. He is editor of Indiana University Press's "African Systems of Thought Series" and is coeditor of the Smithsonian Institution Press's "Smithsonian Series in Ethnographic Inquiry." Dr. Karp is the author of *Fields of Change among the Iteso of Kenya* (Routledge and Kegan Paul, 1978) and the editor of *Explorations in African Systems of Thought* by the Smithsonian Institution Press, 1987.

A woman pours millet beer for a senior guest at a sacrifice in her
husband's homestead. He is the younger brother of an elder, so
that she is the wife of one of the more important hosts.

LUGBARA RELIGION

RITUAL AND AUTHORITY AMONG
AN EAST AFRICAN PEOPLE

JOHN MIDDLETON

FOREWORD BY IVAN KARP

SMITHSONIAN INSTITUTION PRESS
WASHINGTON, D.C.   LONDON

Originally published 1960
Reprint 1987

*This volume is a photographic reprint of the original
edition, which was published in 1960 by the Oxford
University Press for the International African Institute
and reprinted by them in 1964, 1969, and 1971. The
original edition, except for its front matter, has been
reprinted in entirety, and the original pagination has
been kept. A foreword and a bibliography have been
added.*

Library of Congress Cataloging-in-Publication Data

Middleton, John, 1921–
 Lugbara religion.
 Reprint. With new foreword and bibliography.
 Bibliography: p.
 Includes index.
  1. Lugbara (African people)—Religion.   2. Uganda—
Religion.   I. Title.
BL2480.L76M52   1987   306'.6'089963   86–21889
ISBN 0–87474–667–1 (pbk.)

CONTENTS

FOREWORD

This book does not seek to present Lugbara religion as a system of theology, but to make a sociological analysis of the place of ritual and belief in Lugbara social life" is the modest beginning (see Preface) of this pioneering study of ritual and political practices in an African society.

John Middleton's *Lugbara Religion* is rightly acknowledged as a classic in the interpretation of the role of belief and ritual in social and political conduct. Among its many strengths are the author's innovative use of case studies and of Lugbara explanations of their own actions.

In major ways this book goes against the grain of our expectations. Religion should be, we tend to think, more a matter of systematically formulated beliefs about ultimate concerns—theology—than about political practice. Yet *Lugbara Religion* refuses to accept that religious practices can be understood solely as an enactment of belief. The analytic stance of *Lugbara Religion* is thoroughly agnostic. It refuses to treat cosmology as either the primary content of action or its dominating cause. As a result, a significant achievement of Middleton's analysis is that it implicitly challenges our usually unexamined definition of religion as a dogma associated with an institution, such as a church defined in the Durkheimian sense of a specific group with a ritual purpose.

In what must surely be one of the most contentious assertions in social anthropology, the author begins chapter 2 by stating that the "Lugbara have no set of interconsistent beliefs as to the nature of man and the world" (p. 25).

As a graduate student first reading this work twenty years ago, I penciled in the margin, "Really!" My doubt had been raised by more conventional works that sought to describe the beliefs of non-Western peoples as systematic and coherent with respect to their actions.

Yet I had been trained in the social anthropological analysis of religion. I knew that belief and ritual are implicated in the social and political lives of many peoples in a manner that contradicts the

contemporary Western experience of religion as being set apart. I
was prepared from previous reading to accept that religion both
affected and was affected by political organization. What I found
shocking to my orthodoxy was the methodological assertion that
religion could not be set apart from and understood *except* in the
context of social and political life. I was unprepared to accept an
account of another people that refused to draw a radical separation
between political action and religious system. I have since moved
closer to Middleton's position, as has the form of social and cultural
anthropology coming to call itself "practice theory" (Ortner 1984).

By challenging conventional definitions John Middleton in *Lugbara
Religion* does more than describe the political implications of religious
belief. He alters our image of both religion and politics. This book
is neither about organizational politics nor religious systems. What
is revealed in this study is a politics of the self in which the actors
struggle to influence their fate as much as they struggle to control
people and resources.

Fashions in disciplines move quickly. Since my graduate-school
days, social anthropology has become both more skeptical about the
beliefs of other cultures and less so. At the same time that studies
of cosmology have become increasingly popular, we have begun to
realize that describing beliefs as "interconsistent" may tell us more
about the assumptions we bring to interpretations about non-Western
formations and about personhood than it does about the formations
themselves.

In an important article Ernest Gellner shows how the assumption
of coherence, termed the "principle of contextual charity," leads to
fitting items of belief to contexts selected to demonstrate the
assumptions of the observer (1973). He rightly points out that we
often assume coherence in other cultures where we refuse to find it
among ourselves. A literary scholar once described anthropology to
me as the discipline that defines other cultures in holistic terms and
describes the search for wholes among ourselves as Utopian thinking.
Lugbara Religion avoids those errors of translation. It shows the
Lugbara through the fullness of their contradictory assertions, the
conflicts they both create and try to contain, and the difficulties
they strive to manage.

I do not wish to leave the impression that Middleton's splendid
study treats the Lugbara as disorderly and irrational. He amends
his assertion about the absence of ideological order in Lugbara belief

when he states, "Their beliefs are significant in given situations and their consistency lies in the way in which they are used in ritual action" (p. 25). Hence Middleton seeks to discover an order to Lugbara religion that lies not so much in the content of belief as in the contexts in which beliefs are invoked and the uses to which the Lugbara put their beliefs. The analysis seeks to exhibit the order of Lugbara religion by describing three spheres of Lugbara life: social and political practices, rituals, and the Lugbara experiences that are embodied in the extraordinary texts through which the Lugbara themselves describe and explain their actions and rituals.

This study examines Lugbara religion in the context of the multiple interests of the Lugbara as they use religion to lead their lives and the conditions under which they produce their actions. Described this way *Lugbara Religion* might seem to take the form of transactional analysis in anthropology.

It would be naive to relegate *Lugbara Religion* to the category of transactional analysis. Middleton does show that interests affect the way that Lugbara invoke their beliefs, but the Lugbara are not portrayed as cynical or thoughtless entrepreneurs in Middleton's account of them. They are people who combine striving for power with the desperation of the afflicted.

If the Lugbara are not utilitarian entrepreneurs, neither are they the metaphysicians described in the French tradition of African ethnography. Their religion is overwhelmingly pragmatic. The appeals they address to ancestors, their invocations of ghosts, and the accusations of witchcraft so meticulously described in this book are made by people attempting to take some small measure of control over their lives. The Lugbara attempt to understand their fate when that fate seems to surpass understanding. The central theme of Lugbara religious practice is the attempt made by Lugbara to control the evil they see in the world around them. This is surely one of the major conclusions of the splendid final chapter of the book, which explores the Lugbara idiom of evil that is displayed in what Middleton terms "inversion."

The same Lugbara who accuse their ritual elders of witchcraft also appeal to them to interecede with the ancestors to alleviate illness and suffering. One possible description of the Lugbara attitude toward their religion is that it combines skepticism in some contexts with a profound underlying attitude of faith. Malinowski early on described religions in this manner (1962). Yet I think this formulation misses the mark. Middleton certainly portrays the Lugbara as inconsistent, but his analysis of their assertions and actions is more subtle than a picture of mixed faith and skepticism provides. The Lugbara are believers, but at the same time they are also deeply uncertain about their own interpretations and the future course of their lives.

Lugbara Religion portrays people whose actions are ordered by conflicting goals that they combine with strenuous attempts to influence the forces they perceive as affecting their lives. Hence they move in rapid succession from political accusation to healing rite to supplication at the cult of the ancestors.

Portraying the Lugbara in terms of the perspectives and interests of their lives is achieved through the case studies and texts for which this book is celebrated. Middleton's great achievement is that he honestly examines how the multiple and conflicting interests of the Lugbara are related to the inconsistency with which they articulate their beliefs. At the same time, he shows that the kaleidoscopic image of Lugbara ideology can be explained by demonstrating that beliefs are related to external conditions under which they are invoked. During the time that Middleton lived among the Lugbara, population growth and the related shortage of land often brought lineage members into conflict with each other. These are two of the conditions with which the Lugbara are shown in this book to struggle. Their social environment helps to account for how and when they pursue their accusations and interpretations. The Lugbara seek both power over others and autonomy for themselves. Yet when they do so they seem continually to hesitate, always to be afflicted with uncertainty about the validity and outcome of their actions. Contrast Middleton's image of the Lugbara with the certainty of Evans-Pritchard's account of the neighboring Nuer, who were described as having no difficulty "moving from representation to representation" (1956). The Lugbara are pictured in a manner that brings them closer to Meyer Fortes's portrait of the Tallensi, among whom forms of control seem very tenuous indeed. Like the Tallensi, the Lugbara seek to "prehend" and manage innately uncontrollable and unknowable occult forces, which themselves manage to overcome the political interests that seem only on the surface to govern any given moment of Lugbara life. Both the Tallensi and the Lugbara more often choose to seek guides for action in an uncertain world than to maximize advantage and control (Fortes 1966, 1985). Fortes's

writings about the Tallensi and Middleton's *Lugbara Religion* together pose challenges to the relativist assumptions of symbolic
anthropology and the utilitarian assumptions of transactional analysis. Neither the assertion of cultural uniqueness nor the presumption
that all action conforms to the "laws" of the marketplace can explain
the balance between universal problems and contingent solutions
examined in these two studies.

Lugbara Religion also challenges our sense of how a "religion"
might be described in another culture. As I suggested, the Lugbara
case leads to an understanding of religion that moves away from the
account of a systematic theology articulated in an institutional
setting. It forces us to examine religion as a set of beliefs and
practices that people invoke to define evil, alleviate suffering, and
contain an uncontrollable world. I have not meant to suggest that
Lugbara Religion does not describe Lugbara discourse about the
world. That task is left until the last chapter, which provides a
masterful account of how "inversion" and spatial distance are devices
used to define identity and deviance, a Lugbara ideology of self and
other. Even though the description of ideology and belief is left to
the conclusion, this book is one of the few works by an anthropologist
that is truly concerned with religion in its central sense of raising
questions about how being in the world relates to moral concerns.

For the Lugbara, discourse about morality engages questions of
power and discipline. Witches are defined as lacking discipline over
their emotions and desires and at the same time failing to control
their quest for power. *Lugbara Religion* shows the Lugbara to be
almost obsessed with both power and discipline. Their concerns are
displayed through the superb texts of interviews with them found
throughout the book. More than almost any other Western account
of an African religious system, this one refuses to obliterate the
African voices on which it is based. Not only do the Lugbara accuse,
but they also doubt, worry, and vacillate. While I would not call
them philosophers in the sense of being engaged in second-order
reflections on thought, the texts show that the interpretations the
Lugbara make are vital to the conduct of their lives. At the same
time, Middleton demonstrates how conflicting and disparate their
interpretations may be, and it is that which may be the enduring
contribution of *Lugbara Religion*. There is plenty of sociological
analysis here and a fine account of idioms of interpretation. More
important, however, is the book's sense of the complex contours of

life in an African society. *Lugbara Religion* is a work based on careful and sensitive fieldwork. If we read it carefully we can hear the echo of Lugbara voices.

Ivan Karp

REFERENCES CITED

Evans-Pritchard, E. E.
  1956   *Nuer Religion*. Oxford: Clarendon Press.

Fortes, Meyer
  1966   "Religious Premises and Logical Techniques in Divinatory Ritual."
        Philosophical Transactions of the Royal Society of London, no. 251.

  1985 (1959)
        Oedipus and Job in West African Religions.
        Cambridge: Cambridge University Press.

Gellner, Ernest
  1973   "Concepts and Society." In *Cause and Meaning in the Social Sciences*.
        London: Routledge and Kegan Paul.

Malinowski, Bronislaw
  1962   "The Foundations of Faith and Morals." In *Sex, Myth and Culture*. New
        York: Harcourt, Brace and World.

Ortner, Sherry
  1984   "Theory in Anthropology since the Sixties." *Comparative Studies in*
        Society and History 26: 126–66.

PREFACE

THIS book does not seek to present Lugbara religion as a system of theology, but to make a sociological analysis of the place of ritual and belief in Lugbara social life. For reasons which will become apparent, most attention is therefore devoted to the rites and beliefs associated with the cult of the dead. But, since this cult cannot be understood in complete isolation, I have included accounts of some other rites and beliefs.

The cult of the dead is intimately connected with the maintenance of lineage authority. The exercise and acknowledgement of this authority are bound up with the cycle of lineage development. Senior men attempt to sustain their authority against their juniors' claims to independence, and the consequent conflict is conceived largely in mystical and ritual terms. There are few accounts of African religions that are set in the context of the competition for power within the lineage and household. I have found that it is this context that makes intelligible what is at first sight contradictory ritual behaviour among Lugbara. In Chapter IV, which is the central chapter of the book, I show how the men of a single lineage group manipulate the cult of the dead as a means to the acquisition and retention of authority.

Lugbara hold certain particular beliefs, and they have a certain kind of social organization. Their behaviour is intelligible only in terms of these beliefs and this organization. The first three chapters, therefore, give an account of those aspects of Lugbara society and culture which are relevant to the theme of Chapter IV. In Lugbara thought all phenomena that can be called religious are explicitly associated with God, and in Chapter V I discuss the ways in which divine power is thought to affect men.

I have not considered many matters which might have been discussed in an account of Lugbara religion. In particular I should have liked to consider in detail the distinction made so clearly by Lugbara between things that are 'good' and things that are 'bad', a dichotomy which runs through almost all their thinking. Nor have I compared Lugbara religion with other African religions. I hope to do both of these things elsewhere.

Certain sections of this book are based upon previously published articles. Of these the most relevant are 'Some Social Aspects of Lugbara Myth', in *Africa*, xxiv, 3, July 1954; 'The Concept of "Bewitching" in Lugbara', *Africa*, xxv, 3, July 1955. 'Myth, History and Mourning Taboos in Lugbara', in *Uganda Journal*, 19, 2, September 1955. I am grateful to the editors of these journals for permission to reproduce parts of these papers, and Figures 1 and 9.

ILLUSTRATIONS

PLATES

A woman pours millet beer for a senior guest at a sacrifice in her husband's homestead. He is the younger brother of an elder, so that she is the wife of one of the more important hosts

Frontispiece

FIGURES

ACKNOWLEDGEMENTS

My fieldwork, from December 1949 until April 1952, was financed by the Worshipful Company of Goldsmiths and the Colonial Social Science Council, London. I wish to acknowledge my gratitude to these bodies for their generosity, and to certain of their officers, in particular Mr. G. R. Hughes and Mr. A. P. Jenkins of the Goldsmiths' Company and Mrs. E. M. Chilver of the Colonial Office, for much personal kindness. Much of the material in this book was originally presented as a report to the Colonial Social Science Research Council, and I am grateful for permission to reproduce it here. The bulk of the material was written up at the University of Oxford with financial assistance from the Wenner-Gren Foundation for Anthropological Research, New York. I was able to spend a further three months in Lugbara during 1953 with the help of the Oxford University Exploration Society.

I cannot thank all the people in Uganda who gave me help and hospitality, but should like to mention Dr. A. I. Richards, then director of the East African Institute for Social Research; Messrs. P. R. Gibson, J. D. Gotch, and E. A. L. Watts, District Commissioners, West Nile, during my stay; Drs. G. S. Nelson and S. V. Rush, and Messrs. C. P. S. Allen, E. C. Lanning, A. S. MacCombe, I. R. Menzies and A. C. Watson, of the Government of Uganda; Rev. A. S. Maclure and Mr. D. Gilman of the Africa Inland Mission and Father J. P. Crazzolara of the Verona Fathers; Dr. A. W. Southall of Makerere College; and Dr. K. P. Wachsmann of the Uganda Museum. Among the Lugbara who gave me help and friendship I am especially grateful to Sultans Obitre Onyolo, Augusto Agali and Maskini Adua, to Wakils Henry Diko, Khalfan Simandre and Daudi Jurua and to Hon. Gaspare Oda. I should like also to mention my assistants Oraa Oganya, Oguda Eka, and Yukua Efio.

In England Dr. J. H. M. Beattie, Dr. M. M. Douglas, Professor E. E. Evans-Pritchard, Professor D. Forde, Mr. W. R. G. Horton, Dr. V. W. Turner and Professor E. H. Winter have read all or part of the MS. and have given much valued help and criticism. I am grateful to Professor A. N. Tucker, who taught me the rudiments of Lugbara grammar and phonology. I wish also to thank Miss Barbara Pym for seeing the book through the press and for helping me in its final revision.

University College, London
  October 1959

NOTE ON ORTHOGRAPHY

The orthography used in this book is based upon that suggested by
Professor A. N. Tucker in his *The Eastern Sudanic Languages*, Oxford,
1940. I have, after discussion with him, simplified his system of representing vowels, so that his i becomes i

ɪ	i
u	ʋ
ʊ	u

In conjunction with a, i or ʋ the vowels e and o become tense; in
conjunction with i or u they become lax. I have therefore dispensed
with his distinction between e and ɛ and between o and ɔ.

Lugbara makes use of both explosive b and d and implosive 'b and 'd.

Lugbara has semantic tone differences. I have not marked tones in
this book.

I

LUGBARA SOCIETY: STRUCTURE AND AUTHORITY

1. THE PEOPLE AND THEIR COUNTRY

THE Lugbara are a Sudanic-speaking people and are classed by Tucker as members of the Moru-Madi sub-group of the Eastern Sudanic group. Linguistically they are closely related to the Keliko and Logo to the west and to the Madi to the east. To the north are the Nilo-Hamitic-speaking Kakwa and Kuku, who claim common origin with the Lugbara and who are in many ways culturally very alike. To the south are the Nilotic Alur and the Sudanic Ndu (Okebu) and 'Bale (Lendu).[1] The Lugbara recognize clan ties, expressed particularly in inter-marriage, with the Kakwa, Madi and Keliko; they regard the Alur, Ndu and Lendu as being culturally more distant and hostile, although many Ndu live among them as smiths. A sketch map showing the distribution of these peoples is given on page 2 (Figure 1).

The Lugbara live in the present day West Nile District of Uganda and in the Territoire de Mahagi of the Belgian Congo. In 1948 there were about 183,000 Lugbara in Uganda, of whom 160,800 lived in the West Nile District. There are some 60,500 Congo Lugbara, of whom 58,100 lived in the Congo and the remainder were migrants in southern Uganda.[2] They thus number in all about 244,000 souls.

The Lugbara live mainly along the line of the Nilo-Congo divide, which at this point is also the political boundary between Uganda and the Belgian Congo. The centre of the country is between 4,000 and 5,000 feet above sea level, and forms a clearly

[1] See A. N. Tucker, *The Eastern Sudanic Languages*, Oxford, 1940, and my 'Myth, history and mourning taboos in Lugbara', *Uganda Journal*, 19, 2, September 1955.

[2] 1948 Census for Uganda figures; Congo figures are from the Chef de Poste, Aru.

marked plateau. Almost all of Lugbara except the bush-covered area of Aringa in the north-east consists of open and almost treeless rolling plains. The country is covered with a network of permanent streams and rivers, flowing into either the Nile or one of the tributaries of the Uele. Between streams are small ridges, row upon row receding into the distance, many crowned with

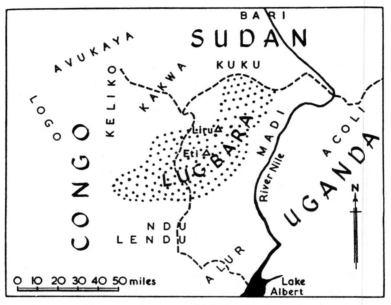

FIGURE I. The territory of the Lugbara and the neighbouring tribes.
From *Uganda Journal*, 19, 2, September 1955.

clumps of eucalyptus trees but otherwise almost unwooded. Unlike much tropical African bush country, this is green and fertile, and covered with farms and homesteads. Across the open country one can see vast distances. In the centre of the country rise the two massifs of Eti and Liru. These mountains are visible from almost every part of Lugbara in clear weather and they have a conspicuous place in Lugbara mythology.

The Lugbara have been administered sporadically since 1900. Before that the area of the southern Sudan was the scene of Arab

slaving, with continual warfare and destruction of tribal organiza-
tions. But the slavers seem not to have reached the Lugbara, and
they escaped the fate of the majority of the small tribes of the
region, who were preyed upon by slavers, Zande and Mangbetu.
The Belgians set up an administration in 1900. The main part
of the Lugbara passed to the Sudan in 1908, and to Uganda in
1914. The western Lugbara have remained under Belgian control.
The Belgians created 'chiefs' in this formerly chiefless society, and
there has developed an administrative system of chiefs and sub-
chiefs. Taxation was introduced in the years of the first world war,
and traders appeared at the same time. Lugbaraland is too high
for cotton, the main cash crop of Uganda, and the people have had
to offer their labour for their cash needs. In 1951 nineteen per
cent of the adult males of the Uganda Lugbara were absent from
the district; the proportion varies from one area to another, the
main factor being land shortage, which is growing serious in
central Lugbara. There were twenty-five per cent. of the adult men
away from the central Lugbara areas in that year.

The Africa Inland Mission and the Verona Fathers entered the
area in the 1920's. They have many small bush schools and one or
two larger stations, the latter with European staff. It is difficult to
assess their influence and indeed it cannot be considered apart from
that of general European contact. Lugbara regard missionaries as
agents of the new power of government which is in many ways
antagonistic to the traditional systems of authority. School
attendance varies considerably from one area to another, and since
most children leave school after only two or three years the general
educational standard is low. But the affect of the missions has been
considerable, as they have acted as a channel through which
European ideas have been introduced to Lugbara. They are the
only source of education, which must be acquired by anyone who
wishes to enter the new power system of the Europeans. But there
is in all fields a very marked separation of European and Lugbara
ways of life. Most Christians, evangelists and others, practice both
some form of Christianity and their traditional rites, and find little
difficulty in reconciling the beliefs belonging to each, as they are
significant in different situations. All but a very small minority of
Lugbara still accept their indigenous religious beliefs and teach
them to their children; and they still practise the rites associated
with them. There has been no government interference in ritual,

except in the rare cases of human offering at rainmaking ceremonies.

Although European economic, political and other activities
impinge upon and affect Lugbara society at all points, Lugbara
still carry on their traditional activities much as they have always
done, and still consider the world of the European as something
quite distinct from their own. Even though in recent years the
effects of labour migration have become more marked, for most
of the population the government is still something extraneous,
although it is by now taken for granted as existing for some purpose
of its own. The most obvious effects have been in the introduction
of taxation and in the prohibition of feud and warfare. As far as I
have been able to discover, life is still basically very little changed
from the traditional pattern. Most heads of families have taken
part in feuding and have killed men in the traditional way, and for
them the activities of Europeans and Indians living in the small
townships of Arua and Aru are distinct phenomena taking place
in another sphere.

II. LAND AND SETTLEMENT

Lugbaraland is fertile, and supports a population of some 240
persons to the square mile in north-central Lugbara. There is a
good and well-distributed rainfall, and seasonal differences are
not considerable enough to lead to transhumance or to have any
marked effect on social life, except that in the dry season there is
little work to be done in the fields and that food and beer are more
plentiful after the main harvest period of July-August than at
other times.

Main crops are millets and sorghums, legumes and root crops
such as sweet potatoes and cassava. Livestock are kept, mainly
cattle and goats, with some sheep, and of course fowl. In general
the domestic residential groups, which I describe below, are
economically self-supporting as regards foodstuffs. And water,
firewood, ochre, clay, reeds, thatching grass, iron, calabashes and
other necessary raw materials are found almost everywhere.
Traditionally there was little exchange of these materials, and men
had no need to go far from their own neighbourhood for economic
reasons.

Lugbara social organization is one of small local settlements in a constantly fluid relationship, within which territorial values are conceived in terms of those of the agnatic lineage. Lugbara social relations are restricted in range, the social field of any group being small. Local communities are continually changing both in internal composition, owing to individuals hiving off as tenants to live in other settlements, and in external relationships, owing to changes in population and locality with shifting of fields and migration-drift of the total population from north to south. Between local groups few ties are long recognized except those of a remote and overall kinship springing from ultimate common ancestry. The society is a fragmentary one, local communities being small and economically and socially largely independent.

The settlement pattern is typically one of dispersed homesteads scattered across the fertile ridges of this upland country. The smallest unit is the hut (*jo*), the home of a married woman. The Lugbara practise polygyny, although over sixty per cent. of the married men have only one wife, and each wife should have her own hut, granaries, and fields. In a polygynous household the husband may have a hut for his own use, which is used for the entertainment of guests. Today it is usual for the huts of one husband to form a distinct compound, separate from other compounds of related families, and usually surrounded by its own hedge of euphorbia, climbing beans, pumpkins, and other plants. Traditionally a compound contained the huts of a joint family, but today this is not common except in the case of the compounds of important men. In many areas, especially in southern Lugbara, it is common for each wife of a polygynous husband to have her own hut in its own separate compound, away from those of her co-wives. Here there is more interspersion of small lineages than elsewhere, and lack of long attachment to a lineage home (these are the more recently settled areas) has resulted in the intermingling of a lineage's huts to a remarkable degree.

The term used for compound in its literal and social senses is *aku*, the empty space of mud and dung kept clean by daily brushing, the floor on which most of the everyday life of the women is conducted. The word *'buru* is also used, especially in a social or metaphorical sense. There is usually only one entrance to the compound; inside are the huts and granaries, under which are the shrines and magical plants. Other shrines are on the hut verandahs, and the three upright stones of the fireplace, the centre of the sphere of women's activities, are somewhere in a sheltered corner of the compound floor. The word *ljco* ('hedge') is often used to refer to a large compound, and especially when talking of those of the past, which were larger than those of today. *Akụ*, *'bụrụ*, and *ljco* refer to a single residential settlement, of any size from a homestead containing the hut of one wife to that containing the huts of a family group of three or four generations. In a large homestead there is no term for a component segment's home, larger than the hut. Besides the living huts there is usually a girls' hut in any group of related compounds, where the unmarried girls sleep with their lovers.

Around the compounds are the fields. This is not the place in which to describe the Lugbara system of farming. It is sufficient to say that each wife should have three types of field, the fertilized home fields, the unfertilized fields away from the compounds, and the irrigated riverine fields. Each type is used for particular crops, and each has its own crop rotations and methods of manuring. The fields of a settlement are scattered, so that all wives may share in all types of available soil. Under indigenous conditions there is thus an optimum size for a single farming group. Once a group's territory has no more of any single type of field within reasonable walking distance then any increase in the number of its wives may lead to the dispersal of its huts and so to segmentation or fission. If some wives find it difficult to obtain all three types of field, the opposition between them leads to quarrelling and often to accusations of poisoning.

Shortage of land may, however, be overcome without the segmentation of the group. Individual households may move away, the husband becoming a tenant elsewhere, usually with a mother's or wife's brother. Land shortage is not the only reason for such attachment, but it is the most common; it was the reason in just over 70 per cent. of cases recorded in two areas. The word *anyị'ba* ('stranger') or a variant of the term, is used for a tenant, as for any attached person: it is the general nature of the interpersonal link that is important, not the reason for the attachment. The rights of a 'stranger' are heritable. Today also many younger men leave Lugbaraland and move to southern Uganda, where they take up plots and grow food and cash crops.

III. CLAN, LINEAGE AND SECTION

Lugbara conceive of their society as composed of clans that have dispersed from the original clan homes where their founders were begotten by the mythical culture-heroes Jaki and Dribidu. There are today at least sixty clans (*suru*), defined genealogically by reference to their founders, the sons of the heroes. These sons, whose mothers were women found by the heroes when they arrived from elsewhere, and whose identity is unimportant and unknown, begot sons in turn. Their agnatic descendants form the clans which Lugbara regard as the basic and enduring units of their society. Clans have clan-names, which are names given to all descent groups, the constituent lineages of clans.

Clans are dispersed and are not corporate groups. Localized sub-clans, for which the Lugbara term is also *suru*, are corporate groups and are the agnatic cores of tribes. There are about sixty tribes, with an average population of 4,000 people. A tribe is a territorial group, and is defined as being the largest group within which fighting is settled by discussion; there cannot be a state of permanent feud between groups of one tribe, but there may be permanent warfare between units of different tribes.[1] The tribe has no single head with authority; there may be a rainmaker in a tribe but he has only sporadic ritual authority over its members. A tribe is segmented into sections, there typically being what I call major, minor and minimal sections. The last is co-terminous with the family cluster, the basic settlement group.

Sub-clans are segmented into smaller descent groups which are in turn segmented; usually there are about three levels of segmentation altogether. I refer to these segments as major, minor and minimal lineages. Each lineage provides the agnatic core for a territorial section, the minimal lineage being the core of a family cluster. A section is a territorial group, a lineage a descent group. Both compose systems in their own right, that of sections comprising the actual groups in which Lugbara live on the ground, that of lineages being a conceptual system by which the former is conceived as unchanging and the relationships between its units validated. Lugbara make no distinction between them, a section taking the clan-name of its associated lineage.

[1] There are no longer feud and warfare, but tribal relations are still discussed by Lugbara as though there were, and so I use the ethnographic present.

The smallest segments are continually segmenting, this leading to realignment of segments at higher levels, but the numbers of levels of segmentation and of generations in genealogies remain more or less constant. Genealogies usually have from eight to thirteen generations from the present day to the clan founders. It would be possible to trace the supposed genealogical relationship of any two members of a sub-clan and even a clan, but this is never done: the range of recognition of kinship ties between individuals is at a much lower level of segmentation. There may be up to a dozen generation-segments in the genealogy of a sub-clan. At any one time only certain of them are relevant as a basis of organization in a social activity, and so associated with a territorial group as its core. It is only these that are generally given clan-names and which I call lineages. If necessary, however, it is possible to refer to any generation-segment by a clan-name. Since there is constant segmentation most generation-segments have been significant as lineages at one time or another and then had a name, and it is this that can be used in these cases. However, if the segmentation rate has been slow, then several generations may have passed without there being segmentation at all, and so these segments will not have been named. They will probably soon be forgotten and the names of their apical ancestors either forgotten with them or placed collaterally as brothers of the main descent line.

A segment is distinguished by reference to the wife of an ancestor three or four generations back. This is Lugbara theory: segments are distinguished 'by the marrying of wives'. The segment takes the clan-name of the minimal or minor lineage of its ancestress. Segments may also be differentiated by full-brother founders, in which case they take the name of the brother concerned or are given a new name composed for the occasion. Later, after several generations, these names are likely to be accepted as the clan-names of ancestresses and genealogies will be changed to fit in with this hypothesis.

Some sections consist only of agnatic lineage kin and their wives, but in most cases there are also attached kin. Within a family cluster's settlement there may be individuals and families of different affiliation. Most of these attached people are cognatic kin of someone in the host lineage or are attached with the tie of client (*atɨbo*). A man may attach himself to a mother's brother or to a wife's brother, usually because of land shortage or quarrelling in his home group. He and later his descendants as a group are known as sister's sons or sister's husbands (the latter tie is kept even though in time it becomes one of mother's brother-sister's son). Or attachment may be made by a man who puts himself in a client relationship to a wealthy individual, either because he is poor or because of famine or war. Such a man is a client, and his descendants may in time be accepted as cognates. At the level of the family cluster these are individuals attached to individual hosts, but at higher levels of segmentation attached kin are numerous enough to form accessory sections. The relationship between them and their host section is that between their founders and the original hosts: almost invariably accessory sections are known as 'sisters' sons' or 'sisters' husbands'. A section has a territory, which has a boundary, and an accessory group is said to live 'within the boundary of another section'. They are known as 'strangers' (*anyi'ba*).

The same generic terms are used for the local and descent groups; these are the words *ori'ba* and *suru*. *Ori'ba* means literally 'ghost people'; *ori* is a ghost, that is, an ancestor for whom a shrine has been placed by his descendants. It consists of people who regard themselves as a group by reference to common ghost shrines. Lugbara see descent by 'blood' as running in both lines, and a ghost may bring sickness to living people related to him through both men and women. *Ori'ba* are primarily those groups under the ritual authority of a single head, who may invoke the ghost against his dependants, or which may be represented by him at sacrifices. They are defined ritually as being composed of people within a single ritual field. They are typically minimal and minor lineages and sections, and the term may also be extended to the speaker's own major segment. *Suru* has the meaning of a group of people who consider themselves a group and are so considered by others because they live in a common territory and have ties between them based on descent by common ancestry, including quasi-genealogical links. The ritual content of the ties which bind members of an *ori'ba* are absent. *Suru* may refer to a specific local or descent group, or to a group such as Europeans or Arabs, or to a category or species.

IV. THE FAMILY CLUSTER AND THE ELDER

Elementary and polygynous compound families are grouped into larger residential units, which I call family clusters. Each has a head, the *'ba wara* or *'ba ambo* (literally, 'big man') which I translate as 'elder'. The composition of the family cluster cannot be understood without consideration of his status, since it is defined largely in terms of his authority.

The family cluster is not a large group. I have figures for about forty, which vary between fifteen and sixty people, with one or two beyond these extremes:

20 and under	21-30	31-40	41-50	51-60	over 60	
7	13	4	6	9	3	=42

This group undergoes a cycle of growth and segmentation or of decline and fusion with another group. But whatever its size it is defined by the possession of one elder. It may be segmented into component groups, to which the term 'joint family' could be given in certain cases. These are segments which would become separate family clusters if segmentation occurred. But such segments may also be simple compound families only. What is significant is not a formal structure of joint and domestic families but the ties of residence, kinship and authority between the various segments of the total group under the authority of the elder. The structure of this total group and the pattern of authority within it will be discussed at various points in the course of this book.

A family cluster is typically based on a minimal lineage; the head of the lineage is the head of the cluster. The lineage is a unit in inter-group systems of relationship, and is represented by its elder. He is the senior living descendant of the lineage's agnatic ancestors, the member who is nearest to the most recent of them and who is expected to die and to join them first. His spiritual status is a dual one; he has two roles which overlap to some degree. He is the ritual representative of the lineage and also the family cluster's head. In the latter role he has religious sanctions over a range of dependants which include both agnates and also people who are members of his family cluster but not of his agnatic lineage.

The status of elder and his authority shade into those of subordinate family heads, who may also be called elders if they are old.

But Lugbara always know whether a man is a real elder or not, and the term is properly applied only to those men who by virtue of genealogical position in the lineage have the custodianship of certain shrines. All heads of domestic families whose fathers are dead have shrines to the ghosts of the recent ancestors. But an elder, besides having these ordinary shrines, also has special shrines for the ghosts of the founding ancestors of the minor and wider lineages. I call these external lineage shrines.

An elder has certain marks of office, of which the most important is a special stool, *ogua*. Only elders may sit on these stools and they are inherited. There are other marks of office found in various parts of the country—certain long sticks or wands are the most usual.

Lugbara define an elder by saying that a man is called *'ba wara* 'because he eats the chest of meat', 'because he eats the tongue', 'because he eats the elder's portion', 'because he sits on the *ogua* stool', 'because he stays with the shrines' (this is partly a reference to his role in war when he stays behind to make offerings to the ghosts during the fighting), 'because he cuts meat at the shrines', 'because he puts the meat into the shrines', 'because he puts his hand into the shrines'. In some parts of northern Lugbara he is known as *ori'ba* ('ghost shrine man'). Only he may eat certain parts of the meat at sacrifices—the spare meat of the chest, the liver, kidney, testicles, penis and intestines. He has ritual authority and the duty of ritual guardianship of his dependants; it is he who consults oracles and performs or supervises at least the more important rites of sacrifice. Also he has secular authority within the family cluster—it is his duty to allocate land, for example—but it is always the ritual aspect of his role that is emphasized.

The elder should be the eldest son of the senior wife of his predecessor. This wife is the first married. If a married man inherits a wife from his father then that wife, if married first, becomes his senior wife with precedence over the wife whom he has already. 'You fear that wife of your father because she is like your mother.' She may not, of course, be a man's own mother, but one of his own mother's co-wives. In this case, the heir is the first-born son of the senior wife, even if the son is younger in years than a son of the junior wife who was in fact she who was first married to this particular husband. This principle permits both filial and adelphic succession.

This rule refers essentially to the ritual succession, to the power of being able to sacrifice at the shrines as the nearest direct descendants of the dead ancestors. 'A widow carries the shrines with her,' it is said. But the ritual successor may not in fact be regarded as the elder in all situations. If he is young, or weak, or poor, he may be ousted by a close agnate who is senior in years, strong-willed or wealthy. This man becomes the holder of over-all secular authority. He should only be a guide and teacher to the 'true' elder, and act as a guardian. Sometimes he will act as elder in secular matters until his death, and may also be referred to as an 'elder'. At his death then his own son may wish to succeed, and a dispute occurs between him and the true elder. The group may then segment.

The form of Lugbara genealogies is not fixed, but easily changeable. It depends merely on the consensus of opinion, in particular on that of the more senior men, at a given time. The genealogies given by the senior men of a lineage may often be at variance with one another, since genealogical validation is the only accepted criterion for *de jure* as distinct from *de facto* eldership. Besides genealogies being changeable in this respect, there are other criteria. A man may invoke the ghosts of the dead to bring sickness to a dependant who flouts lineage authority. The dead are said to 'hear the words', in particular those of men who are genealogically 'true' elders. So that a man who can successfully invoke the dead may be accepted as the true elder. I argue in later chapters that part of the significance of the cult of the dead is that its operation may validate the claims of elders and would-be elders in this way.

The process of lineage segmentation is not clear cut. There is rarely a moment at which it can be said that a new segment has been formed. Lineage ties are not significant at all times but only when called into operation at a given occasion. In Lugbara a segment is significant primarily when its elder's role becomes significant, on ritual occasions. Therefore a new segment may not become significant in the sense that its elder acts as head of a social group until an occasion of sacrifice. Sacrifices do not take place every day, and there may be a space of many months between the death of an elder and the first time that his successor actually plays his role at offerings made at the shrines of families in the lineage, and is by doing so affirmed in his new position by his dependants. The elder is the custodian of the external lineage shrines. Sacrifices at these shrines are rare, only once in every two or three years; until the occasion arises the elder of a new segment will probably not build a shrine. He may do so but it is unusual and smacks of over-eagerness and ambition. If, of course, he inherits the eldership of a lineage which does not segment on his predecessor's death, then he does not need to build a new shrine but merely uses that of his predecessor, although he may move it to a place near his own homestead if it is some way away. In north Lugbara these shrines are usually the centres of rain-groves, which cannot be moved, and near which the segment of the lineage with rainmaking powers must stay. Essentially it is not the physical possession of a shrine which is an attribute of his status but the possession of the necessary spiritual qualities which enable him to approach the ancestors and to represent his lineage to them on the one hand and to represent them to the living on the other. The possession of a shrine is in theory secondary; but as might be expected, the actual possession of the principal sign of eldership becomes important. Lugbara say

because he is big, he is near his father who told him the words of the ancestors

and the emphasis is on the fact that only he knows of those mysteries unknown to ordinary men, the 'men behind' as adult family heads who are not elders are called.

The elder holds domestic authority over all members of his family cluster, to a greater or less degree. It is complete over his agnatic dependants but less so over their wives (who remain in some spheres under the authority of their own agnatic kin) and over attached kin who have agnatic ties with lineages elsewhere. Those elders who are also genealogically the heads of minor and major lineages have no domestic authority over any but their own family clusters, but they may act as representatives of the minor or major lineage on occasions, primarily on ritual ones. They are still called only elders (*'ba wara*). They may wield very considerable influence by virtue of their position and also of their personal qualities, but it is not formally recognized that they are superior in internal authority to genealogically junior elders of the same major lineage. I was told of one senior elder of a major lineage, Maro of Andruvu, an extremely respected elder whose presence was enough to silence any normally obstreperous gathering of quarrelling kinsmen, that

> We fear the words of Maro. He speaks slowly and is never angry or quarrelsome. Truly he is an elder and we little men follow his words. He leads us as a bull leads his herd of cattle.

But when I asked whether he would be expected to intervene in a bridewealth dispute going on in a minimal lineage other than his own, I was told that

> He is the elder of that lineage there, and we here do not listen to what he says. Here our elder is Draa and we follow him.

Maro's influence was considerable enough for the local government county chief, a very powerful man, to ask for and to heed his opinions; but it did not extend to the internal affairs of lineages other than his own minimal lineage, or at most to his own minor lineage.

In all societies authority within a given group may be exercised by different persons only so long as it relates either to different people or to different matters. There is for Lugbara an ideal pattern of authority within the family cluster, consistent with an ideal pattern of internal structure of the cluster. The distribution of authority is expressed in terms of seniority which is in theory based upon differences of generation and age. In theory there is only one elder, and he and other senior men who are the heads of large family groups within the cluster are generically known as 'big men' (*'ba amboru*). A very senior and respected man, especially if an elder, may also be known as *atalao*, which might be translated as 'father-elder' (*ata*=father). Other men who are heads of domestic families are the 'men behind' (*'ba vele*). More junior men are *karule* ('youths'), a middle-aged man who is still formally a youth being known as 'big youth' (*karule wara* or *karule amboru*). These terms are used loosely, since age and genealogical status are not always commensurate, and the ranking may in any case be upset by factors of personality and wealth.

The 'big men' are the heads of component segments of the minimal lineage. These segments are usually distinguished by virtue of having separate 'grandmothers'; that is to say, by the wives of a common grandfather or great-grandfather who is the apical ancestor of the lineage. Lugbara theory holds that a segment divides after three generations, but this is by no means always so and the actual number of generations is not important. What is important is distinct maternal origin and this is effective at the range of grandmother or great-grandmother. A segment of smaller depth rarely contains enough adult men for it to be considered a distinct segment. Usually this group is a joint family, but at times it may be only a single compound family. Since in this context it is its segmentary status that is important, rather than its size or internal composition, I call it a family-segment. It is not based upon a lineage, but upon an incipient lineage; and properly it bears no clan-name. It may in fact be distinguished by the clan-name of its apical ancestress in intra-minimal lineage affairs, but is not so known beyond the minimal lineage. It is not called a lineage (*ori'ba*) but a compound (*akʉ*). It is under the general domestic authority of its head. An example of the way a family cluster is segmented into family-segments is given in Figure 6. Later, in Chapter IV, I discuss the operation of the cult of the dead in this particular group. This figure shows the generally accepted situation as it was at the beginning of my stay.

This ideal distribution of authority is rarely found, however, due to population increase and decrease and changes in the age distribution of members of the cluster. Lugbara consider that ideally their society is one without internal change; yet they recognize that lineages segment and proliferate and that quarrels and disputes are signs of incipient segmentation. Lineages increase in what may be called critical population, either by rise in numbers or by shortage of land. There is an optimum ratio of people to available area of land, and when this is exceeded then segmentation is likely to occur. The precipitating factor is usually the death of an elder whose authority has hitherto kept the segments together. The phase before his death and the subsequent segmentation is usually marked by disputes over his authority to allocate land and other resources. During this phase efforts are made by other senior men, and by their juniors, to change the existing pattern of authority. They try to assert authority over members of domestic families other than their own, and in situations, especially ritual ones, in which the elder is ideally the only person to exercise authority. Lugbara hold that any threat to the existing distribution of authority is to be resisted. An elder wishes to retain sole authority within his family cluster, except in matters of domestic importance only which do not affect the cluster as a single group, and Lugbara values support him in this endeavour. Yet within the cluster the head of a family-segment has the duty of pressing the claims of his members against those of co-ordinate segments. He is expected to do this and his dependants complain if he does not. But from the viewpoint of the total cluster he should not do this, but should discuss matters in amity with his fellow heads of family-segments. These two courses are not easily compatible and the head of a family-segment finds himself in a dilemma. The ideal of a responsible man's behaviour—and *a fortiori* that of an elder—is that he should be quiet, dignified, slow in decision, just and ready to act in union with his 'brothers' of the same grade as himself. The unity of the lineage is the ideal. But not all senior men are like that, and younger men are still less so. Younger men are thought to be more disruptive, since they lack the social maturity and experience of elders. The expected (but not perhaps the ideal) behaviour of junior men thus fits the position in which they find themselves—that of heads of junior segments, exhorted by their dependants to gain benefits for them but subject to the over-all unity of the lineage and the authority of its elder. A young man who shows 'slowness' is pointed out as a man of promise, a future elder, but he may find himself disliked by his equals of the present and even disowned by his own juniors, who attempt in their turn to usurp his authority. However, juniors see themselves as separated strongly from their seniors. Younger men 'fear' to eat with their seniors, especially on ritual occasions. A younger man who succeeds an elder of senior generation 'fears' to step into his place. The elder is a person whose status involves him in dangers and responsibilities which younger men do not want. An informant told me that he was glad he was not a first-born son, since otherwise he would have to become an elder. During my stay his elder brother succeeded to the eldership very hesitantly and apprehensively, and told me that he hoped he would not have to act as ritual representative for some time to come, until he had grown used to his new status. He 'feared' to sit as equal with older men whom he had formerly regarded with some awe. My informant told me that should his brother die he himself would run away as a labour migrant to south Uganda, since he 'feared' the status so much. This should not be taken to mean that younger men do not have ambitions to become elders. But if their ambition is marked they are condemned by public opinion. The situation is really that a man wants the power that the status holds but is afraid of the ritual responsibilities involved. The same informant said on another occasion:

> It is good to be a big man. People fear you and you are strong. You are big, like a leopard or like an elephant, and other people fall beneath you. It is like a man cutting grass: he cuts grass with his knife, *tu tu tu.* So an elder speaks to smaller men.

The importance given to the identity of the lineage means also that an elder should try to increase it in size, both by natural increase and by attracting uterine kin and clients. The larger the group the more able it is to maintain its rights in land and resources against others, the wider is the elder's domestic authority and the higher his status and that of his lineage. The members of the lineage expect their elder to be ambitious, and support him in his claims in much the same way as the subjects of a king support him in his efforts to increase the importance of their kingdom and the kingship. An elder is very conscious that he has duties to living and dead members of his lineage, and that the maintenance and increase of his authority is synonymous with the well-being of his lineage and family cluster. The ideology connected with the cult of the dead supports such a view. Thus just as the relations between component segments of the family cluster should be both competitive and co-operative, so should those between family clusters and minimal lineages, and so between their elders. A man once said to me:

> Elders often quarrel among themselves like young men. They are men and all men have bad hearts. But the ancestors do not quarrel among themselves.

Although it is often said that the dead do in fact quarrel, in this context the meaning is clear. The 'elder' who really joins under his own authority two co-ordinate minimal lineages is an ancestor— at least he is usually so and is so thought of by Lugbara, as it is said that a lineage segments after three generations. I am here discussing authority: minimal lineages may together be represented in ritual contexts by a senior living elder, but he has no secular authority outside his own family cluster.

In short, there is a conflict in the system of authority, both within and between family clusters and minimal lineages. Lugbara see this conflict as something liable to disrupt the ideal pattern of local and kinship relations and authority, and so to be minimized; values of the unity of the lineage and of the identity of interests of men of equal seniority in generation and age sustain their view. This conflict is inherent in a segmentary system of this type: the balance of authority alters with changes in factors of population and land and with the death of the holders of authority, events which are outside the control of the living. Much of my exposition of the cult of the dead will deal with attempts of the living to control the effects of these factors.

V. AUTHORITY, RESPECT AND SIN

Lugbara society, traditionally at any rate and to a large extent today, is singularly lacking in any effective sanctions for the maintenance of proper authority within the field of social relations of a man or family. Modern chiefs and sub-chiefs are concerned mainly with taxes, labour and other matters that are outside traditional everyday life for most Lugbara. Force, expressed in feud and warfare, was exercised against distant groups at the limit of a family cluster's field of direct social relations. Within that field it was, and still is, soon stopped and subject to considerable disapproval. There are exceptions—a man may beat his wife and children—but even there force must be exercised in moderation and never persistently. Today feud and warfare are prohibited by the government and have been replaced by chiefs' courts, but to take a close kinsman or neighbour to court leads to disapproval expressed in ridicule, rudeness, assault or even ostracism.

Open violence is wrong between agnates and close uterine kin. This applies especially to members of a group part of whose corporateness lies in the recognition of a single elder who has authority within it, and to a less degree to members of a wider group which recognizes a lineage head with powers of representation. Where mutually recognized authority breaks down, then self-help is used in its place; and the recourse to self-help destroys the recognition of common authority and representation. When two agnatically related lineages resort to violence it shows that their formerly recognized common authority and representation no longer exist; certainly the former does not, although the latter may persist to some extent. A strict line of demarcation cannot be drawn between recognition of an elder and the resort to violence, since the recognition of a new inter-lineage relationship develops slowly over a period of time.

Disputes over rights in land, women and livestock occur at all levels of the lineage, although they may be settled differently and may take different superficial forms. The minimal lineage recognizes the internal authority of its elder; wider segments recognize no such authority. But the minor or major lineage, depending on its size or recent history of segmentation, has other attributes which minimize the risk of overt hostility. One is that it is exogamous. It may not be the widest exogamous segment of the sub-clan, but the prohibition of intermarriage within it is rigidly maintained, whereas that beyond it may occasionally be broken and the segment concerned soon split into two. This is not common but every sub-clan has a few cases within the last generation or so. Within this segment sexual relations, as apart from marriage, are true incest; beyond it Lugbara accept them as taking place but unless followed by pregnancy or too flagrant it is unlikely that any action will result, either by the living or the dead. But incest within it is a sin, with mystical sanctions sent by the dead and by God. Adultery within this segment, unless performed at the request of an impotent or absent husband, is also sinful, being a breach of close fraternal relations. Beyond it adultery is regarded more as a normal offence to be dealt with by fighting or compensation. It is also the group within which homicide is fratricide, for which there is no human punishment. Assault, especially if against an older man, is also more of a sin within this range than beyond it; the latter case leads to counter-assault, the former brings mystical sanctions into play. All these offences within this segment are in the nature of sins, their sinfulness lying in their rejection of true agnatic kinship values. They are contrasted to the commensality, mutual help and identification of interests that comprise ideal agnatic kinship behaviour. At this range sanctions for orderly conduct are mystical, to do with ghosts and ancestors; accusations of witchcraft may occur as alternatives to violence. Relations with more distant agnatically related lineages of the same sub-clan are generally sanctioned by show of overt violence, the feud, in which an ultimate peaceful settlement is sought since after all the parties are still agnatically related. This is the range within which personal kinship terms are used. It coincides with either the minor or major lineage, usually with the former. Which segment it is in any particular sub-clan depends upon the size of the groups involved and on how long ago lineage segmentation took place. For convenience I shall refer to this range of segmentation as being that of the inner lineage.

The family cluster is not an isolated unit, since its members have relations of neighbourhood with nearby clusters and of kinship beyond its borders. Individuals have personal ties with individual cognates and affines over a wide area, but the most intensive are within the inner lineage and the territorial section associated with it. Some of these relations are sustained by only the most diffuse sanctions. These are those which apply to unrelated persons in everyday informal relations—meeting at markets or on the road, at beer drinks, and so on. But most of the social interaction of any Lugbara individual or family is with kinsmen, and these are essentially relations of authority, for which there are more formal sanctions. The network of authority relations must be sustained if Lugbara society is to continue and its members to live in amity and peace. Every person has some status or set of statuses in this network, although it is accepted that persons may change their statuses over time, as they increase in social maturity and as persons die or move away from one local network of relations into another. Also people try to acquire power, try to exercise authority that is not theirs, try to disobey the authority of others or to exercise power in a subordinate status when to do so would destroy the authority of the holder of superordinate status. I was once told

Those ants there run along in lines like soldiers, and all carry their food and thatch grass. Perhaps there is one ant who is a chief, who knows these things? The Banyoro have a Mukama and they obey his orders or they are put into prison and beaten and their wealth taken by the chief. But we Lugbara are not like that. We have no chiefs and there is no one to give us orders. So every man tries to become 'big' and strong and men's hearts are bad. There are some men, like the rain-makers, who have good hearts, but they are not many. Is it not good to be strong? Then one has much wealth, and wives and children, and becomes a big man.

Lugbara have an ideal conception of their society and of relations between God, the living and the dead. The dead are members of their lineages with their living kin, and they retain ties with non-agnatic kin also. The dead are kin, but in most cases they are senior kin, and the living should behave towards them as towards senior living kin. Despite the statement I have just quoted, which shows that Lugbara may see their society as an almost anarchic one, they are very conscious of the need for the proper exercise of authority at the lower levels of the system, those of family cluster and inner lineage. They merely recognize that the ideal may not be practised.

For Lugbara the essence of the exercise of authority, whether between agnates, cognates, affines or neighbours, is for the relationship to be one in which the junior obeys, 'fears' or 'respects' the senior. 'Fear' and 'respect' are contained in the term *ru*. The word is used in many contexts but respect towards a senior kinsman is the most important. Respect involves politeness to senior kin, listening to their opinions and observing their wishes. Towards affines of the opposite sex and senior generation it involves the obligations not to eat in their presence, not to meet them on a path, not to sit with them alone in a hut or on the same papyrus mat, not to address them by other than the correct terms of affinity, and generally to obey their demands and wishes. Not to observe 'respect' leads to 'shame' (*drinza*, literally 'head hanging'), and is more than a mere breach of manners, although the dividing line is often difficult to draw. A man is said by others to be 'with shame', and they remove the shame by stroking his head four times (three if a woman) A man is felt to be shamed by others regarding him as deserving of it, rather than spontaneously feeling it himself. Although an occasional demonstration of lack of respect may not be considered very important, if it is persisted in it marks a man out as being 'bad' (*onzi*), a man who 'destroys' (*eza*) the lineage and community. Obvious breaches of respect by overt aggressive behaviour are more serious than the mere non-observance of the rules of respect To kill or strike a senior kinsman, or to shout and quarrel with him, are the worst offences against individual kin. To commit incest with a close kinswoman, or adultery with a close kinsman's wife, or to cause the death of close kin by foolishly and pointlessly causing feuds, are the offences that really 'destroy' lineage and community.

Most of these offences, of which the worst are incest and fratricide within the inner lineage, are categorized by the term *ezata*.

Eza is to 'destroy' or 'spoil', and *-ta* is the substantive suffix. *Ezata* is 'destruction' or 'destroying'; it was given to me as 'the deed that destroys good words', and a Christian pastor translated it for me as 'sin'. A man who persistently offends and insults his close kin is a 'man with sin'. *Ezata* are contrasted with 'bad deeds' (*yeta onzi*), which need not be concerned with lineage and kinship values, although less important offences against kin may be so called. Sins are mystically punished by the dead and by God, especially by the former. Bad deeds are met by human response such as fighting or beating, although the dead may also be indirectly concerned.

Sins affect a man or his immediate dependants, particularly his wife and children. The usual response to their commission is for sickness to fall upon the offender or his family. The sickness is likely to be that of 'growing thin' (*oyị*) which is known to come from the ghosts of the dead. It does not lead to death, but 'shows' the offender 'his words and the words of the dead'.

Besides ghostly sickness and other more usual consequences, which I discuss in later chapters, sins may lead to a condition known as *nyoka*. This is sent, or at least is approved, by God. *Nyoka* is unending trouble or disaster which follows a man and his lineage. Its usual form is sterility of women, livestock and fields, and its most serious consequence is the dying out of the lineage. It may be preceded by omens. Although the distinction between sin and *nyoka* is not always easy to find, it is said that God is much more concerned in cases of *nyoka* than he is in those of mere sin, and so are the distant lineage and sub-clan ancestors; the more recently dead are not thought to bring *nyoka*. *Nyoka* does not affect merely the offender and his immediate family, but his entire lineage, not only in its wealth and prosperity but even in its very existence as a discrete entity. Lugbara say that a lineage becomes small in numbers and will soon die out. Then it is known as a 'remnant lineage' (*sụrụ acepịrị*)

because it has forgotten the words of the ancestors; it has forgotten the words of God the creator; it is alone and dies out; its words are finished; *nyoka* is with it for ever.

It was said of one such lineage:

Long ago the men of Anguruku were many. They had strong hearts and they brought much fighting to us here, and because of that many of their children and our children were killed. There was hunger and the men went to the fields and said 'Where are our brothers? We are without hoes.' God was angry at those men and brought *nyoka* upon them. *Nyoka* struck them because of the words of God.

Sins are moral acts committed knowingly by individuals, and they are usually followed by ghost-sent sickness. *Nyoka* is seen as the end-result of a long series of sins: it was destroying Anguruku because of the troubles brought upon the community by the ceaseless feuding of its members at the end of the last century. This is not the fault of its present members, but is due to their fathers' sins. *Nyoka* affects the whole lineage which is considered as a single entity to have committed persistent sin. In the past the members of Anguruku have made offerings to their ancestors to try to remove their trouble, but now it has been recognized as being due to God, who has decided that the lineage shall die out. *Nyoka* is the consequence of sins, but also something more: it is the result of a long-standing disregard for ties between men and the dead and men and God. There is an ideal relationship between the living and the dead, breach of which is caused by sin and leads to ghostly sickness of the individual concerned. Persistent sin leads to a breach of the ideal relationship between God and his creatures, and this leads to the state of *nyoka* affecting the lineage which has shown that it harms not only its own internal system of authority but also the well-being of its neighbours and the whole local community. It must be stressed that such actions are immoral ones: disasters that affect the entire community, such as drought or famine, are not considered the consequence of immoral acts and so are not *nyoka*.

Sanctions for the maintenance of the system of authority are mainly mystical. There is a wide range of mystical sanctions, some thought of as operated by God, some by the dead, others by witches, which are brought into play in various situations in which the pattern of local authority is disturbed. God and the dead do not live on the surface of the earth as do men, but come into contact with the living in certain ways. These include consultation at oracles and diviners, and dreams and visions. God enters into contact with men by means of spirits and other manifestations, and the dead affect men by sending sickness in response to which men offer sacrifice at shrines set up for the dead.

God, the dead and witches enter into the system of authority, as well as living men. Lugbara conceive these agents as supporting or opposing men in their attempts to acquire, exercise or throw off authority. These agents are believed to be able to send sickness—and in the case of God, death—as signs of their approval or disapproval of the behaviour of living men, and the living appeal to them for support in the ever-changing pattern of authority relations. They are said to have certain characteristics and to behave in certain ways on account of certain motives. Beliefs about them cannot be placed within a single logically consistent framework, as can the religious beliefs of many peoples. But there is a sociological consistency in the ways in which these beliefs are used in social interaction between persons. This will be demonstrated in the course of this book. But first I must give an account of the main beliefs held by Lugbara about themselves, their society and the world around it; it will be easier for the reader to follow the later discussion if the main details of the cultural background are given first.

II

THE CULT OF THE DEAD: ANCESTORS
AND GHOSTS

1. THE LIVING AND THE DEAD

LUGBARA have no set of interconsistent beliefs as to the nature of man and the world. Their beliefs are significant in given situations and their consistency lies in the way in which they are used in ritual action. In addition, every local area has differences which set it apart from its neighbours and act as factors of local integration and self-awareness. This is true of all aspects of Lugbara culture. The instability and fragmentary nature of the total system is apparent in religious usage as much as, if not more than, in any other part of social behaviour. This is seen both in differences in ritual and in the nomenclature of shrines and mystical agents.

Lugbara religion comprises several cults, that of the dead being the most important. Most sacrifices are made to the dead. This cult is concerned mainly with relations within the family cluster and the inner lineage. It is primarily a lineage cult, in that agnatic ancestors are the most significant. Non-agnatic ancestors are important in some situations in which the interests of the cluster and the lineage as groups are not essentially involved.

The lineage includes both living and dead members:

Are our ancestors not people of our lineage? They are our fathers and we are their children whom they have begotten. Those that have died stay near us in our homes and we feed and respect them. Does not a man help his father when he is old?

The main part of Lugbara ritual is concerned with the relationship between living men and their dead kin. This relationship reflects that between men and groups as they are at the present moment, a relationship which is conceived as controlled and sanctioned by the dead. Lugbara beliefs about their world validate their ritual and secular behaviour in the sense that they provide an ideal of Lugbara society. This is not a utopia but an ideal of what Lugbara society actually is. The ideal does not change from the form supposed to have been given to it at its beginning by the hero-ancestors and their sons, who were the founders of clans. All Lugbara hold that this is the only form in which their society can exist. They do not conceive of another. Even though some educated Lugbara are becoming aware that today their social system is in certain contexts part of a wider system, this does not alter the belief that Lugbara society is an unchanging one and independent of outside change. They are aware of change today, but see it as leading to the breakdown of an orderly distribution of authority and power, a breakdown that should not be permanent. This brings the ideal form of their society into higher relief than ever. Those Lugbara who are concerned about the moral aspects of the Christianity they learn at school are attracted to it as much because it seems to approximate to traditional Lugbara morality as because it sets a new standard; but such people are very few.

For Lugbara, living and dead of the same lineage are in a permanent relationship with each other. The dead are aware of the actions and even the thoughts of the living, 'their children', or at least they may be so. The living act as temporary caretakers of the prosperity, prestige and general well-being of the lineage, on behalf of the ancestors who did the same during their lives. 'Our ancestors' are seen as good people who set an example that men should follow and who maintained the ideal of the social order and of social behaviour merely by their having lived as they are said to have lived. A man who squanders lineage property or who by his actions weakens this system of authority is blamed as much for having failed to keep faith with the dead as for offending his living kin.

Men relate the doings of the ancestors in vivid and dramatic detail, describing features, tone of voice and gestures. They picture them as men like themselves, as have been all men since the time of the heroes. It is usually implied that they were not stupid or weak as are men today, but always had the interests of the lineage at heart and behaved as senior and respected men should do, 'slowly' and with dignity. 'Our ancestors' are considered to have been men of integrity and worth. Offerings made to them are made with sincerity and their right to send sickness to their descendants is not begrudged them: it is proper that they should do so.

Lugbara are not aware at every moment of the day of their ancestors watching them, either to chide or to guard them. It is only when sickness appears, if sent by the dead, that the more or less latent relationship between the living and the dead is actualized. It is expressed then in ritual. Generally speaking in everyday life people merely know that the dead take an interest in them and expect to be respected by having meat and beer placed for them at their shrines. The living should speak well of them and follow their precepts, and especially the words said on their death beds to their children. The proper relationship between dead and living is for the former to stay quietly under the huts, which they will do so long as they are contented and well treated. The latent relationship becomes precise and meaningful at sacrifice, when it acquires a social content by becoming part of the set of ties that compose an actual network of relations of authority between living men.

Although most of Lugbara ritual is concerned with the dead, God is nevertheless associated with almost every relationship between living and dead. God is 'the creator of men' (*'ba o'bapiri*), who long ago created the world. He is conceived of in two aspects, as God in the sky, remote from mankind and 'good' (*onyiru*) and as God in the streams, close to mankind and 'bad' (*onzi*). His power may be manifested in many ways, in natural phenomena such as lightning and in the form of spirits which are given shrines by men. He is the ultimate fountainhead of all power and authority, of all sanctions for orderly relations between men. But custom, the rules of orderly observance of those rights and duties that compose the status of a member of society, is decreed and sanctioned by the ancestors. God made the world, but the hero-ancestors and their descendants, the ancestors, formed Lugbara society. The rules of social behaviour are 'the words of our ancestors'. A client (*atibo*) is a man without a lineage, a refugee from elsewhere. Before acceptance by a host or sponsor he has no kin, and is a 'thing'. When he is accepted he becomes a kinsman. Before this he may be killed as a 'thing', without fear of vengeance. Yet he is still regarded as a creature of God, and indeed as a Lugbara, even though his clan is unknown or unrecognized. God even made the Europeans.

God is, for Lugbara, a concept that links together several activities that at first sight might appear to be quite unrelated. The relationship between God and the ancestors is difficult to discover. It is never made explicit. Every lineage has its own ancestors, but God is everywhere, in a relationship of equal intensity with all lineages. Since Lugbara never conceive of themselves as forming a single social unit they never come together to sacrifice to God, except that wide communities may occasionally unite to send a ram as a scapegoat to God. It is sent to the mountains. Lugbara say 'we forget our ancestors and send a ram to the mountains'. Mountains are both the abode of God and of the two hero-ancestors, who are common to all Lugbara also; they lived before the formation of Lugbara society and were near to God. But the relationship is not considered to need clearer expression than that.

II. THE NATURE OF MAN

Living people are 'people of the world outside' or 'people who belong to the world outside' (*ba oro drị amve*). *Oro* (world) is on the surface of the earth, the visible world in which living men are. It is contrasted to the earth itself (*nyakụ*). When people die they become 'people who have died' ('*ba drapị 'borị*), or 'people in the earth' ('*ba nyakụa*). The dead are still 'people' ('*ba*) but they live under the surface of the world. Details of the ways in which they live are irrelevant to the living, since it is only when they are actually in contact that they become significant and at those times they come near to the huts and shrines in their descendants' homesteads. It is said 'People say our ancestors live as we do, but we cannot see them and we do not know'. They do not bear further children, but otherwise it is assumed they live human-like lives. They talk among themselves and discuss the activities of the living: 'now our child gives us food, and we are glad'.

There are no beliefs in heaven or hell, nor of any belief of award or punishment after death for the life lived on earth. Offences and sins are punished while the offender is still alive, or, if he has died, punishment falls on his living kin. There are no beliefs in reincarnation nor in any mystical connexion between a certain ancestor and a certain descendant, for example a grandson, of the kind often met with elsewhere. Certain people are thought to

become animals, or more accurately their souls are thought sometimes to occupy the bodies of animals, after death. But this is an
attribute of certain people as holders of specific statuses and has
nothing to do with reincarnation. Such are rainmakers, who may
become leopards at death. This is an attribute that helps to
describe and make understandable his status and power. The
leopard is a symbol of 'slowness' and dignity. A leopard is like a
chief, not a chief like a leopard. The belief is like that of witches
using certain night animals as vehicles; it is a general attribute of
a particular status.[1]

The dead are buried in certain ways, but as far as I know this
has nothing to do with preparation for a future life. Although
much of the symbolism associated with burial has significance with
respect to changes in status of the man from living to dead, there
is certainly no overt idea of preparing the body or the soul for an
after-life. Neither the posture of the corpse nor the objects which
are buried with it have any purpose of this sort.

I wish here to describe, very briefly, Lugbara notions as to the
composition of man, since they are relevant to what follows. A
man has a body (*ɽua*). When he dies and is buried his corpse (*avu*)
is put into its grave and there rots; it 'goes' nowhere. After death
the physical body loses importance and graves are soon forgotten,
except that those of senior men and women are marked with a fig
tree (*larɨ*) which later bears the name of the dead person and is part
of the complex of external lineage shrines of a minimal lineage.
But otherwise the grave site is soon hoed and planted over.

When alive the body contains breath (*ava*).[2] At death the breath
leaves the body and 'just goes', no one knows or cares whither.
It 'wanders here on the surface of the earth and does nothing',
nothing, that is, to affect the living. *Ava* is the breath as sign of
life, not its essence. Once life has gone then the breath is lost and
no longer of significance.

Breath is sometimes equated with the concept of *orindi*, but they

---

[1] The Moru, a closely related people, are said to have totemic beliefs (Nalder,
A Tribal Survey of Mongalla Province, pp. 157ff.). But I have found no trace of
such beliefs in Lugbara. The nearest are the taboos on eating certain foods such
as mushrooms, which are accepted by certain clans. But these are not totemic.
They refer to legends that are used to distinguish sub-clans which are parts of
a former clan, the fission being explained in terms of disputes over food.

[2] This word is used for air which makes a noise while going in or out of its
container (as when being pumped into a tyre). The word for 'air' in general is
oli ('wind').

are usually distinct. Breath is in the lungs, *orindi* is in the heart, and it makes the heart swell and contract. *Ava* and *orindi* leave the body together at death, but are distinct. I translate *orindi* as 'soul'.[1] It is not an impermanent thing, but survives after death and can affect and contact living men. It is not thought to enter the body at birth, but 'just comes'. It cannot be seen and is 'like the wind'. It is said to go to God in the sky after death, and later to be contacted by a diviner and then to come to the shrines and live under the earth, beneath the compound floor.

Before contact it may come to earth, especially at night, and is to be seen in dreams. If a man dreams of his dead father then it is his soul which is seeing his father's soul come down to earth, 'to walk about'. If a man dreams of a living person he says 'my soul met with so and so's, in a dream', and it is a pleasant thing if they are normally friends. But to dream of a bad person, someone with whom a man is quarrelling, a stranger, a man who changes face, or of any of the night animals associated with witches, is an evil omen (*o'dụ*), a sign that sickness, death or witchcraft are coming to the home. But the soul is not an evil thing in itself, and it is only seeing the soul of an evil person or creature that is an evil omen.

The soul can thus become visible, and I have heard it said that in the still of the night the souls of a man's dead kin may be heard grunting and muttering to one another; they meet near the huts and shrines to discuss their living kin. The soul can think and behave wilfully and consciously. It is often said that children have no souls, and certainly those of women are not as powerful as are those of men. This reflects their lack of authority when alive. The soul has responsibility, especially in kinship matters, and neither women nor children are fully responsible human beings.

Besides breath and a soul a man has a shadow (*endrilendri*). It is sometimes said that the shadow and the soul are 'the same as' or 'together with' one another, and that souls, when visible, have no shadows. Also witches can harm their victims by treading on their shadows.

The soul may appear at night in a dream, and also in the day-time if only recently dead and not yet contacted by a diviner. But if a long dead ancestor is seen in the daytime, it is a spectre (*atṛ*). A spectre is an evil omen, especially of disaster sent by God, such

[1] Linguistically it is a compound of the words *ori*, ghost, and the intensive particle, *-ndi*: so that it means 'the essence of the ghost'.

as lightning. A spectre may appear in a whirlwind (*oliriku*), which is also said to be a manifestation of God. But these concepts are vague and unimportant.

Lastly a man possesses *adro* and *tali*. I translate these as 'guardian spirit' and 'personality' respectively. They are given to each man at birth by God, and are associated with divine power. The personality is in the brain and the heart, *culu*, which is together with the *asi*.[1] Only men have personalities. *Tali* is attributed to a man according to his actions during his life and it tends to increase as does his social status in the community. It is associated mainly, however, with his own actions, apart from his lineage status, and so is seen as due to the power of God, who is above and outside considerations of lineage position. *Tali* is a word used in other contexts also: it refers to the mystical power given by God to rainmakers and diviners, and is used to refer to those places at which divine power has been manifest to men (as at the snake oracle of the prophet Rembe, which I discuss in Chapter V). *Tali* refers to the manifestation of the power of God in his transcendent, creative, 'good' aspect. *Adro* refers to that of God in his immanent, 'bad' aspect. I have heard it said that 'a man has *adro* and *tali* because men were made by God in the sky.' They are the signs of his divine creation. At death the *adro* leaves a man (it may not dwell inside him but is 'in the home' near him) and goes to dwell in the streams with God in his 'bad aspect; there it becomes part of a collectivity of 'God's children' (*Adroanzi*) and is said to be 'in the bush' (*asea*). The *tali*, however, is not associated with a man as an ancestor, as it is not associated with lineage status, and goes to dwell with God in the sky.

Lugbara notions as to the moral nature of man are not very explicit. Babies are not social beings, and have no souls; they have neither authority nor responsibility. As men grow adult their authority and responsibility increase into old age and ancestorhood; those of women are always less than those of men. In Lugbara myth, which I discuss in chapter V, there is the implication that before the creation of Lugbara society by the hero-ancestors men were asocial and amoral. They were without kin and without kinship authority and responsibility. Clients are like this today, as they come from outside society and are 'things', without kin ties; as they acquire kin links they become social and

---

[1] *Culu* is the anatomical organ, *asi* the seat of the emotions.

moral members of a new field of social relations. Men are in general responsible creatures, who recognize norms of orderly behaviour towards one another, the dead and God. As their status increases, especially after death, so they become more responsible: the dead are thought of as being beneficent and kindly senior kin. But a man may deliberately abuse the authority that he exercises as a responsible member of a kin-group or neighbourhood. He is then a witch, a man who reverts to an asocial, amoral, 'natural' and evil type of behaviour. I discuss witches later in this book; here it is enough to say that they are men who pervert their powers to their own selfish ends.

III. ANCESTORS AND GHOSTS

The 'ancestors' are not physical entities. To express their nature, and their significance for the living in the various situations in which they come into contact with them, Lugbara use certain terms. These express what might be called different aspects or qualities of the status of ancestor, relevant in different contexts in the relationship between living and dead. A difficulty for the observer is that the concepts denoted by these terms are not explicitly defined by Lugbara: definition is possible only by analysis of the situations in which they are significant. The most important of these concepts are those denoted by the terms *a'bi* and *ori*. It is to ancestors in one or other of these aspects that most sacrifices are made.

A'bi is a term used for all the forebears of a person through whatever lines of descent. Lugbara know that their ancestors are many, and no one man knows the names of more than a limited number of the ancestors of his clan, let alone of those related to him through women. He knows only those who are significant to him as points of reference for the articulation of descent groups. But all, whether known by name or not, are 'ancestors'. The word *a'bi* is used also for certain living kin, both as a term of reference and of address. These kin are the mother's father and wife's father, and the term is used for classificatory kin also. It is often used, as a term of reference, to include the father's father, but he is addressed as *baba*. This is to say, *a'bi* is used for the forebears or progenitors of any line of descent of *ego* or *ego's* children. I shall translate the term as 'ancestor', since in the situations described in this book this is the most common meaning, and alternatives such as 'forbear' or 'progenitor' are less adequate translations of it. The concept includes the notion of 'progenitor', but it includes also that of a kinsman to whom is due respect, deference and obedience. 'Respect' (*rụ*) is at the centre of the attitude towards anyone referred to as *a'bị*, whether living or dead. They might appropriately, though cumbersomely, be called 'the respected ones'.

Ancestors thus include all the dead and living forebears of *ego's* lineage down to *ego's* son's generation. They are both male and female and include both those who have begotten or borne children and also those who have died childless.[1] The dead among them are important in ritual as the objects of sacrifice. These are thought of as forming a collectivity, in which individual ancestors are not significant *qua* individuals. They send sickness to the living, but they send it collectively, and shrines are erected for them as collectivities also.

Shrines are also erected for *ori*, and these are the more important. Ancestors are thought of as *ori* when individual shrines are placed for them by agnatic or uterine descendants; it is said that an *ori* shrine cannot be placed for a man who has no male children. An ancestor with such a shrine does not change his status from *a'bị* to *ori*: the extra status of *ori* is acquired by him while he continues, in other contexts, to be *a'bị* as well. The essence of the status of *ori* is that he is an individual ancestor, who is in personal and responsible contact with living descendants. *Orindi* (the soul) is the essence of the *ori*, and the soul is a representation of the socially responsible *persona* of a living person. Only adult men and old women are believed invariably to have souls. Ancestors as a collectivity can send sickness to the living, and are said to do so if offended by lack of respect and consideration by their descendants. But *ori* are said actually to listen to the words of their living kin, to know their thoughts and to observe their actions. It is especially the more recently dead *ori* who do this; the individual relationships between them and the living that they had while alive are continued after their deaths. *Ori* are individual ancestors in certain

[1] The verb *tị* means both to beget and to bear children. It also is used to refer to succession to status, for example a man's succession to the status of his brother. In Lugbara thought a childless ancestor may thus be in the line of succession to lineage status, even though he was not a forebear in the strict physical sense. I should add here that Lugbara do not practise ghost marriage.

situations which are significant in relation to responsible kinship behaviour and authority. Lugbara use different terms for these concepts and I wish to do the same. I call *a'bi* 'ancestor' and *ori* 'ghost'. This is at variance with common English usage, in which all the dead, or their spirits, are ghosts. In my usage all ghosts are ancestors but not all ancestors are ghosts.[1]

The ghosts are those ancestors who are remembered in genealogies, or at least the more important of these; whereas the ancestors include all the ancestors, whether their names are remembered or not. The ghosts' position in genealogies does not mean that they are remembered as individuals and their personal qualities while alive attributed to them when dead. But it means that they are given as the apical ancestors of segments and lines of descent, and are so seen as having been 'big' men. It is axiomatic that such men were responsible and conscientious: even those who have recently died are so considered, in spite of the fact that in some cases I was told that while alive they were not greatly respected. I was told that while alive a man may not be respected by his son, or at least may not be obeyed by him, because the son wishes to acquire the father's status for himself. 'But this is because sons do not respect their fathers, who are "big" men.' It is also said that a man puts shrines for his dead father 'because he respects him'—the contradiction is a situational one and needs no explanation for Lugbara. It follows that a ghost, who is defined by his having a shrine for himself, is a respected ancestor and so also a responsible one.

IV. GHOST INVOCATION

Men come into contact with the dead primarily at the rite of sacrifice. The dead affect men by sending sickness to them to express displeasure at actions considered to weaken the harmony and unity of the lineage and the local group based upon it; these are the actions considered to be sins. As a response the living make offerings to the dead at shrines set up for them. The shrine is the local focus of the relationship between living and dead members of the agnatic lineage. Today some homesteads, where the head of

---

[1] I could call *a'bi* 'ancestors' and *ori* 'ancestor spirits', since *orindi* might be translated 'spirit' as well as 'soul'. But I think it better to keep the word spirit to refer to manifestations of divinity.

the household is a Christian, have no shrines. An elder said to me, speaking of such people:

These people are not real Lugbara. Have they no ancestors? Do they not respect them? Do they not even respect their fathers while they are alive? What will happen to their children if they do not respect their fathers?

And another elder, a Catholic, said:

I do not 'cut' at the shrines of my lineage. But when my people 'cut', I sit near, since it is my work to 'cut' meat. Some say these things are of Satan, but that is not true. They are good, the things of our ancestors.

The values that are at the centre of social life, those of kinship and the lineage, are sustained in the cult of the dead.

I have said that the ghosts are the more important in Lugbara ritual. Sacrifices to them are more frequent than others and are of living animals, whereas those to ancestors and other agents are usually of grain or dried meat; their shrines are placed in the centre of the homestead, and Lugbara talk of the ghosts more often than they do of ancestors when discussing ritual. The relationship between the living and the ghosts is a latent one; it is made actual or immediately significant for the living, in two ways. They are known as *ole ro*, to which I refer as the process of ghost invocation, and *ori ka*, to which I refer as that as ghostly vengeance. Literally *ole ro* is to 'bring sickness (because of) indignation', the bringing of sickness referring to the action on the part of a living person who invokes his ghosts to bring sickness to one of his kin or dependants whose behaviour he wishes to control. *Ori ka* is 'the ghost brings sickness' on its own account, without prior invocation; it may be said that the 'ghost shrine brings sickness' (*orijo ka*). Sickness comes from the ghosts, in their shrines under the granaries, through the operation of these processes. In the case of ghost invocation the sickness is caused by someone invoking his ghosts. The ritual guardian of the sick person consults the oracles to discover the identity of the agent concerned and the cause of his anger, and the oracles also state whether sacrifice is to be made and of what it should consist. The sacrificial object for ghosts is usually an animal; it is consecrated and dedicated to them, with a promise to sacrifice if the patient should recover from his sickness. If he does not recover, then the oracle was mistaken and there is no point in making the sacrifice. If he does recover the sacrifice is made at the shrines, the meat shared among the members of a congregation, the patient anointed and blessed, and the matter is regarded as closed.

The typical situation of ghost invocation was given to me on many occasions in words such as

> Ghost invocation is like this: a man cries to the ghosts that his son is bad, and they hear his words and send sickness to strike that son.

This, the father invoking his ghosts against his child, is always the example given. I was told that in face of an insult or offence by a dependant a man makes no open move; he should stay silent.

> Then this man goes home. He sits and thinks: 'if I complain at the shrines, the ghosts will do that son of mine much harm.' So he sits and thinks, but he does not say words at the shrines. But the ghosts, his father and his father's father, see him sitting and see his heart is heavy and that he wails. They think among themselves and bring sickness to that son. To say words with the mouth at the shrines is bad. If a man, or an elder says words thus, his child will surely die. If he does not say words the child becomes sick and learns to obey his father, but he will not die. If he does die people will grumble and blame his father. Then the father would think later: 'I did badly to ask the ghosts to bring trouble to my son' and he must give two bulls to the child's mother's brother, because those people there are angry because he harmed their sister's child. These are the cattle called *avuta* (corpse things).

A man invokes the ghosts against a kinsman whom he considers to have committed a sin, and he 'thinks these words in his heart' in his hut at night while he lies thinking about the matter or sitting near the granaries in the daytime. He thinks about it quite deliberately; if he merely muses idly while elsewhere or discusses it with friends over beer, this is said not to be ghost invocation. It may lead to 'bad luck' (*drilonzi*), 'striking' the offender, but that is another matter. Because invocation is thought and not said aloud, I do not use the word 'curse' for it. A curse is a deliberate utterance of words against an offender, and especially it includes the words 'you will see' or 'we shall see'.

For an elder to invoke is part of his expected role. He conceals his action until sickness seizes the offender, and when oracles point out his part in the affair will acknowledge it. Indeed, it is usually he who puts the case to the oracles and so actually suggests

himself as responsible, although Lugbara do not see the importance of this aspect of oracles. Certain actions are expected to lead
to the process being set in motion. After a long quarrel between
Abaloo, an unruly and conceited young man who had become a
government headman and had shamed his seniors by lording it
over them as the chief's local representative, and his dead father's
brother, Ozua, a man of considerable importance and prestige,
I was told:

> Now Abaloo has shamed his 'father' on many occasions. Now Ozua
> has gone to the ghost shrines to cry to the ghosts and to Abaloo's father,
> his brother. But sickness has not yet taken that child. So Ozua has not
> yet told people because at first you hide those words.

The assumption was made that after such a quarrel it is incumbent
for the senior kinsman to invoke his ghosts, although there is no
way of knowing whether he really does so consciously. Since the
process in fact comes into being only after an oracular diagnosis of
the sickness that occurs some time after the action that is said to
have led to invocation, a specific case of invocation cannot be
discussed before then. I have asked men who were in the position
of Ozua whether they intended to invoke the ghosts, and have been
told 'perhaps; it is good that I should do so', but since a man does
not know whether he has succeeded in invoking the ghosts over
a specific offence until the sickness appears and the oracles point
to him as responsible, it is clear that some such answer is the only
one possible. A man later remembers that he had been thinking
about the offence and concludes that he had invoked the ghosts,
but he cannot know at the time of his anger whether or not he has
succeeded in doing so. If later the oracles point to him, then he
can in all honesty admit to having invoked the ghosts by the mere
fact of his having been angry in his homestead. Since invocation
is done by 'thinking' and not by 'saying the words by mouth',
there is no contradiction. In many cases of which I know a man
had both threatened the offender and has also mentioned this to
a close kinsman. The latter later remembers this and the name
of the man concerned is among those first put to the oracles and
may easily be accepted by them. However, I remember two or
three cases in which the oracles pointed out men who were clearly
taken aback at the diagnosis and who argued, saying that the
oracles had lied—always an accepted possibility. They were not

willing to admit that they had put their feelings into action. As I
show later, and as the statement quoted on page 36 shows also,
there is considerable ambivalence in the position of a man who
invokes the ghosts against his own son.

Lugbara do not say what is the actual power of invocation, nor
how it develops in a man, except that his father should be dead.
Details of this sort are not directly relevant to the process of which
ghost invocation is a link. Although even a child may have the
power, if his father is dead, it is mainly old men who exercise it.
It is akin to the power of witchcraft in that the older a man is the
more likely he is to have it; and indeed as I show in chapter IV
an old man who invokes too often will easily be considered to be
a witch. A man of great personality is likely to invoke and to be
heard by the ghosts. It is the man whose status is such that insult
to him is seriously disruptive to the family-cluster who is thought
to need to do so. It is clear that such a belief needs no elaboration:
it is the situation that defines the invoker, as it is the situation
that defines a witch, rather than any intrinsic characteristics.

The motive for a man's invoking the ghosts is the sentiment
called *ole*. This is difficult to translate by a single word but the
nearest is perhaps 'indignation'. *Ole* is usually defined by Lugbara
as the sentiment aroused by seeing a man eating rich food, with
succulent relishes, and who does not invite one to share with him.
Or the feeling of seeing a rival at a dance showing off his agility
and impressing girls while one is standing at the edge of the circle
alone. It is this same sentiment that motivates witches, as I shall
show in a later chapter. So that in this sense it might be translated
as 'envy'. But 'envy' is not sufficient for the sentiment that is
supposed to be felt by an elder invoking the ghosts against a
dependant. He does so because he is outraged, in his role as head
of the kin group and *not* as an individual, at the anti-social behaviour of the offender. His authority as an elder has been flouted
and the kinship relationship of which this is a part has been
weakened. If the invoker is not an elder he is outraged at behaviour
towards him that is unfitting from a kinsman. The sort of action
that leads to *ole* is striking or fighting with a kinsman older than
oneself—this is perhaps the worst offence possible, and although
it is comparatively uncommon it is frequently given as the example
of an offence that leads to ghost invocation; to swear or shout at a
kinsman; to deceive a close kinsman by stealing or cheating or

lying; to quarrel with a kinsman; for a woman to quarrel with her husband, or to strike him or deny him the exercise of the rights he holds in her; for a man to fail to carry out the duties of a guardian or heir. They are all offences which affect the social relations that are at the basis of orderly family and community life, and the non-observance of which brings a man 'shame'.

A person is said to have ghosts invoked against him because he 'destroys, the words of the home' (*'buru*). *'Buru* is the word for home or homestead in its social rather than physical sense. The purpose of ghost invocation may be seen in the statement that the work of an elder is 'to purify the territory (of the lineage), so that the home may be all clean' (*angu edezu, 'buru ma ovu alaru*). I have been told

> The work of an elder is to keep the territory without trouble, so that the home may be clean, so that death, sickness and 'evil words' do not enter into the homesteads and people live peacefully and quietly. Then their wives will have children and they will be many there together.

'Evil words' (*e'yo onzi*) refer especially to witchcraft, part of the elders duty being to see that rancour and quarrels are controlled so that witchcraft does not appear. The statement continues

> It is good that an elder invokes his ghosts against his disobedient 'sons', who do not follow his words. A man stands in place of his (dead) father, and if a wife or child does him ill he will cry to that father and trouble will seize that child. This is good. This is what we call *ole*. *Ole* does not destroy the land. It is bad for a man to strike with his hand, or with his spear; now the ghosts strike on his behalf. These are the words of the lineage. . . . See, a client cannot invoke the ghosts; he has no clan. But I, and that elder there . . . we have our kinsmen, and it is good that we invoke the ghosts against our sons.

It seems correct to translate *ole* as a feeling of indignation or outrage at sins or immoral behaviour, using 'immoral' in a limited sense to refer to behaviour directed against recognition of orderly ties of kinship and lineage.

V. THE RANGE OF INVOCATION

In the typical example usually given by Lugbara—apart from actual situations—it is the elder of a family cluster who invokes

the ghosts against certain of his close kin and dependants, especially against a disobedient 'son'. However, it is not only elders who
may invoke the ghosts, although it is certainly they who are said
to do so more than other people and most cases of invocation
demonstrated by oracles have elders as invokers. Any man whose
father is dead may do so: when his father is dead he may erect
ghost shrines and so acquires the power to invoke ghosts as part
of his new status of head of a family segment. With this position
of authority goes the accepted right to invoke ghosts against a
dependant who arouses the sentiment of *ole* by his unseemly
behaviour. The ghost cult is essentially a lineage cult, but in the
context of authority and invocation it is the family cluster based
upon a minimal lineage that is a ritual unit. It is subsumed into
the network of ties that compose the field of lineage relations, as
indeed the taking by a local group of the name of its dominant
lineage would lead us to expect.

The ritual unit is at the centre of the congregation that assembles
for the sacrifice that follows ghostly sickness. This congregation
is composed of kin; and it is the immediate kin that are concerned
in invocation. The range of relevant kin varies in different situations, and in that of invocation it is narrower than in that of
sacrifice to the ghosts. In the former situation the kin who may be
invoked against by an elder include his sons and daughters, his
wives and his sons' wives and children, his brothers and their
wives and children, his sisters, and his mother if she is a widow
living under her son's protection. All these ties include classificatory kin within the minimal lineage. He may also invoke against
a sister's children and a daughter's children. Usually it is agreed
that he should not invoke against them if they are living elsewhere,
although he may invoke against a married daughter living with
her husband at his home 'because he married her mother with his
wealth and begot her.' Other close kin within the minimal lineage
may be added, such as a father's brother. The range of invocation
is said to be limited by kinship through 'blood'; unrelated clients
living under a man's protection are controlled by the threat of
violence and not by mystical means. A ghost is said to be able to
affect its living kin through both men and women, and women
under the domestic authority of close 'blood' kin are included.
Most cases of ghost invocation occur within the family cluster;
and the process is definitely connected in Lugbara thought with

the maintenance of authority within the cluster, in particular when it is set into motion by an elder.

Sickness is directed against an individual, not against a group as a whole. But the offender may not himself suffer sickness. It may fall upon a member of his family who is junior to him—a son, daughter, wife or junior sibling. If the offender is a woman, sickness may fall upon a child or sibling, but not on her husband.

A man rarely invokes against male agnates who live outside his own family cluster. He may do so against female agnates and kin traced through them by 'blood', but to do so is to invade the sphere of authority of another elder and is not done without ample justification. Much depends on the personal relationship between the elders, but it is rare for them to be on such terms as to permit this cross-invocation. I know of no case at first hand, but have heard of cases occurring and leading to much argument, dispute and sometimes counter-invocation between the elders. I was told that if an elder invokes his ghosts against a sister's son elsewhere the sister's son's own elder will

be angry and say 'That mother's brother is bad, why does he invoke ghosts against my son?'. Then the mother's brother says 'Those are not my words, it was my ghosts which brought sickness' (that is, without being invoked by himself). The other elder says 'No, you have said evil words, it is your fault. Long ago you ate my bridewealth, now why do you bring trouble on my child like this?' Then the brothers-in-law, (applied to all men of the two lineages) quarrel, but that mother's brother fears and thinks to his ghosts 'They quarrel at my words. Now, my ghosts, help that sister's son to get well, then he will come by and by to give you food at your shrines'.

The point is that such invocation has nothing to do with the maintenance of authority within the family cluster. A man who is insulted by his sister's son over some personal matter should not invoke ghosts: there are other and accepted ways of bringing sickness to an individual kinsman outside this particular context, which I discuss later. A man has a legitimate reason to invoke against a sister's son if the latter is an attached kinsman at his mother's brother's homestead; and in this case it is only the elder's duty to invoke the ghosts, not the concern of other men of the host group.

A man invokes ghosts against a sister's child as part of the kinship relationship between them. It is said that a man would rarely invoke against a sister herself. But a man may invoke against his daughter or his daughter's child (who is really a substitute for the daughter) in the homestead of her husband, which is typically in the territory of an unrelated lineage. This is done either if bridewealth has not been transferred, or if enough has not been given, or, less commonly, if she or her husband's people do not observe the rules of affinal etiquette as regards regular visiting and sending of gifts of food and beer. A man cannot invoke against his son-in-law, since he is not related by blood and 'because you are friends and you gave him your daughter.' But the daughter and her children are close kin by blood. It is said that the result of invocation against a married daughter is that she has insufficient milk to suckle her children—and so it affects the health of the members of the guilty lineage, her children. The invoker is acting in his role of head of the lineage in that he is concerned to ensure the transfer of cattle with which his sons will later get their wives and children; and to a lesser extent he is acting as leader of the kin-group in a situation that might develop into one of fighting—most fighting is over bridewealth and women; he is thus protecting his lineage against the possible death of its members in feud. The case differs from those that occur within the family cluster and are concerned primarily with domestic authority; and this is reflected in the fact that the sickness is lifted by the father merely asking his ghosts to do so. Ghostly sickness is usually removed by sacrifice, but in Lugbara sacrifice is associated with a congregation of kin assembled to remove sickness and discord within the group; such sacrifice would be inappropriate in this situation.

Both invocation against a son's wife and against a married daughter's child are recognized to be ways in which men whose children have married may score off one another. Such men call one another 'my friend' most punctiliously and act in a formally friendly manner. This involves the giving of beer to each other, which often leads to an open competition as to who can supply the most beer in order to shame the other. It is said that they call each other 'my friend'

because always you stay together with him. You sit together to talk if you visit each other. You fear to quarrel with him, since it brings great shame.

This is one facet to some cases of invocation against a son's wife or against a daughter's child. It is one of the few ways in which pressure can be brought to bear upon an affinally related lineage to fulfil their bridewealth obligations, or in which displeasure may be shown at the way in which they have carried out the marriage negotiations, without coming to open fighting, which is the last resort in situations of this kind.

Invocation is in most cases by an elder, and in any event it is usually done by an adult man who is head of a family-segment. But it may be performed by a minor, and still be motivated by the approved sentiment of *ole*. Any male whose father is dead may invoke the ghosts; even a child may do so against an old man. It is rare, since such a child, while still unmarried, is 'still at home'; he is not yet fully socially responsible. But since a child may formally inherit widows—if old and past child-bearing, at any rate, they may go to a child—there is nothing in Lugbara theory to prevent a child from holding formal status as head of a family segment. A man in Mbaraka was the successor to his dead brother's status and was the guardian of his brother's infant son, for whom he had left sufficient cattle with which the child could later obtain a wife. The brother used these cattle to obtain another wife for himself. Later he became sick and it was said by the oracles that his dead brother's son had invoked his father's ghost against his uncle. The child was then about ten years old, and it was said that he was motivated by the sentiment of *ole* because his uncle, in abusing his powers of guardianship, was destroying the unity of the family group. It might have been expected that the dead man would have brought sickness upon his brother himself, but it was said to be a case of ghost invocation by the boy because he had told others that he was angry with his uncle and that he would try to invoke his dead father's ghost. The father had been dead for several years and had become a ghost in that time—that is, the son had had to place a shrine for him on account of other sickness and so he actually possessed a shrine in his homestead, where he was looked after by his own mother, a woman past child-bearing. The child thus had a formal status in the kinship system as the head of an incipient line of descent and so could represent it ritually. To invoke against his father's brother was to use the right means of countering the latter's abuse of his powers as a senior kinsman of the same minimal lineage. It was not regarded as being any kind of insolence on the part of the boy. As in all cases of invocation, the personalities of the people concerned are important: in this case the brother who had used the cattle for himself was a bad tempered and unpopular man, unlike his dead brother, who was universally respected.

Women may also invoke the ghosts. A woman may place shrines if her mother is dead, and she invokes her own mother, her mother's mother and her mother's sisters. The agnatic lineage is thus not significant in invocation by women. It is rare, but I know of two cases, both by old women who invoked their dead mothers against their sons who had struck them, a terrible offence. I was told that in one of these cases the woman invoked against her son 'to show him her words; he had brought shame upon her and upon his home'; that is, the invocation was considered to be concerned with lineage well-being rather than with the personal affront to his mother. Lugbara say that a woman may invoke the ghosts against her children and younger siblings only. Even if she has left her natal home to go to her husband she may invoke them against siblings still at home or married elsewhere in their turn. Thus actual distance is not a factor. Invocation by women is not very important. Men deal with matters that affect the lineage and women with household affairs only. In both these cases the invoking women were important in status—one was an only child, without brothers, and the other the eldest sister of a family. They were assumed therefore to have lineage interests at heart and not to have acted merely from personal anger. Also they were old, past child-bearing, and so 'like men'. But their invocation was not thought to merit large sacrifices with a numerous congregation: the matter was not concerned with lineage alignments as are cases of invocation by men.

VI. GHOSTLY VENGEANCE

The lineage consists of both living and dead, and lineage authority is thought to be exercised by the dead as well as the living, their representatives. That the authority with which ghostly sickness is concerned is essentially lineage authority may be seen from the process of ghostly vengeance. This is the bringing of sickness by the ghosts on their own account, without invocation, if their living kin neglect them by not placing meat and beer at

their shrines for a long time. The dead are said to murmur together 'Our child is bad, he does not care for us now', and they
cause sickness to visit him. It is said that the dead watch one
anothers' offerings jealously, 'as our elders do'—the motives
attributed to the dead are those attributed to the living too.

A ghost watches a man giving food at sacrifice to him. A brother
of that ghost begs food of him. The other will laugh and say 'Have you
no sons?' Then he thinks 'Why does my child not give me food? If he
does not give me food soon I shall send sickness to him.' Then later
that man is seized by sickness, or his wife and his children. The sickness
is that of the ghosts, to grow thin and to ache throughout the body;
these are the sicknesses of the dead. You go to the rubbing-stick oracle,
and it says 'Your father is sending sickness (*ka*). He wants to eat food
of yours. For many days you have not given him food, now he is begging
food from you'. People do not grumble at the ghosts, because it is the
living man who is selfish. He makes a sacrifice and the dead are joyful.
He gives them beer, a he-goat, or a bull.

This is how Lugbara describe the process, but there is a difference between this account and actuality. Lugbara describe an
ideal, in sociological isolation; but in reality the offerings made as
a consequence of ghostly vengeance are made within a social
context of disputes over lineage authority. A small offering is
placed on the ghost shrines at every meal, a child usually being
sent with a piece of the cooked food; and at a beer-drink beer may
be poured on the stones also. This is not 'sacrifice' (*owi*), and there
is no congregation as there is at a proper sacrifice. A sacrifice is not
made except for a specific purpose in response to a specific case
of sickness of which the agent is said by the oracles to be a ghost.
In fact it is the living members of the lineage who may grumble
in this way ('as our elders do') and it is thought that the ghosts
then hear them. This is not invocation, which is a deliberate and
conscious 'thinking' by a man near the shrines. In ghostly vengeance the living are thought merely to talk or to grumble among
themselves about the behaviour of a kinsman, and the dead then
hear them and take the decision to send sickness themselves, as a
result of their own discussion and not at the specific request of the
living. The point of the difference is that in ghost invocation a
man takes the responsibility upon himself for causing sickness,
even though indirectly. In ghostly vengeance it is the dead who are
believed to be responsible for the decision, and they make it upon

the grumbling of many people and not on the invocation of a single person: responsibility is thus shared both among the dead and among a group of living kin.

VII. GHOST SHRINES

The shrines, in and near the compounds, are the visible foci of the relationship between living and dead. Each type of shrine, that is the shrine for a particular ancestor, ghost or spirit,[1] has its own specific name. Shrines in general are called 'pieces of granite' (*eramva*). They are of various shapes and sizes, found on the ground and near outcrops of rock in all parts of the country, and are 'just stones'. They may be shaped roughly or set up as they are found. But once erected and used for sacrifice they become shrines and acquire a sacred character as the huts for their incumbents, as I shall call the ancestor, ghost or spirit who may occupy them. They are 'the things of men', and women have little to do with them. A shrine never loses sacredness, and if still in use will be moved to the new site of a compound, whereas other pieces of granite, such as those that support the granaries, may be discarded.

In the compounds of a family cluster there are several different shrines. The most important, those of the ghosts, are placed under the main granary. This is 'the granary of the ghosts' and is that for eleusine, the traditional staple. Other shrines are under the eaves of the senior wife's hut, inside the huts, in the compound hedge, in the nearby cattle kraal, on the paths, and lastly the external lineage shrines, the 'biggest' and the most sacred, are hidden away in the long grass and bush, where only the elders who hold rights in them may see them.

The shrines of the agnatic ghosts are called 'ghost huts' (*orijo*) or merely 'ghosts' (*ori*). Their construction varies considerably but they are always made of small granite slabs. These may merely be placed flat on the ground so as to form a kind of paving, or each shrine may be built as a 'house' of five stones carefully fitted together to form four walls and a roof. Sometimes they are built as miniature round huts with roofs of stone or even thatch. They are usually kept swept and clean, although outside ritual occasions

---

[1] I discuss spirit shrines in Chapter V. They are placed for forces which are manifestations of the power of God.

they may become overgrown and chickens, goats and children wander over them unconcernedly. Differences in shape of these shrines is not significant except as an index of the degree of cultural variation in Lugbara. The building of shrines in a certain way in one area is seen by the people as a sign of their distinct identity and of their being the centre of 'true' Lugbara culture.

Usually each shrine is for a particular ghost—'one stone one person'—although at sacrifices blood, meat and beer are scattered over all of them. Often, especially in southern Lugbara, one shrine may house two ghosts, either brothers or father and son. The actual means by which the ghosts use their shrines and take the offerings made to them there is considered unimportant and is not known. Lugbara do not regard discussion of such matters as fruitful; any questions on these subjects meet with the invariable reply of 'How do we know these things? Only our ancestors know them.' Lugbara say that a certain ghost is 'in' his shrine. It is difficult to determine the exact sense in which this is meant; it is certainly not meant literally. Nor is it merely that a ghost occupies his shrine only at the time of sacrifice. He is there always, in the sense that he is believed to 'know' what goes on near the shrine, as when an elder invokes him or when he hears many of his living kin grumbling about one of their number. A ghost may have more than one shrine, in different compounds, so that no single one is considered to be his home. Ghosts live 'in the ground', but they are also 'in' their shrines and can be contacted there.

These shrines are placed for the ghosts of lineage ancestors rarely further back than the inner lineage founder. The more remote ancestors have other shrines, the external lineage shrines outside the compounds. The ghosts who are more frequently invoked and who are considered to bring sickness are the recently dead, who may be still remembered by the living. They are the fathers, grandfathers and their brothers; more distant ghosts are not so troublesome. It is said that just as a father disciplines his son and expects respect from him, so does a man expect his dead father to take a close interest in his activities, whereas other ghosts are not especially concerned. A man 'fears' his father and is always willing to believe that he is acting harshly and unjustly towards him. This attitude tends to be exaggerated in the case of a classificatory 'father'. More ghostly sickness is said to come from a man's own dead father than from other dead kin; but sacrifice is made to all the ghosts in all the shrines under one granary and not merely to the one responsible for a specific case of sickness. The role of the father's ghost needs to be qualified in the light of this fact. Just as a living elder is the living representative of his juniors, as intermediary for them with the dead, so the youngest dead senior kinsman is the intermediary between dead and living. He may be the one who brings sickness, but he does so in his role as intermediary—Lugbara compare him to a chief's court messenger in this respect—rather than out of personal grievance. This is the theory; in practice he is more likely to be thought to have a grievance since he personally knows the living. A man Okwaya told me that if his elder brother Olimani, the head of his family segment, invoked against his son, the oracle might say:

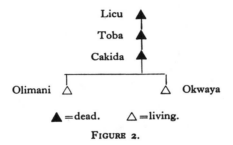

FIGURE 2.

O Okwaya, your child is sick. Olimani has cried to the ghosts and they have brought sickness. Olimani has cried 'My child has done me ill.' Cakida hears and cries likewise and Toba hears. Then Toba cries to Licu. Then that Licu listens and thinks slowly and says that they should send sickness. These words are like the words of government. You go before the headman and he says 'You do ill.' Then you are taken to the sub-chief and he says 'You do ill.' Then you go before the county chief and he says 'You do ill.' Then you get a fine. It is like this with the ghosts also.

The more senior ghosts are said to bring less sickness than junior ghosts because they delegate to their juniors the task of watching over the living.

The agnatic ghost shrines are of two types, properly called *orijo ambòru* ('big ghost shrine') and *orijo andesia*; *andesia* means 'I refuse to give' because only the sacrificer eats, without a ritual congregation among which sacrificial meat is shared as at the 'big' shrine. In everyday speech the former are usually called *orijo* and the latter *andesia*, although there are several variant names. Lugbara have told me that they are like elder and younger brothers, and I shall refer to them as senior and junior internal ghost shrines respectively. The relationship of ghost to shrine is not one of one ghost to each shrine. The same ghost may occupy both senior and junior shrines; that is, a shrine for a specific ghost may be found among both the senior and junior ghost shrines of the same family. Since every segment of a family cluster has its own shrines a particular ghost may have several shrines of both types in the various homesteads of a single cluster. The ghosts will move from one to another, and are thought to like to do this and to visit their shrines in turn. Part of the work of oracles is to discover their whims in this respect.

The relationship between these shrines is based on difference of lineage status of their owners. The 'owner' is the person who erects and has general ritual interest in a shrine in or attached to his own homestead. He may not necessarily make the actual sacrifice at it—many people own shrines at which sacrifice may be made only by elders—but it is thought of as his. He is the 'owner' or 'possessor' (*eipi*), a term used for the owner of livestock or wives, that is, who has general rights in them as against other people.

A man places a ghost shrine only when his father is dead. Before that sacrifices on his behalf are made at his father's shrines. After his father's death he may 'put' (*'ba*) ghost shrines on the advice of a diviner, depending on his position within his sibling group. Only the senior of a set of full brothers may put the shrines, his juniors using his shrines since they are under the ritual authority and protection that was formerly part of the status of their father. A set of full brothers is a close ritual unit in this sense.

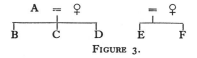

FIGURE 3.

Thus while A is alive only he, as head of the homestead and the compound family, has the shrines. On his death, if the group does not segment his eldest son B puts the senior ghost shrines for the use of himself and all his brothers C, D, E and F; while E may put his own junior shrine for the use of F and himself. E and F might move away a short distance to their own compound: they are a single matrisegment and an incipient new minimal lineage which may be referred to by the lineage name of their mother. But they are ritually under the guardianship of B, and sacrifices at their junior shrines can be carried out only by B. The principle is that a segment consisting of the sons of one man which has not yet split into two or more new segments has only one senior shrine, but that each junior set of full brothers has its own junior shrine— the senior set (B, C and D) does not have a junior shrine at all, unless they inherit one. The converse of this principle is that each compound of a single segment consisting of the sons of one man should have its own ghost shrines, senior or junior, the whole segment comprising one ritual unit. But in cases where full brothers separate, as they often do in late middle age, the reason usually being given that 'our wives quarrel', then the seceding party places a new junior shrine in the new compound. An adult living in his senior half brother's compound will, of course, put his own junior shrine in his part of the compound.

If however segmentation occurs and both B and E later become elders or heads of distinct segments, then B will keep the senior shrine that was formerly owned by their father A, and E will set up another senior shrine for the use of his own segment. Since once a shrine is erected it should not be 'forgotten' E will then have both senior and junior shrines. This situation is a reminder of the juniority of this segment to that of B, especially in a ritual context, the one in which seniority and juniority are most significant; and it will remain until E's segment can be divided into matrisegments by the separation of sets of full brothers in the succeeding generation. Then E's eldest son would take the senior shrine and a junior son the junior shrine. The way in which such a shrine is maintained and remembered depends on its sacrificial history. A shrine at which sacrifices are never made is soon forgotten and although the shrine itself will not be discarded so long as the homestead remains it may be left behind at a later move to a new compound.

These shrines may be newly placed or inherited. A man whose father has ghost shrines may succeed to his status. He inherits his father's shrines and unless he moves the compound he does not interfere with them. He waits for sickness to appear in his family and then consults a diviner to contact the soul of his recently dead father. This is usually about a year after the death. The rite of 'putting the ghost shrine' (*orijo 'ba*), is then performed. Ghost shrines are only placed for men who have begotten children and for women who have borne them. But the soul of every dead person is contacted by a diviner at the rite of 'contacting the soul' (*orindi tį zįzu*). Both rites are often done together but they are distinct. An important point is that a shrine is not merely a sign of status, as such, but its possession validates that status. The ghosts accept a shrine and their acceptance means that the owner's status is accepted and agreed to by them. No other validation is needed. At the rite of 'putting the shrine' a diviner contacts the soul of the dead man to ask him whether he is willing to drink beer at the new shrine:

> Today your father enters the home, yesterday he was outside. Now he wishes to drink beer, he wishes to enter the home.

Although many informants told me that they knew of no cases of refusal to drink beer on the part of the ghost, he is always formally asked and his acceptance is a sign of approval. He is then given beer on the new shrine, and the beer is shared by all the other adult males of the inner lineage if it is a senior shrine, by those of the minimal lineage if it is a junior shrine. These are 'brothers' in this context and must drink together only if there is no anger or disagreement in their hearts. In this rite they are accepting a new shrine owner as one of themselves. The ownership of a shrine validates the owner's status, both from the view of living and of dead kin.

After placing a new shrine for his father a son may use all his father's shrines. A man who inherits shrines from a brother who had a son might not do this. But by the rite of 'contacting the soul', which he as well as the deceased's son performs, the dead man shows approval of his inheriting the shrines. Formal approval of the living is not needed. A son takes the place of his father and so moves up into his father's generation, as it were; this is not so in the case of a brother, and so validation by other members of that generation is not necessary. Oracular statements are assumed to indicate the ghosts' wishes; the oracle decrees who will offer and at which shrine: a verdict that the new inheritor's shrine will be used is a sign of the ghost's approval of his acquisition of the new status.

VIII. ANCESTRAL SHRINES

Besides the internal ghost shrines placed under the main granary there are other shrines which are erected for ancestors as collectivities. The principal ones are closely linked and found in all compounds. They are called *a'biva* and *anguvua*. *A'biva* is the name both of the shrines and the incumbents, and means literally 'the ancestors beneath'. This refers to the ancestors who live beneath the huts of their decendants. 'A man lives above in his hut, his *a'biva* live beneath him.' The *a'biva* are said to be the souls (*orindi*) of the dead; they stay in and near the huts and at night can be heard grunting as they talk with one another. They are a collectivity of the souls of male ancestors who have begotten children: this is the general consensus of Lugbara opinion, although it is sometimes said that they are 'just ancestors' without qualification. These souls form a collectivity in which individual personality, responsibility and kin relationship to living people are irrelevant. They are not the entirety of souls of any man's cognatic or even agnatic ancestors, but those of the ancestors of his direct line of descent within the minimal, or sometimes the inner, lineage. *A'biva* shrines are inherited within the matrisegment only, and do not pass to half-brothers. It is clear that since the minimal lineage and its constituent segments segment continually the actual identity of *a'biva* in the shrines of any particular line of descent would change with segmentation, but their identity is not relevant and it is merely axiomatic that a man's *a'biva* are those of his descent line. Each set of *a'biva* comprises the souls in a particular line; these lines, of course, descend from a common apical ancestor, but their interconnexion is never stressed. Women do not become *a'biva* 'because they do not give food or beer to the dead, they are things of the grass only'. Women bear their children away from their natal lineage homes, and since they own no shrines they own no homes and are not full lineage members with full responsibility in lineage matters.

A special shrine is placed for *a'biva* on the verandah of the senior wife's hut. It consists of two flat stones, one upright, the *a'biva* proper, and beside it a flat stone, the *a'biva's* 'wife'. It is said to bring sickness on its own account, in the form of swellings of the body. The oracles decree that the sickness is brought by *a'biva*;

Then you call a diviner, to divine with a gourd. She contacts the souls with her gourd. The souls say 'We have waited many years, now hunger conquers us, our child has not given us food.' Then the diviner says 'Oh, I awaken you with my divining gourd, all you *a'bɪva*, say words. Say truly if it is you who seize this man with sickness.' Then those souls say that it is they and say that if he gives them food then they will remove the sickness.

Then food is offered to them. Ghosts, as ghosts, do not need a diviner to contact them, since their souls have been brought into permanent and individual contact with the living at the ghost shrines. But *a'bɪva* can only be contacted by a diviner, like a man who is recently dead.

Men who die childless become neither ghosts nor *a'bɪva*. They join a collectivity of childless ancestors called *anguvua*, people who are said to be 'forgotten' or 'lost' to their kin. Barren women do not become *anguvua*, however; 'they are nothing'. *Anguvua* are very similar to *a'bɪva* and Lugbara usually speak of them as being 'together'. They bring sickness to children, 'because they wanted children and got none'. They are contacted by a diviner as are *a'bɪva*, and are given food, although of a different type. The sickness they bring is similar, a swelling of the body, and 'their sickness comes with that of *a'bɪva*'. There is no actual shrine for *anguvua*. They are 'in the ground, and are like *a'bɪva*, but of a different *sɪrɪ* (clan or type)'. The offering is placed just inside the doorway of the senior wife's hut, on the ground. Having had no children, 'who will put a shrine to them?'; the erection of a shrine is a visible sign of piety towards a dead kinsman. Although the *anguvua* are a collectivity of childless ancestors, there is nevertheless always assumed to have been an original childless ancestor in each minimal lineage, and the others 'follow' him. He is typically a brother of the lineage founder or a founder's son. His name is no longer known and is 'forgotten'. *Anguvua* of a single minimal lineage are thus related, since they all 'spring' from an original childless ancestor. Since they lack lineage and kinship status they do not have responsibility towards the living, and lacking male children they are not significant as points of segment articulation and are soon forgotten.

A third shrine associated with the dead is the *talɪ* shrine. I have already mentioned this concept and translated it as the 'personality' of an individual. Shrines are placed for the collectivity of 'personalities' of those ancestors who have left male children. The shrine is known as *talį* or *talįjo* (*jo*=house). It is a small cocoon-like shrine of dried mud, six or nine inches high, with a single hole, the '*talį* house door'. Although every man has his own personality, only one shrine is placed for all the shrines under one granary. That is, the collectivity of personalities of the lineage dead come into contact with the living at a single shrine. If an offering is made at the ghost shrines then food must also be placed within the *talį* shrine. There is the concept of a single lineage personality, participation in which is expressed by the living in their actions. The personality is, however, wider than the lineage itself. Every *talį* shrine, although associated with the collectivity of ancestors for whom offerings are made at it, is associated specially with one ancestor from whom this joint personality originated. This ancestor is either the apical ancestor of the inner lineage of the shrine 'owner', or the first ancestor of his mother's lineage. The joint personality is thus linked with those of other lineages elsewhere. This shrine is sometimes called *angumatalį* ('the personality of the territory') of the inner lineage. The agnatic ancestor concerned is the same in all the shrines of the inner lineage.

Lastly there is the shrine called *abego*. This is placed for a man or woman who had been dead about a year and who died very old and helpless. The old and weak are glad that God has spared them, yet are angry at their helplessness, and if neglected while senile they will later send sickness to their living kin. The shrine is placed at the same time as the soul is contacted by a diviner. It consists of a small flat granite stone, the shrine for an agnate being under the main granary and that for the mother's lineage members under the verandah of the senior wife's hut.

As I have stated earlier, ghosts enter into direct, personal and responsible contact with the living. The contact occurs when kinship norms are breached. An ancestor *qua* ancestor is a symbol of common ancestry and descent and so of unity of kinsmen, but is not so concerned with controlling kinship behaviour. The specific kin ties between individual ancestors and with living kin are not significant in action; they are relevant rather as foci in the articulation of lineages and lines of descent.

The ancestors in these internal ancestral shrines send sickness on their own account, by vengeance (*ka*). They cannot be invoked by living persons. The offence that leads to sickness from them is considered to be impiety, usually expressed as not offering food to them. In fact Lugbara do not always make periodical offerings without first being struck by sickness; yet this is invariably given as the reason, and it is part of Lugbara belief about the dead that they demand such propitiatory feeding. For Lugbara, the feeding of the dead at their shrines is part of the general complex of obligations towards kin, and lessens the conceptual distance between living and dead kin. Visiting kin (*wa'dį*) must formally be offered food and drink as a material recognition of the bond of kinship, both cognatic and affinal. To offer food at the ancestral shrines is to recognize kinship ties with the totality of the lineage dead, a duty recognized to be important and even essential. The contact thus made is different from that made with the ghosts. The latter is with individuals, who are concerned with responsibility for maintenance of orderly lineage ties, especially between living kin. This is the role of the dead as ghosts. Contact with ancestors is with a collectivity, whose members are not thought of as being responsible for orderly relations between living kin. There is no moral content, in this sense, in the sending of sickness by the ancestors. This may be seen from the fact that they are contacted by diviners. First consultation is at the rubbing-stick oracle, which decrees that contact must be made by divination. Oracles are said to know the motives behind the activities of both living and dead, but diviners can 'know' the dead only, and then only in certain of their aspects.

The rituals connected with the ghosts are said to be 'big', whereas those to do with the ancestors are 'little'. The congregation that attends ghostly sacrifice is larger and consists specifically of a wide range of kin, whereas those at ancestral sacrifices are smaller and the lineage-kinship element is less important. Lugbara make the distinction also in terms of the food offered to them: ghosts 'eat' meat and beer, but ancestors 'eat' bloodless offerings only.

IX. WOMEN'S SHRINES

The shrines so far described are for paternal or maternal agnatic ancestors and ghosts. There are also shrines placed for the ghosts of women in the mother's mother's line. These, the 'woman ghost (shrines)' (*okuori*), are placed under the eaves of the hut of the senior wife in the compound. A man cannot place a shrine to his agnatic ghosts while his father is still alive. But he may put women's ghost shrines while his mother is still alive, since she has no ritual status which he may usurp, nor is his father interested in these shrines; they are placed for the ghosts of his wife's people, with whom he has no ritual relationship. A man usually has shrines to his mother's mother and to his mother's own sisters. A junior full brother uses his senior brother's shrines; they distinguish matrisegments. When his mother dies a man will sooner or later put a shrine for her in the same way as for his father; he waits until a diviner shows sickness to have come from the dead parent.

Although 'owned' by men, the ghosts in these shrines are usually invoked by women, or they may send sickness by ghostly vengeance. For example, if a child persistently strikes its mother, she may invoke the ghost of her dead mother to bring sickness to it. This is Lugbara theory; in practice it seems not to happen unless the child is at least a responsible adolescent, who then places a shrine or who has his brother place one. In such a situation the child's mother's brother would be expected to be angry also and could send sickness on his own account. But he is not concerned with invocation at the women's shrines, through which his own mother may bring sickness. The distinction is that invocation is concerned with lineage and family authority, whereas the curses of a mother's brother are concerned with relations between himself and his sister's child as individuals. I was told that a man can invoke his mother's or grandmother's ghosts against his own full siblings and their children, but I know of no case of this happening.

Offerings are made on behalf of a man by his sister or his wife, although the latter 'does not know well the words of his mother': but a woman must make the offering. It consists of gruel with milk, or sometimes the meat of a female goat.

These shrines are not of great importance, since women rarely play much part in lineage affairs. The exceptions are old women past child-bearing who are considered to be in close contact with the dead, either because they are the elder sisters of heads of lineages or because they are sisters of heads of lineages who have died before them. Being old, they are 'like men', and may exercise considerable family authority. Their powers represent, on a ritual plane, the belief that a woman may be important because 'she should have been born a man, but God chose her to be born as a woman.' A woman has no ritual importance in the lineage of her husband, but only in her own natal group.

X. MATRILATERAL SHRINES

Besides the internal shrines for the agnatic ghosts and ancestors, there are three shrines associated with the mother's brother, two of them with his ghosts. The latter are in Lugbara theory not very important, and are said to 'follow' the agnatic ghost shrines. Offerings are not made to them very often, but they are none the less much feared since they are 'strong' (*okporu*), as are one's mother's brothers themselves. Patrilineal ghosts are feared and respected as guardians of lineage prosperity, but the attitude to matrilateral ghosts reflects that towards living matrilateral kin. They are seen as having a strong sense of what is proper in their sisters' sons' behaviour, and thus are feared. But they are also seen as being tender and solicitous towards their sisters' sons, and as guardians over them as individuals, without regard to their suitability as lineage members. Part of this ambivalent attitude is the sense of grudging that a mother's brother is said to feel towards the lineage of his sister's son. He loves his own sister's son but resents the latter's loyalty to his agnatic lineage, of which the other members are seen by the mother's brother as brothers-in-law, unrelated by 'blood' and so potentially hostile. Only the sister and her own children are linked to him by 'blood'. At the basis of this ambivalence is the position of a man's married sister, who might have been born a man, but being born a woman had to go elsewhere and bear children for others; these have negotiated the terms of bridewealth payments and are seen as potential feud-enemies.

The most important and the most common of these shrines is called *lucugo*. It is intimately connected with another shrine called *drilonzi*, a word for 'bad luck' or 'misfortune' in general. Bad luck in this context refers particularly to lack of fertility of wives, livestock or crops, and to lack of success in hunting.

Lucugo sickness—lack of fertility of the kinds I have mentioned—is caused by a man's true mother's brother thinking or speaking 'bad words' against him. There is no invocation of ghosts involved;

merely for a man to think angrily of his sister's son is enough. The
mechanism by which sickness occurs is not known. Lugbara do
not consider it a problem: it merely is so. The motivation is not
that of *ole*, as in ghost invocation, although it is assumed that the
mother's brother has justification in the behaviour of his sister's
son. The oracles are consulted and it is indicated that a *lucugo*
shrine be erected and a ritual meal shared by mother's brother and
sister's son, when the sickness will be removed. Later offerings
may be made at the shrine.

The oracles may then decree the placing of another shrine,
called *drilonzi*. Normally it is set up as physically part of the
lucugo shrine. Offerings are not made at it apart from the *lucugo*;
when the latter receives an offering so does the former, 'because it
follows the *lucugo*'. *Drilonzi* can affect only adult men and women,
who have sexual intercourse, and it is usually connected with
impotence and menstrual disorders.

Sickness brought by the *lucugo* shrine appears to be capricious,
in the sense that it is caused by a mother's brother thinking
angrily, but with no justification by appeal to community well-
being such as is given by the invoker in the case of ghost invocation. Yet it is felt to be quite right and understandable that a
mother's brother should be capricious in this manner. The underlying ambivalence in the relationship is expressed clearly in the
ritual situation. The indispensability (in theory, at any rate) of
the sister's son to his mother's brother as cutter of meat at an
important sacrifice; the capriciousness of a mother's brother
causing *lucugo* sickness; the withholding of fertility, a thing of the
greatest importance to Lugbara; and the notion that this and the
ambao and *adroori* shrines (see below) 'watch over' their owners
as well as bringing them sickness; these are all in certain ways
mutually contradictory.

Any adult man may have sickness brought to him by his
mother's brother's ghosts. He places a shrine, 'mother's brother's
ghost' (*adro-ori*), or 'mother's brother's ghost hut' (*adro ma orijo*),
the latter being used especially for the shrine set for the ghost of
a true mother's brother. It is placed under the eaves of a man's
mother's hut, if she is still living in his settlement; if she is dead
or has moved away he puts it under the eaves of his senior
wife's hut. This sickness is the result of ghostly vengeance; it is
not associated with invocation. I was told

Every day that mother's father says 'Oh, I want food from that sister's son.' Then he seizes me, or my wife, or my child. I go to the rubbing-stick oracle. It says 'The ghosts of your mother's brothers are angry. You just live lazily, you never put food there for your mother's father or your mother's grandfathers.' So then you go home, you take a he-goat, and cut it.

A last type of matrilateral shrine is that called *ambo* or *ambao*, which is found only in the north of Lugbaraland. It is erected for the ancestor—not the ghost—of a man's father's mother's brother; it causes dysentery and diarrhoea, and affects men, women and children. Its erection is the concern of the elders of the two lineages concerned only, who together eat beans and simsim provided by the elder of the father's mother's brother's lineage; he also brings the stones and erects the shrine. It is placed in the compound hedge, and can then later bring sickness of its own accord within the family cluster, usually against a thief. It is said to be very strong and dangerous, and this is the reason given for its being put in the hedge: 'if it were under the granary it would seize people every day'.

These matrilateral shrines are all 'placed' by a mother's brother or one of his lineage, and they provide the offering. There is thus no notion of reparation or restitution made for an offence committed towards them. In ghost invocation the elder, who is usually the invoker, may supply the offering, but he does so in his role of head of the group and controller of its livestock: the invocation is made on behalf of the entire group. It might be argued that in the case of these matrilateral shrines the mother's brother's group regards the sister's son as one of their members and that in this sense the situation is analogous to that of ghost invocation. But there are important differences. In cases of 'matrilateral' sickness there is no ritual congregation and there is no local community involved. The reason for this is clearly that the persons concerned do not form the core of a local community, nor of any corporate group.

These shrines bring 'bad luck' and sterility. Sterility is the consequence of the most serious curse one can make against any-one, and it is significant in two ways: it is not commonly a curse made against a member of one's own lineage, and it concerns the whole segment as well as the actual individual immediately affected. When it is made by a man's own ancestor it leads to sacrifice at the external lineage shrine, the 'biggest' shrine of all, and is regarded as something extremely serious and dangerous. The hostility felt by the mother's brother's group against the sister's son is directed against him not as a sister's son, a relative by 'blood', but as a representative of the potentially hostile affinal lineage. He is the victim merely because, being connected by 'blood', it is only he who is liable to be affected in this way, according to Lugbara belief. Ghostly sickness, like all mystical sickness except that brought by witchcraft and sorcery, travels along the path of 'blood'.

Two points emerge from this. The underlying tensions in the mother's brother—sister's son relationship are those resulting from the affinal element of that relationship. It is this element that gives rise to one side of the ambivalent content of the tie. This tie is one of hostility, that was often expressed in open fighting. Its expression in the mystical bringing of sickness does at least minimize the occasions of open hostility, which are extremely disruptive. By the resolution of the tension by mystical means and the recognition of its existence by the oracular verdict the relationship between the two lineages concerned is kept in being, even after the original negotiants and even the connecting woman are dead. Fighting destroys it, as does the fighting that may follow divorce to ensure the return of the bridewealth—in fact, the fighting is a recognition that divorce occurs. Resort to mystical processes may be made without the tie being destroyed—indeed, by definition it must still be recognized for these processes to be set in action at all. Just as ghost invocation between agnates reflects tension in the structure, which is recognized and resolved ritually—without the use of force—so the processes I have been describing in this section do likewise with regard to the ties between lineages originally related affinally, and so temporarily or potentially, but now related permanently after the birth of the child who is related to both by 'blood'.

The loss of fertility of the women and livestock of the entire lineage is considered to be due to the powers associated with external and fertility shrines, which I discuss below. Matrilateral shrines are associated with loss of fertility of a matrisegment only. It is a sign of the desire for independence of that segment. Such a desire is disruptive to the agnatic lineage and cannot easily be admitted by a responsible member of it. But he may safely point to loss of fertility as a sign that his mother's ancestors wish for his increased independence. This wish is typically a consequence of his increased social maturity, coincident with increase in number of his dependants and their need for more land. This usually follows their marriages, as new children are born; the vagaries of conception and birth by these wives coincide with their demand for more resources, and is interpreted as validating that demand.

XI. EXTERNAL LINEAGE SHRINES

The internal ghost and ancestor shrines are set within the compound. Those other shrines to the ghosts and ancestors which are set outside it I call external lineage shrines. This follows Lugbara usage; they are said to be 'outside', because they are 'big'. They are placed in the long grass or bush outside the compound of the elder, usually some yards away from the nearest path. Only the elder may have custody of these shrines and none but the elders may attend sacrifices at them, or indeed even look at them. Those owned by the senior elder of a sub-clan are often rainshrines also, and are then set in groves which are the most sacred places in Lugbara. External shrines are regarded as very sacred, and contrast markedly in this respect with the internal shrines.

There is a variety of names for these shrines. They are known as *rogbo* or *rogboko* in the south, as *kᶙrᶙgbᶙ* in the west, and as *orijo* in the north and east;[1] and there are other terms. The shrine varies considerably in form. Usually it consists of two flat stones— one for each ghost, there usually being two—and an upright stone, this being 'like a policeman who is sent by a chief to seize a man'. It is said that the external shrine has 'struck' a man. At sacrifices the blood is poured over the upright stone first, 'because it passes these words to the others'. The stones are rarely found by themselves, there generally being other shrines associated with fertility, which I describe below.

Only elders of minimal lineages have these shrines. Although the senior elder of a minor or major lineage, and sometimes of a sub-clan, has superior ritual powers in certain fields he has no special shrine other than that of his own minimal lineage. There is no hierarchy of shrines corresponding to a hierarchy of lineages.

[1] In the south *orijo* is used for the internal ghost shrine.

Lugbara say that the identity of the external ghosts is disclosed by oracular utterance, and it may change over time. The history of any particular external shrine shows this. Unlike an internal shrine, which is set for a particular ghost and remains his over several generations until it is finally discarded, an external shrine may change its incumbent ghost within a comparatively short period. The oracles state that food is required by a certain ghost and so he is then considered to be 'in' the shrine, and whichever ghosts were there before are said to have lost interest in it. They may have internal shrines as well and so be fed there also. Lugbara say that the ghosts are jealous of each other and demand to be fed in turn, so that if the sickness associated with external shrines occurs frequently it is taken as a sign that a distant ancestor's ghost is jealous of those in the shrine. The identity of the incumbent is then changed, after oracular consultation.

This is how Lugbara see it. But the identity of these ghosts is not as haphazard as their theory might indicate. The shrines are placed for two distinct ghosts of the lineage, who share any one shrine. They are usually father and son. This is by no means

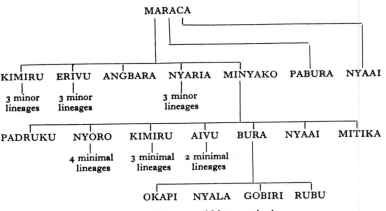

FIGURE 4. Lineages of Maraca sub-clan

invariable, and where there is a contradiction between the relationship of ghosts and genealogies it is a sign that the lineage is in process of segmentation and that genealogies are being telescoped and altered to become consistent with actual distribution of segments and of authority. There may be only one shrine for an

entire minor lineage, although sacrifice may be offered there to
different ghosts by each component lineage. And a shrine may be
shared by a major lineage also: it depends on the recent history of
segmentation of the group. The principle is that the external shrine

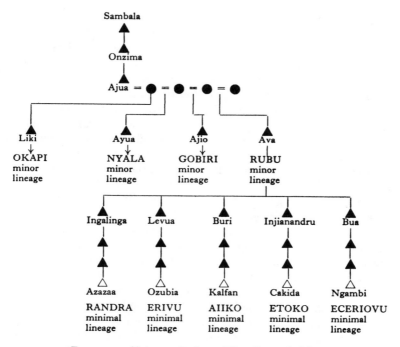

FIGURE 5.   Skeleton genealogy of Bura lineage in Maraca

symbolizes the unity of the inner lineage and its cult maintains this
unity. The sharing of the same external ghosts is a sign that the
group is a single ritual unit and that open fighting within it is a sin.

An example of this process is in the major lineage Bura in
Maraca. This group has increased at a greater rate than its closely
agnatically related lineages, and it has also increased unevenly,
one of its component lineages having grown faster than the others.
Its present genealogy and position are shown in Figures 4 and 5.
Only relevant names are given and collateral lines are omitted. It
was formerly part of a lineage called Minyako that has segmented
and is no longer an effective lineage segment, although it is often

referred to by that name. When Bura had been a minimal lineage
for some years it had a single external shrine and a single elder;
the ghosts in the shrine were Sambala and Onzima, and they
were also in the external shrines of the other lineages that were
co-ordinate with it—Padruku, Nyoro, Aivu, Kimiru, Nyaai and
Mitika. These are all still in existence except Kimiru, which
has split into the three lineages of Ombavu, Ambidro and
Randra; and the others vary in span and in numbers of subordinate
minimal lineages due to different rates of increase in population.
Today they do not share ghosts in common, but are split up into
different ghost-sharing groups—Padruku and Nyoro, Aivu and
the three groups that were once Kimiru, Bura, Nyaai on its own and
Mitika on its own, although these last are very small and are being
absorbed ritually into groups related more distantly but territorially adjacent. An intermediate stage was when Aivu, Kimiru,
Bura and Nyaai formed a ritual group—although as far as I can
discover never a formal political group—called 'Baria. Here we
are concerned only with Bura, which has undergone several stages
in the process of segmentation.

1. The stage I have mentioned was followed by Bura segmenting into four minimal lineages and so becoming a minor lineage.
These four were named after the clans of the four wives of Ajua,
the founder of Bura: Okapi, Nyala, Gobiri and Rubu. Whether
or not these segments actually originated in this manner we can
no longer tell, since the half-brother relationship between minimal
lineages is the conventional one and genealogies change over
time to validate this assumed relationship. At this stage there was
only one shrine in Okapi, the senior lineage, in the care of the elder
of Okapi who was the senior elder of the whole minor lineage. In
the shrine were Onzima and Ajua.

2. This stage was soon followed by one in which each minimal
lineage owned an external shrine, each under the care of the
lineage elder. Onzima and Ajua were still the incumbent ghosts
in all of them.

3. In order to balance the political segmentation properly,
there followed a change in the identity of the ghosts, and gradually
Onzima was 'forgotten'. His place was taken by the respective
sons of Ajua who were the founding ancestors of the four minimal
lineages, Liki of Okapi, Ayua of Nyala, Ajio of Gobiri and Ava
of Rubu. This process, which can be seen today at a lower

level (see stage 5 below), clearly took some time and was presumably sporadic, the changes occurring according to oracular utterances.

4. The lineage Rubu has increased at a greater rate than the others, and today consists of five minimal lineages, of which one, Eceriovu, was probably originally a client lineage but of which the ancestry is now fitted into that of the rest of Rubu. This segmentation took place in the youth of old men now alive. At first the new lineages, Randra, Erivu, Aiiko, Etoko and Eceriovu, shared one shrine, that formerly held by the elder of Rubu in stage (3). In this shrine were three ghosts, Ajua and Ava, as before, and Ingalinga, the eldest son of Ava. Ingalinga was brought into the shrine by the then elder of Rubu-Randra in an effort to show that his line of descent was the most important; it was an effort to prevent segmentation from being validated ritually and so to maintain his own unique status as elder of all Rubu.

5. His efforts were unsuccessful and today all the lineages of Rubu have their own external shrines in which are two ghosts, Ajua and his son Ava. Randra also has a stone for Ingalinga and Erivu one for their distinguishing ancestor Levua, although this is a very recent stone. As yet the other lineages have not added stones for their own special ancestors, but this will occur sooner or later. They are not yet of sufficient size or generation depth for them to wish to assert their ritual, and so political, independence. Erivu has one mainly because its elder, Ozubia, is ambitious and jealous of Randra's elder, Azazaa. It is Azazaa's prerogative to supervise sacrifices at any of these shrines, but for one at Erivu's shrine there would be disagreement as to who should supervise. Ozubia has managed to do so once, but Azazaa says that although it was at an external shrine and so 'big', the particular occasion was only a 'little' one since the sickness concerned was only 'little', and so he did not trouble himself to assert his authority and risk too open a rift in lineage harmony.

The external ghost shrines thus link the basic lineages of the system into groupings at the next higher co-ordinate level. There may be inconsistency in formal lineage levels, as in Bura, where Rubu has one more level of segmentation than do its co-ordinate lineages. In each external shrine there are always at least two ghosts, one representing the wider lineage as a single unit and the other representing the smaller lineage of which the custodian is the elder. Where there are more than two shrines the principle still applies.

It is usual for the junior ghost in an external shrine to be differentiated from the other junior ghosts in co-ordinate shrines by their being regarded as half-brothers; they have different maternal origins, and co-ordinate external shrines represent on a ritual or ideal plane segments that are so differentiated genealogically. This differentation may also be reflected more directly in external shrines set up for the ghosts of ancestresses. These are known as 'grandmother' or 'ancestress' (*dede*), a term used for any woman two or more generations senior to the speaker, and including agnates, other cognates and affines.

The *dede* shrine typically consists of three flat stones, set for the ancestress herself, her mother, and her sisters collectively. The ancestress is she by reference to whom the minimal lineage is differentiated. It is her status in this respect that is significant and not her personal name as such, which is usually not associated with the shrine, although it may sometimes be mentioned in genealogies.

I have described shrines set for 'mothers' brothers', of various generations, that is, for members of the agnatic lineages of the lineage's ancestors' wives. The *dede* shrines, however, are set for these wives themselves, individually, and for their mothers and sisters (although the latters' names are very rarely known). That is, they are set not for their agnatic line but for the submerged lines of descent through women. Lugbara say it is for women only because generally only women of the lineage may sacrifice at it; they are not concerned with lineage offences, the concern of the agnatic ghosts. I have heard it said that the *dede* shrine is 'like a wife' to the external agnatic ghost shrine. The *dede* is placed near the latter shrine, but is not so important, and is never found alone whereas the agnatic shrine may be found by itself.

The complex of external shrines includes also the burial trees of the ancestors concerned. These trees are called 'ancestors' (*a'bi*). They are the fig trees planted at the heads of the graves of important men and women. Not all are shrines, but only those of the founders of minimal lineages. The tree that has a shrine has a stone set under it; properly it is this stone that is the shrine, but Lugbara speak of it and the tree as being one. Like all burial trees it is sacred and may not be cut, nor the ground beneath it cultivated, so that it may stand in a small thicket. On the unwooded Lugbara plateau these thickets are often the haunts of snakes and leopards, beasts with mystical associations with both the dead and with God. The external shrines are placed close to the *a'bị* tree of the lineage founder and there is a close ritual relationship between them. The tree marks the grave of the lineage founder. Burial trees are conspicuous landmarks; their distribution on the open Lugbara landscape shows the past of the lineages dispersed across it and give a visible sign of a single tradition of development from the founders to the present members.

Together these three shrines represent the ancestors whose genealogical relationships with one another correspond to those of the minimal, minor and often major lineages of which the minimal lineage is a segment. The ancestors in the *a'bị* tree shrines are also ghosts in the internal ghost shrines and provide a direct link with them. The ghosts of the external shrines have formerly, of course, been in the internal shrines. As generations succeed one another and an original minimal lineage segments and becomes first a minor and then a major lineage, even a sub-clan, so the original ancestors become more remote. The ghosts that are significant in ghost invocation and ghostly vengeance, especially in bringing of sickness to specific individuals, are those of the more recently dead, and sacrifice, although made to all the ghosts of the lineage—not as a single collectivity however—is made especially to those who have brought the sickness. As compounds move over time the shrines of the more recent ghosts come to be more important than those of the more remote, until in time the latter are said to be 'outside a little'. They leave the compounds and the granaries and move to the external ghost shrines and burial trees.

The 'outside' ancestors, however, still demand food. So when their 'children' are fed at the internal shrines some of the food and beer is placed also at the burial trees. The ancestors say:

Now we are big ancestors. We live outside. If you give our children food you should give us food also, some at the internal ghost shrines and some at the burial trees. Now our children live in the internal shrines, in the compounds. Now we have no children (i.e. no living children or grandchildren) to give us food every month. We live outside.

The reference to food 'every month' should not be taken literally: ghosts are not fed regularly. A small portion of the offering is taken by the elder's ritual assistant who places it on the stone at the *a'bi* tree. Meanwhile the elder performs the sacrifice proper at the internal shrine, where there is a congregation; there is none at the burial tree, where there is merely an offering of food.

Food is offered to the ancestors at the trees because they represent the unity of the entire minimal lineage on a ritual plane. The congregation at the internal shrine consists of representatives of segments of the lineage; and most offences which lead to sacrifice at the internal shrines arise from tensions and quarrels within these groups; thus the sacrifice has as part of its function the cementing of the group's solidarity. The congregation assembles and at the rite various actions are performed which symbolize their re-unity. On a ritual level this is done by a duplicatory offering at the burial tree of the founding ancestor of the minimal lineage concerned. This ancestor's being placed 'outside' the compound symbolizes his not being 'owned' by any single head of a segment. The founding ancestor is related to all lines of ghosts and living, and so above segmentary interests, conflicts over which are the basis of dissensions that set off the process of ghostly sickness and sacrifice. The repetition of the offering to an ancestor at the burial tree is to bring the remote ghosts 'outside' into the sharing of ritual food, which stands for the re-affirmation of lineage ties.

Sacrifices made at the external shrines are in response to ghostly vengeance only. The ghosts cannot be invoked by the custodian elder. They are said to be too far away to be easily aroused by what are to them the comparatively small offences to do with lineage discipline and order; these are more the concern of their 'children', the ghosts in the internal shrines (even though in fact their identity may be similar). Internal ghosts send the sickness of 'growing thin' to 'show' the offender their anger. The external ghosts bring the far more serious complaint of sterility, so that either a man's wives or his cattle do not bear. The offence is said to be the non-specific one of impiety—the ghosts have not been offered food and drink for a long time. Their anger grows and finally they 'seize' a member of the group in this way. Sterility is, apart from total extinction in warfare or epidemic, the most serious harm that can befall the group. The fertility of its women, livestock and land is its greatest asset. The cases of which I know were all of sterility,

A Lugbara homestead. Shrines may be seen under the centre granary. Unlike most homesteads, this has no surrounding hedge. The fields are beyond, near the borassus palm.

The boiling medicine oracle. Using a snail shell, the operator pours medicine from the pot into the small clay cups, which are set in a smouldering fire. The smaller cups represent suspected agents and the larger one with a handle confirms their verdicts.

together with a kind of general malaise over a long period. Both external ghosts and ancestresses may bring sterility; it is not brought by the ancestors in the burial trees; offerings here are made as repetitive offerings only, and not to remove sickness brought by the shrine itself.

XII. FERTILITY SHRINES

The external lineage shrines are erected for the ghosts of the more distant ancestors of the lineage, including those beyond the apical ancestor of the minimal lineage. These are also fertility shrines, associated with distant ancestors, but the forces within the shrines are regarded as almost independent of any ancestral power. Like the external lineage shrines, these shrines are said to be 'big', and are concerned only with fertility of women and cattle and success in hunting, that is, with the processes on which the prosperity of lineage and kin-group depend.

The main shrine of this sort is usually called *rogbo* in northern and central Lugbara; in southern Lugbara it is merged with the shrine called *tįrį* and the word *rogbo* is used for the external lineage shrine. In it is 'our first ancestor', in this case the father of the ancestress by whom the minimal and often the minor lineage is differentiated from other co-ordinate lineages. The same ancestor is also 'in' a shrine called *eralengbo*,[1] which is erected inside the cattle kraal outside the compound. Also, of course, this ancestor is also in the external lineage shrine of his own agnatic lineage elsewhere, so that he provides a tenuous mystical link between the two lineages.

The *rogbo* shrine is also called *rįdį* or *rųdų*, and with it is associated a shrine called *tįrį*, which is placed together with the external lineage shrine outside the compounds. In some areas *rįdį* is also called *orubangi*,[2] and is placed near the kraal gate, next to the *eralengbo* shrine. *Eralengbo*, is, however, used only for the shrine inside the cattle kraal. The shapes of the shrines vary. *Eralengbo* consists of an old grinding stone of granite, with a hole worn through in the centre, set upright in the kraal hedge. *Tįrį* consists usually of a large aloe-like plant. *Rįdį* or *rogbo* is usually

---

[1] There are many dialectal variants of this word.

[2] *Orubangi* is presumably connected with the Madi word *Rubangi*, God, and the word *rųdų* is used for ordinary ghost shrines in Madi.

a single flat granite slab, with *asįtį* grass planted near it and the whole surrounded by a miniature fence of *ekaraka* sticks, the whole being about a foot across. It is set in the centre of the compound floor. I have been told that *asįtį* and *ekaraka* are 'things of God'.

The force or power in the *rįdį* shrine is associated with ancestral power. I was told:

Rįdį is a thing which looks after our women and our cattle. It makes them conceive and bear children and calves, and then we are many and 'big'. If a man has wealth, he is said to be 'with *rįdį*; if a man is poor, he is 'without *rįdį*'. And *tįrį*, it is the brother of *rįdį*. Do we not give them food together? The plant of *tįrį* is a bulb, *ojoo*, a thing of great power—do not diviners use *ojoo* bulbs? These words are difficult to understand. They come from our first ancestors, the fathers of our ancestresses, whose shrine (*dede*) you see there in those trees.

All these shrines are offered food at an offering made at any of them. Offerings are made at *rįdį* or *rogbo* primarily in cases of barrenness of the wives or daughters of the lineage; it may affect them even when they are living elsewhere at their husbands' homes. An offering is made at *eralengbo* primarily for barrenness in livestock, especially in cattle. But all are said to be able to 'close' both women and cattle so that they do not bear.

Rįdį and *rogbo* also affect success in hunting. Before a hunt a cock, of any colour, is beaten to death on the stone, and eaten by the men and children of the minimal lineage. After the hunt the horns and leg-bones and hoofs of the game killed are placed on the shrine and left there; often they are hung later under the granary.

These shrines are all 'big' and much feared, but there is little explicit theory about them. Their 'genealogical' relationship to the *dede* ancestresses' shrines is recognized but is not thought of as being of any great significance. In discussing these shrines with elders I was always impressed by the fact that an elder would point to his main external ghost shrine and to his *dede* shrine and speak of them as being merely the places at which their incumbents could be contacted, whereas the *rįdį* shrine, usually erected with these others, was clearly regarded as having a different kind of power, of a non-ancestral kind, even though the ultimate ancestral connexion is known. The former are said to send sickness as a consequence of anger at impiety and at general lack of responsibility of elders and senior men; the latter are said to send sickness without such motivation, without understanding of the guilt or otherwise of the living men concerned.

These shrines are owned not only by elders but also by the heads of component family segments of the family cluster. It is usual for such a man to make an offering at them as soon as he sets up a new compound after reaching the status of head of a family segment. Offering is made once only, so that the shrine is erected, and then many years may pass before another offering is made, since they are said to fear to come into contact with the power of the shrines. The first offering is made on account of a fear that the owner's wives are not conceiving or his livestock bearing calves. This would seem to be a stock fear of a man who considers that he is head of a segment that should become independent (at a lower level the same applies to matrilateral shrines, as I have mentioned). I was told that a man offers at the fertility shrines 'so that we shall know he is a big man'. To be affected, however slightly, by these powers is a sign that the owner is a responsible and senior man, with responsibility to his segment for its wealth to be perpetuated and increased. He is then a holder of the status junior to that of elder but senior to that of 'big youths'. He is in contact with a power that can cause sterility, a power greater than that associated with the ordinary dead.

XIII. SHRINES AND STATUS

There is thus a multiplicity of shrines; the same ancestors and ghosts may be contacted at many shrines, both of different types and at those owned by different living men.

A single ancestor may have several shrines associated with him, as an ancestor, a ghost, a possessor of 'personality' and so on. Together they add up to a representation, on a ritual plane, of his complete social personality. The shrines of a minimal lineage together add up to a ritual representation of the totality of social personalities of the dead members of the lineage. Some aspects remain individual while others are collectivized. In the totality of shrines is represented what might be called the total lineage personality as it is relevant to the members at the present time. In them the living members see their lineage past incapsulated, with differences in the importance (for the living) of the ancestors made clear. They see themselves as having reached a particular point in lineage history or development. Every man has a different view of this history, as it is symbolized in the shrines, and also has a different ritual view, as we may call it, of the present. The contemporary alignments of intra-lineage authority and power and of ambition and rivalry between family segments and their heads are reflected in the distribution of shrines. Men see their lineage past and present in a similar way in genealogies, which are manipulated in order to qualify the owners of shrines for that status and to validate it. The difference is that a shrine is the focus of an actual relationship between living and dead members of the lineage. In this relationship the living see the dead as kinsmen, as the holders of social personalities; these aspects of these personalities that are relevant to the living are divided among the shrines.

The past development and present distribution of lineage authority is represented in these ritual terms. Other types of authority are represented also in ritual, but not in terms of authority of the dead. For example, the relation between a man and his uterine kin is represented ritually in the relationship associated with the *lucugo* shrine, in which the dead have no part.

The actual placing of the shrines has certain significance. Their typical physical distribution is:

Under the main granary	internal ghost shrines
	lucugo (mother's brother's shrine)
	agnatic *talį* shrine
	agnatic *abego* shrine (for recently dead senile old man)
Under the eaves of the senior wife's hut	*adroori* (for mother's brother's lineage ghosts)
	okuori (women's shrines)
	shrine of 'contacting the soul' of recently dead
	abįva ancestral shrine
	matrilateral *talį* shrine
	matrilateral *abego* shrine
Inside the man's hut (or wife's hut if no separate man's hut)	*anguvua* (site for offering, although no actual shrine)
	yakani and other spirit shrines

In compound hedge	*eralengbo* fertility shrine, if no cattle kraal
	ambao matrilateral shrine
In cattle kraal	*eralengbo* fertility shrine
On compound floor	*rįdį* and *tįrį* fertility shrines
At edge of path	*drilonzi* 'bad luck' shrine, certain spirit shrines
Outside in bush	external lineage ghost shrine
	ancestress shrine (*dede*)
	burial tree shrine

It is said that shrines placed under the eaves of the wife's hut are put there so as to be out of the rain, as are those placed inside the hut. Those placed inside the hut include the *anguvua*, for which there is no stone, and two spirit shrines: the *yakani* shrine is said to be there for concealment because of the connexion of the *yakani* cult with anti-government activity (see chapter V), and the other is a small shrine called *joajoa* ('in the hut in the hut') which consists of wooden objects which are placed in the actual thatch.[1]

Generally the shrines are placed in a certain order of importance. The 'big' shrines are the external lineage shrines, which together form a single complex; they are placed outside the compound because they are dangerous and also to signify that they stand above segmental differences within the family cluster and stand for the unity of the total minor or major lineage. After them are the *rįdį* and *tįrį* shrines, which are connected with the father of the lineage ancestress in the *dede* shrine and which like external shrines send sterility to the lineage. Often they are placed together with these external shrines, or they may be put in the centre of the compound, because they are 'big' and 'bad' or dangerous. Third come the internal ghost shrines beneath the granary. Opinion is uncertain as to the relative importance of other shrines. But a pattern emerges in which the four shrines beneath the granary are at the centre of ritual activity, and those under the eaves and within the hut are of less importance and their power is some way derived from those beneath the granary. Lugbara say that they 'follow' those shrines, or sometimes that certain shrines are 'like wives' of those central shrines. Thus the ghost shrines

[1] Illustrations and descriptions of many of these shrines may be found in a paper by Fr. E. Ramponi, 'Religion and Divination of the Logbara Tribe of North-Uganda', *Anthropos*, xxxii, 1937.

'lead' the agnatic ancestral shrines, the *lucugo* leads the other matrilateral shrines, and the agnatic *talį* and *abego* lead the matrilateral *talį* and *abego* shrines. Outside, their distance from the granary, the centre of the homestead, reflecting the degree of danger inherent in them, are the fertility and spirit shrines.

I have already mentioned the grades of seniority within the lineage and family cluster: elder, 'big man', 'man behind', 'big youth', youth and child. These statuses are associated partly with the position of their owners' segments in the lineage, partly by their ownership of shrines, and partly by their ability to invoke the dead, which is demonstrated by oracles. An example is seen in the lineage Araka, shown in Figure 10. Here there is a difference of status between the men Ondua, Draai, Olimani and Otoro. In some situations their segments are seen as four equal family-segments; in others, the segments are headed by Ondua and Olimani only, Draai and Otoro dropping to a junior position.

When regarded as equal, in various situations, family-segments are linked by their respective heads being regarded as 'brothers'. All the 'big men' 'of a cluster are 'brothers' (the elder included, although in certain contexts he stands alone), as are all the 'men behind', and so on. Also, and there is usually inconsistency between the two sets, all owners of senior internal ghost shrines are 'brothers', and so are all owners of junior ghost shrines, whatever their differences in accepted genealogical generation that might in another context define one as a 'big man' and another as a 'man behind' or even a 'big youth'. Even an attached sister's son, who would normally be differentiated strictly from the main agnatic kin in ritual situations, and who would usually be regarded as junior in matters of interest to the cluster as a whole, may become a 'brother' of the 'big men' if he owns a senior ghost shrine, even though his ghosts are different from those of his hosts.

The application of these terms is therefore never very strictly defined, but none the less there is a clear sense of seniority and juniority between their respective members. Lugbara stress the duty of the juniors to respect and 'fear' their seniors, and there is veiled but well recognized hostility between them.

In this society, with few distinctions of rank and wealth and little differences of authority other than within the family cluster, men compete for the ownership of shrines because a shrine is a symbol of status and a mark of ancestral approval for exercising the authority associated with that status, whatever his formal generation status may be. The visitor in Lugbara soon learns that the status of the owner of a compound is assessed not so much by size and number of huts as by the shrines beneath them. An old man may have only a few dependants living in tumbledown and dirty huts; but his status is measured by the number and diversity of shrines visible in his compound. Signs of material wealth, especially if very marked, may enhance status, but they count for little compared to shrines. There are, of course, exceptions. The elder of a small remnant clan has many shrines but few living dependants and his general status tends to reflect his weakness in this respect. But certainly the men whom I know to have the highest status are elders who possess many shrines. Their status is far higher than that of government chiefs, who are far wealthier than other men but who may be little more than 'youths' in ritual status.

Shrines are signs of ritual status *vis-à-vis* both the dead—the higher the status the closer the contact with them and the more numerous the shrines—and the living. The ownership of a shrine confers certain rights and obligations upon the owner, towards both dead and living. Sacrifice at a senior shrine may be as a consequence of either ghost invocation or ghostly vengeance, but at a junior shrine it is only a consequence of ghostly vengeance and never of invocation. In theory any one whose father is dead may invoke the ghosts; in practice it is usually those who own senior shrines. The oracles decide the nature of the process and they are consulted by the head of the family-segment, or by the elder himself if the sickness is especially virulent or persistent. The diagnosis of the oracles depends on the suggestions made by the consultant, and he selects the names to be submitted to them from his knowledge of family and lineage dissensions and tensions.

It is not usually any difference in the identity of the ghosts in these agnatic ghost shrines that is important; this merely reflects the difference in the type of shrine owned and in any case the same ghosts may be in both types of shrine. The important thing is the pattern of rights and duties that ownership implies, and these lie largely in the difference between the processes of ghost invocation and ghostly vengeance. Most invokers are heads of family-segments; that is, it is mainly the owners of senior shrines who invoke, and conversely invokers are seen as having some accepted

right to the ownership of these shrines and so the headship of a
segment. Since a first son, especially of a senior brother, is 'like a
(junior) brother' to his father, any junior brother is in some
respects like a son to his senior brother. So that junior shrine
owners rarely invoke. When they do, especially if on several
occasions, it may mean that their seniors have admitted their
claims to seniority by letting the oracles imply that they have the
social responsibility of invoking. And since the oracles give this
verdict it is a sign of ancestral approval of their claims.

There is thus a struggle to acquire the status of invoker, since
this shows ancestral approval for the exercise of responsibility in
lineage matters. To be shown as invoker by the oracles shows this
responsibility, and also permits a man to speak at the sacrifice that
follows the sickness. Those who speak are again 'brothers', and
only senior men may do so. Such an invoker may come to be
accepted as a member of the higher status grade, and later on
genealogies may be changed in order to eliminate contradictions
between his status in various secular and ritual situations.

Every man who owns internal ghost shrines typically also owns
the 'little', ancestral, shrines, *a'bjva* and *anguvua*. They are for
collective and not for individual ancestors and are not significant
in the rivalry to obtain ghosts that represent the individuality of
the segment. It is axiomatic that each set of ancestral shrines has
originated with a particular ancestor who is at the head of a descent
line, but it is rather a conventional belief that this is so, and his
name is unknown. The incumbents of all ancestral shrines of this
type are in this sense equal in identity: they are as it were something that every constituent descent line possesses as part of the
total social personality of its members.

The position of the *talj* shrine is different. The incumbent of
each *talj* shrine is known and expresses a higher level of lineage
segmentation than junior ghost shrines and ancestral shrines. This
level is that of the sons of minimal lineage founders, these sons
being conventionally given in genealogies as half-brothers. These
are the segments that will become independent minimal lineages
at the next stage of the development of the lineage, earlier than
the present day family-segments in the typical lineage where there
are the two levels of segmentation. The *talj* shrines are, as I said
earlier, associated with a single far-back ancestor's personality,
which is thought to be in some way perpetuated in a whole line of

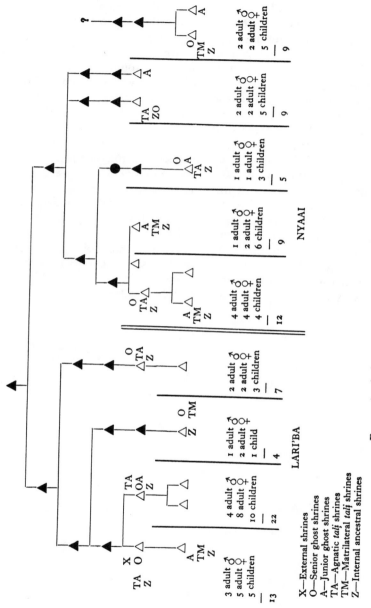

X—External shrines
O—Senior ghost shrines
A—Junior ghost shrines
TA—Agnatic *talj* shrines
TM—Matrilateral *talj* shrines
Z—Internal ancestral shrines

FIGURE 6.   Araka—family segments and shrine distribution

his descendants. The *talį* shrines in the compounds of these potential new lineages are associated in this way with the founder of the entire inner lineage. Those of junior men in these segments, men who are nevertheless heads of family-segments and so owners of ghost shrines, are associated with the founding ancestors of mothers' agnatic lines and not with their owners' agnates. Thus they are not in competition with the *talį* shrines of the segment heads, and also they emphasize the distinctness of the segment from other like segments which share the same agnatic ancestor in the head's *talį* shrine. The situation may be seen in Figure 6.

To own a shrine is a sign of a man's social responsibility, of his headship of a unit—minimal lineage, component family-segment, set of full brothers—or of his fitness for such a position. Attainment of these positions is in theory by genealogical status acquired by birth. But in fact the re-alignment of these small segments is due to other factors also, and genealogical validation will follow any *de facto* re-alignment. The relative position of segments is shown by the shrines owned by their heads. In Chapter IV I shall consider the ways in which men try to acquire shrines and higher status by the operation of the cult of the dead.

III

THE CULT OF THE DEAD: SACRIFICE AND PURIFICATION

I. SICKNESS AND ORACLES

FOR Lugbara the cult of the ghosts and ancestors is concerned with the curing of various mystically caused sicknesses that are the consequence of offences which have aroused the disapproval of the dead. Sickness may also be brought by other agents: living kin may curse, living men may bewitch, disease spirits may send disease, God himself may send sickness which leads to death. Lugbara theory is that specific illnesses are associated with specific agents, and there is a fairly elaborate aetiology of disease. A man aches and grows thin and so knows that the ghosts have sent sickness to him; he aches in his stomach or his bones in the early morning and knows that a witch or sorcerer had affected him; he aches in his head and knows a kinsman has cursed him; his wife does not conceive and he knows a grandmother has cursed him; and so on. He may then consult the oracles to discover two things: the identity of the agent and the remedy. Only agents of certain sicknesses are known by oracles. They do not know, for example, the actual identity of a witch or sorcerer; and certain specific diseases, such as meningitis, are known to come from disease spirits and are not always referred to oracles. Other sicknesses, such as obvious forms of venereal disease, are not referred to oracles since their origin is known. This last category of sickness consists of newly introduced complaints, and they are neither diagnosed nor treated by traditional means: the patient goes to the European hospital for treatment, or obtains Ganda or Congo medicines from men who have returned from southern Uganda, whence these diseases have spread. In the case of traditional sicknesses which are not known by oracles, especially those to do with witchcraft and sorcery, diviners can discover the identity of the actual agent: I discuss them in Chapter V.

In actuality, however, and despite Lugbara theory, the nature of the sickness is determined not by its symptoms but rather by the identity of the agent as decided by oracular utterance. Ghostly sickness is always referred to in general discussion as 'growing thin' (*oyįzu*). But specific cases of sickness for which I have information, for which the cause was given as ghost invocation, included other ailments besides many cases of general lassitude and weakness; the 'growing thin' is not necessarily observable but an assumed physiological concomitant to any general physical or even mental malaise. These included temporary sterility, impotence, many undetermined chest and stomach complaints, toothache, earache, persistent headache, failure of lactation, and others. All of these are also associated with witchcraft, with curses by kinsmen, and other types of agent. Most sicknesses are in fact non-specific enough for them to need to be defined by oracles rather than by their physical symptoms. The actual sickness itself, let alone the responsible agent, is not usually defined clearly until after oracular consultation. I have been told 'we consult the oracles as the Europeans go to see the doctor at the hospital', to discover the cause, the remedy and also the actual nature of a complaint. Lugbara say that the nature of the sickness is a sign of the type and identity of the agent. In fact it is the latter that are the more significant in the total situation and the definition of the sickness is relatively unimportant and is contingent on them.

There are five main oracles used, all generically called *andrį*. Here I do not need to give details of their construction and operation. They are the rubbing-stick oracle (*acįfe*); the boiling medicine oracle (*onda*); the chicken oracle (*buro*); the rat oracle (*gbagba* or *kumuno*); and the poison pod oracle (*e'a*). There are others found in some areas, but they are less important. The rubbing-stick oracle is the common one; it consists merely of a sorghum stalk which is rubbed by the operator with a twist of grass. When the grass sticks, it has 'known' the name given to it at that moment. It is thus open to conscious or unconscious control, but I should not like to decide how far either sort occurs. The other oracles are used mainly as confirming oracles for the rubbing-stick; they are all more mechanical and are less open to control.

The first consultation is made with the rubbing-stick oracle operator. Details of the method vary from one operator to the next, but the general course of the consultation is always the same.

The case is described to him, he may ask certain questions as to its course, then the client puts forward names of persons, either alive or dead, whom he has reason to suspect may be guilty. If the victim is so sick as to have to lie down in his hut, if 'he is thrown', then sticks are laid before the operator to represent the suspects, but in any case the actual names may not be given to him. When the oracle has shown that it 'knows' the agent, then oracle operator and client discuss the case further and the operator informs the client what must be done. Usually this involves an offering to the agent if dead or reparation to him if alive. The oracle itself is not consulted on this point, which is decided by the operator from what he knows of the history of the case and of the situation generally. Many cases have a past history of earlier consultations at oracles and offerings that have been unsuccessful in removing the sickness, and in many cases also the client suggests the offering having regard to what he knows of the agent's personal tastes in meat and beer, his own poverty in livestock or in wives to prepare beer, and of course the agent's reasons for bringing sickness, which may have been the result of a quarrel over livestock. Often, therefore, an offering to a ghost is partly reparation for an injury involving theft or misuse of property, which can now be put right in this way. The important thing is that just as it is the client who submits the names of suspects to the oracle, so it is he who in fact suggests to the operator the kind of offering required.

The oracles should be consulted by the elder of the sick person, although a senior man who is not an elder may consult them himself on behalf of his own dependants, especially if the elder is away or if the patient is only a wife or child. If a man who is not an elder goes to consult the oracles independently he is expected to consult his own elder's oracle later, as a check. If the patient is himself an elder he usually sends a brother to consult elsewhere for him, for he cannot consult his own oracle on his own behalf. A man may consult his elder's rubbing-stick oracle on behalf of his wife. If his consultation shows that it is her father's lineage which is responsible for the sickness, he will tell her father who confirms it at his own oracles. A rubbing-stick operator does not consult his own stick on behalf of himself or his dependants, 'because it will tell him lies'. It is usual to consult the oracle of an operator who is not closely related and so not involved in lineage conflicts.

For certain shrines consultation with the rubbing-stick oracle is sufficient. For the more important shrines its findings should be confirmed by other oracles, especially by the chicken oracle. It is said

If you go only to the rubbing-stick oracle, perhaps it will tell lies. If you go to the chicken oracle, you think 'perhaps this oracle does not enter the hearts of people, it may say lies.' Then you go to the boiling medicine oracle, and you think 'perhaps this oracle also tells lies.' You go to the rat oracle. Perhaps this can also tell lies. But if it confirms the others and all have shown the same way, then you know they are telling true words.

This statement implies that it is the individual choice of the client which decides whether confirming oracles will be consulted, and if so which ones; and this is true in fact, although in theory it is mainly the diagnoses that have reference to ghosts that need confirmation.

When straws or sticks are placed for the rubbing-stick oracle it is common for the two most favoured by the oracle to be placed to the first confirming oracle or to the poison-pod oracle. In this way the chances of open contradiction are minimized. Another minimizing factor is that the confirming oracles may be operated by the original client and not necessarily by the original rubbing-stick operator.

It is recognized that the rubbing-stick oracle often lies. In fact I have been told on several occasions that the chances are about equal whether on any one occasion it tells the truth or lies. This is the fault of the oracle itself and not of its operator. If people say that his oracle often lies, he will be 'with shame', but it is no reflection on his personal integrity. Any man may practise the rubbing-stick oracle: he has merely to dream that he has the skill. The power may be inherited, and a son will not practice while his father is still alive, especially if the latter is an active operator. Inheritance is in a single line only. As with mystical powers such as rainmaking, this means that brothers may not both practise. All operators are senior men, and many are the brothers of elders, who do not themselves practise as operators. Often men who are feared for suspected witchcraft or who are in some way uncanny or unusual may become operators. I was told that women occasionally practise, but I have never met one. There is a contradiction in this situation. The lies of an oracle are attributed to the oracle itself, not to its operator. But the power or skill of the operator is inherited and he is regarded as responsible for the success of the consultation and is paid for it if the client is of another lineage. 'The operator thinks in his heart, he thinks of all the words of the matter as he operates the stick.' That is, his skill lies in the interpretation he gives of the stick's behaviour in his hands. The failure of the oracle may thus be attributed to either the oracle or its operator. The power of the oracle and the skill of the operator come from God, who originally gave oracles and the skill to operate them to the first ancestors; oracles are therefore lawful and 'good' things. The confirming oracles are all considered to be more reliable than the rubbing-stick oracle, and their efficacy is due to their own nature, since they may be made and operated by anybody, whereas the rubbing-stick oracle is operated only by those men who have acquired the skill by dreams or inheritance. Payment is made to the operators of confirming oracles but this is for their skill in making the artifacts required and not for the actual operation of them—the chicken oracle is therefore consulted without payment, since there is virtually nothing to make.

Lugbara say that a good oracle may lie if it is deceived by 'the words of sickness'. The lying is demonstrated either by the other oracles failing to confirm its findings, or by the sickness not responding to the treatment prescribed by it. Usually it is then said that there are two agents responsible, so that in fact the patient is suffering from two sicknesses and that the oracle has 'heard' only one of them. If its finding is not confirmed the client may return to the same oracle, although he will probably take the precaution of consulting other oracles as well; or he may ask his mother's brother to consult on his behalf. If the elder consults another oracle he will of course tell its operator the history of the case and may not place the name approved by the first oracle to be considered at all. Such a double cause usually consists of the occupants of two linked shrines, such as the *anguvua* and *a'bjva* ancestor shrines. And there is always the chance that the sickness comes from God, and oracles cannot 'hear' his words. God is said to be especially likely to confuse the confirming oracles.

The rubbing-stick oracle can 'know the words' of only the members of the consultant's own minor lineage, his mother's brother's people and his wife's brother's people, and in these latter categories only closely related kin. The oracle consulted may be operated by a man far beyond its consultant's minor lineage, however. They know spirits of specific diseases and may occasionally know the identity of witches within this range, although this is not usual. Oracles are supposed, in Lugbara theory, to know the words of the ghosts and ancestors. But Lugbara recognize that it is the living kin who invoke them, directly or indirectly, that are important. Even though oracles may be given the names of the dead who are thought to have caused the sickness, the dead are considered to be primarily the instruments of living people with a grudge. It is the relationship between the living that is primarily significant, the relationship between living patient and ghostly agent being expressed in terms of that between patient and invoker.

The most common situation of ghost invocation is that in which a man's elder invokes the ghosts against him for anti-social behaviour. Invoker, ritual guardian and consultant of oracles are the same person, the elder. Since he places the names of suspects before the oracle it is clear to the outside observer that he in fact determines the choice it makes. Lugbara recognize that this may be so in two ways. First, they say that many elders are witches, who bewitch someone and then say that they have invoked the ghosts to maintain their authority, and that in some way that ordinary people do not understand they are able to cheat the rubbing-stick by their witchcraft. This, of course, may be the stock response of the offender. The second is the fact that in sicknesses which the rubbing-stick decrees are due to invocation of ghosts—that is, the sicknesses in which the elder is most likely to be personally involved as invoker—all three confirming oracles should in theory be consulted. It is thought that whereas the rubbing-stick may both tell lies and perhaps be open to cheating, this is much less true of the confirming oracles. The rubbing-stick is manipulated by hand; the others are more mechanical and their authority therefore comes more directly from God. The rubbing-stick also decrees through the mouth of its operator whereas the others show their verdict openly. The rubbing-stick's verdict is accepted without confirmation only in cases of sickness to do with 'little' shrines, those in which the elders are not concerned either as invokers or as supervisers of rites of sacrifice that follow. The importance of confirming oracles is not, of course, merely that they minimize the chance of an elder consciously manipulating oracles for his own ends. In any case I doubt whether there are such elders—certainly I have not met one who did not believe in oracles. It is rather that in matters of little structural significance—that is, the chain of events connected with sickness brought by ancestor and spirit shrines, the sicknesses of which are usually easily diagnosed—there is little choice of alternative agent and no kinship morality involved, and in any case the choice is comparatively unimportant. But in regard to the sicknesses considered to arise from ghosts there are a great many alternatives which may be put to the oracles, and the choice they make may reflect tensions and conflicts in the local community.

II. SIN AND SACRIFICE

A shrine is a symbol of its owner's status, which involves certain kinship rights and obligations, with respect to both living and dead kin, and also certain ritual and spiritual powers. Through his spiritual power and his ritual activity, which only he can possess and only he perform, the intimate relationship between dead and living, which may be latent, may become one in which actual authority is exercised. It is by the rite of sacrifice that the complete status of shrine owner is realized. It is here that the full significance of the relationship between living and dead, focused in the shrines, can be seen.

Sin temporarily destroys the ideal relationship between living and dead kin. By sacrifice the parties restore this relationship, which is seen as a perfect, ideally unchanging and unchangeable one; after sacrifice order reappears. This ideal relationship is apparent in the ways in which Lugbara speak of the dead as the source of order, right relationships and behaviour between kin, even though in a total framework provided by God. This right behaviour is broken by offences that give rise to the sentiment of indignation between kin, which I have called 'sins'. Sacrifice associated with the commission of sins and the resumption of kinship ties involves immolation of animals, whereas oblations not concerned with sin in this sense are of non-living objects. Immolatory sacrifices are 'big' and they have the widest and most formal congregations. Lugbara do not sacrifice at 'natural' crises, such as harvest, sowing, marriage or death. They do make sacrifices at fertility shrines, in order to cure sterility in women or livestock. But sterility is often regarded as a consequence of persistent sin.

Lugbara say that it is by the giving of meat and beer that the living contact their dead kin:

> We cannot see our ancestors with our eyes; but we speak with the ghosts at the shrines beneath the granaries. We give them meat. It is like saying 'welcome', and they say 'thank you' to us for the meat which we give them. And we say 'thank you' to them because the sickness is cured.

By the sharing of food an intimate relationship is affirmed, or rather re-affirmed, between living and dead. Both are present not as two distinct groups but rather as members of a single community, the agnatic lineage. The dead are not members of the local section, the territorial group as it is living today on the Lugbara plateau; but they are members of the agnatic clan and lineages whose living members compose the actual local groups. It is at sacrifice that all the lineage members are present or represented.

To sacrifice is *owi*, meaning to give food to the dead or to spirits, to place food in the shrines, whether to ghosts or not. The verb is always used with the object of the sacrifice: *ori owi* ('sacrifice to the ghosts'), *dede owi*, ('sacrifice at the *dede* shrine'), and so on. In particular the term means to offer meat or other food which has been consecrated for this purpose, to the agents who have sent sickness to a living person, but the use of the word is extended to cover the whole rite or set of rites of sacrifice. *Owi* is quite different from making reparation for injury, by giving food and drink to a kinsman who has caused sickness by a curse, or to a witch or evil-eye man. These gifts are not the object of *owi*, but of mere 'giving' (*fe*). The agents in the latter case are living and can be approached directly and given a gift. This brings them into sympathetic relations with the giver. But there is nothing sacred about such gifts.

Sacrifice is never performed without prior consultation of at least the rubbing-stick oracle. It is said:

> The words of sacrifice are that a man has begun to get a little better, and now we cut a beast to say 'thank you' to the ghosts. Now he gets better and we are joyful. We give food to our fathers and say 'thank you' to them, so that they may rejoice also with us.

Lugbara say that an offering made to the ghosts is to show them that the offender has had his offence brought home to him and repents in his heart, and that his living kin have forgiven him and all wish to resume normal relations with one another and the dead. Sacrifice is not made in order to propitiate the agent who has sent the sickness, as may be seen from the fact that it is made after the sickness is cured. Lugbara say that it is not to cajole or to propitiate the ghosts but to thank them and to rejoice with them. This thanking and rejoicing is compared by them to the thanking and rejoicing by the members of the lineage who assemble to dance death dances at burials. They 'rejoice' in order to mark the reaffirmation of ties of kinship which have been disrupted by the death. It is the same with sacrifice; it is made to mark the restoration of normal relations between living and dead.

Sacrifice is made after the sickness has been removed by the ghosts upon a promise, by the consecration of an animal, that an oblation will be made. It is not made immediately because it is thought impossible for the oracles to know whether God is involved or not. If he is, then the patient will die and it is pointless, wasteful and even presumptuous to make an offering. The promise is made and if the patient recovers it is carried out; if he dies then God is the cause and the promise loses its validity. At death there is no breach of relationship between the dead man and either God or the ancestors. There is no sacrifice because there is no broken kin tie to be mended by the rite, and there is no moral offence involved (kin ties are broken by death between living kin, but these are marked by mortuary rites which do not include sacrifice).

A promise to sacrifice is only valid if the promiser possesses the necessary animal, which is then consecrated, the act of consecration being in itself the promise. A promise that a man will merely find an animal later is pointless. A poor man told me that he had been told by the oracles to sacrifice a goat on behalf of his sick son, but he had no goat and so was waiting:

If God wants him to die, then truly he will die. If God wants him to recover then truly he will recover.

Only if his son's sickness continued to grow worse would he try to find a goat quickly and consecrate it; but he would do nothing hasty. Although his attitude was condemned by a few people, it is a common one, and his condemnation reflected personal dislikes as much as true opinion. It must be said that his son was not very ill. When a person is seriously sick then Lugbara are quick to find and consecrate the necessary animal.

Offerings made to the ghosts consist of domestic animals and beer. The animals are bulls and oxen, he- and she-goats, rams and ewes, and cocks, and both blood and meat are placed in or on the shrines; they are also consumed by the members of the congregation. And blood is sprinkled on the patient and on the homestead. Rams and ewes are also 'the animals of God', and when they are used for oblation it is thought that God is concerned as well as the dead. Beer is placed on the shrines and drunk by the congregation; it is not sacrificed but is merely 'given'. Its use marks the resumption of normal relations—beer is consumed at all rites and ceremonies to mark or to reaffirm the existence of friendly relations between the parties, and especially friendly kinship relations. For certain shrines grain, dried meat or milk are offered, but never for agnatic ghost shrines. Unlike some African peoples the Lugbara do not 'cheat' the ghosts by offering a small object of little value but calling it something of greater value, as the Nuer, for example, may offer a wild cucumber saying they are offering an ox. Lugbara were incredulous when I told them of this and remarked that their own ghosts could see and taste as well as anyone and were not as stupid as those of other peoples.

III. CONSECRATION

The ritual of sacrifice contains certain elements: the consecration of the sacrificial animal, which takes place before the sacrifice proper; the ritual addresses; the killing and offering. All this is *owi* proper, which brings the living into direct relationship with the dead or spirits. There is then the blessing and anointing of the patient on whose behalf the sacrifice is being made. This is part of the purification, which includes both that of the individual who has been sick and that of his family and community. Finally there is the distribution and partaking of the meat, blood and beer among the living members of the congregation, which brings them into a new and re-created relationship with the ghosts and with one another. The last part is properly called *awi*, a word which appears etymologically to be unconnected with *owi*. However, the whole is often loosely called *owi* by Lugbara.

The animal is first consecrated for a particular sacrifice; the ghosts, and God, then show in various ways that they accept it; it is then sacrificed. I use the term 'consecrate' in the context of its being set aside, promised to the ghosts, and so becoming sacred. I do not use the term 'dedicate', since all domestic animals are in fact dedicated to sacrifice, but are sacrificed only after being consecrated for a particular occasion. Consecration is in two parts: the laying on of hands by the elder and the subsequent acceptance of the beast by God and the ghosts. Without the acceptance the former act is invalid.

When the oracles have been consulted, the sick patient's elder,[1] or whoever is acting as his ritual guardian, takes the animal which is to be sacrificed and leads it round the homestead of the patient. If the patient is a male, it is led round four times, if a female, three times. Four is the number appropriate for men and three for women. I have heard that it should be led round in an anti-clockwise direction, but this seems to be unimportant and I have seen it led in either direction. This is known as 'encircling the hut' and its purpose is said to be to 'show', it to the people of the lineage, both living and dead. If the offering is to be a cock it is not taken round the homestead but encircled round the patient's head, four times if a man and three times if a woman.

Before taking the beast round the compound the elder places his hand on its back, and 'speaks words', saying that it will be sacrificed and its meat and blood placed on the shrines. These acts and words comprise the first part of the consecration. In some parts of Lugbara the right hand is used, in others the left: it is the hand that is later used to place the meat inside the shrine. By using this particular hand the elder shows that he is speaking with formal authority as elder of his lineage, and not as a mere individual. He and his assistants are in a spiritually pure condition, in that they have not washed their faces in the morning and have kept certain taboos. The 'words' are usually few, and may even be unsaid but merely thought in the elder's own mind. It is the 'showing' that is important and not an actual series of words and phrases. The promise is invariably kept. If broken it becomes one of a category called *o'yo*, promises made (usually to oneself, in thought only) to expend property or wealth in a certain way; if the

---

[1] I use the term 'patient' for the sick person for whom the sacrifice is made, and the term 'victim' for the animal which is sacrificed.

promise is broken it is soon followed by death, which is sent by God.

The encircling puts the individual or group whose relationship with the remainder of the lineage has been weakened by the offence into a particular relationship with the sacrificial victim, which might be called identification. The laying of hands creates a relationship between victim and the community; encircling creates a similar but more intense relationship between victim and the patient and his immediate family, the members of which are ritually and morally responsible for him.

Once the encircling has been done then the beast must be sacrificed when the patient has recovered or the sickness will return to him again. If he dies then it is not sacrificed since God has taken him in death. But should this happen it is suspected that nevertheless the same sickness will take another member of the same family, in a year or so. The oracles will then be consulted and if they say that it is the same sickness and the same agent then the beast will be sacrificed immediately without waiting to see whether the second patient recovers or dies. It thus happens that if a beast is consecrated and if it is accepted, in the way I describe in a moment, then it will sooner or later be sacrificed on account of the same sickness sent by the same agents, even if the original patient has died. This is significant as an indication of the essential purpose of sacrifice, to re-create ties of lineage kinship that have been weakened by sin. If the offender in fact dies, as a result of the intervention of God, the breach may still remain and is repaired by a later sacrifice for a different patient. A beast is thus in fact consecrated for the re-creation of a breach in a specific set of lineage ties, rather than for the recovery of a particular individual patient.

When the beast has been led around the compound to 'show' it to the lineage, it is stood by the gate to urinate. If it does so while being led around the homestead or immediately afterwards it is a sign that the patient will recover and the sacrifice be acceptable. But if after some moments by the gate it does not urinate, if it defaecates instead, or if it refuses to be led docilely and becomes stubborn, then it is 'bad'. It is a sign that 'God refuses'.[1] God is

[1] Urination is said to be a sign of God's approval in other contexts. A person who is affected by certain types of sorcery is treated by a doctor who applies magical medicines to the patient's body. During the treatment the patient suddenly urinates, or sometimes sneezes, and gets up cured. This is a sign that God has 'refused' sorcery to become effective.

also said to 'refuse' if rain should fall during the rite, or even the sky grow very dark. The matter is then left; it is pointless to try with another animal. There is then no consecration of the animal, for sacrifice on a later occasion. God has shown that he is directly concerned, that the dead are not concerned, that there is no outstanding breach of lineage ties. 'Perhaps that man will be taken by God in death; perhaps the oracles have not followed his words. We do not cut that beast.' Lugbara say that if the ghosts disapprove of the beast then they may let the patient recover—since he has in any case shown his repentance—and will later send more sickness to the same homestead as a protest against the meanness of its head in selecting for them a poor undersized beast. This is a different situation from that described above, since in this case there are two distinct oblations made, even though they are connected. Lugbara see the situation in terms of the ghosts' longing for meat, which can provide an explanation for whatever actually happens to the patient in the course of his sickness. They say that the ghosts refuse because the promised offering is too small. It is not said that it may be refused because the sin has not been atoned for or because certain living members of the lineage have not yet forgiven the culprit. It is, however, God who is said to accept or refuse, and not the ghosts. The role played by God here is that of controller of all nature, including men and ghosts: they are all his creatures.

IV. THE RITE OF SACRIFICE

The victim for the sacrifice is thus consecrated and God and the ancestors show their approval and acceptance of the oblation promised. The elders and important men concerned show that the groups which they represent associate themselves with the purpose of the rite by laying their hands also on the victim's back. The beast is then left in the herd and may not be used for another purpose, such as bridewealth. Later, depending on whether or not the patient recovers, his ritual guardian, usually the elder of his minimal lineage, decides that the sacrifice shall be made.

Sacrifice takes place at the homestead of the patient, who must be present. In charge of the rite and supervising everything, although he may not perform every sacrificial action, is his ritual guardian, even if he is the person who originally invoked the ghosts against the patient. The members of the congregation assemble, without having washed their faces or rinsed their mouths that morning, a sign that they are ritually pure and able to take part in their formal ritual roles. They are the heads of closely related agnatic and accessory lineages and segments; I discuss the composition of congregations, which varies for every sort of sacrifice and offering, in a later section. For a sacrifice at the internal ghost shrines there may be up to twenty or so old men, who come into the homestead and seat themselves in the shady places under the eaves, granaries or shade trees on papyrus mats set for them. They are given beer to drink by the women of the homestead and sit waiting for all to be present before starting the sacrifice. The case of the sickness is discussed and the sacrificial animal inspected to see whether it will provide enough meat to go round. The unmarried girls of the homestead and those girls born into the lineage concerned but now married elsewhere attend if they can do so. Wives and women neighbours prepare vegetables and squeeze beer for the men. Children, goats and dogs sit about in the sun and fowls peck at the food and dust themselves among the shrines in the shade of granaries. At first sight the atmosphere is one of excitement and there may be much laughter and joking. But one soon becomes aware that there is an underlying tension. The assembled elders are conscious that this is an occasion on which they must clear their hearts of animosity towards one another, and unsettled and festering quarrels must later be aired and made up. Since the sacrifice is itself the consequence of an offence on the patient's part which led to quarrelling and then to invocation or ghostly vengeance, there are bound to be some animosity, sulkiness and self-righteousness. The elders do not sit haphazardly but by generation. Nevertheless, there is usually quarrelling between elders of different segments. Much depends on the amount of beer drunk and the degree of hunger for meat, but Lugbara tend to become truculent and aggressive on very little pretext, and I have never seen any rite of this sort performed without some show of hostility. The cause of the sickness has, of course, already been determined by the oracles, so there is no notion of seeking out an offender at these gatherings. They are met together for communion—for ritual, not for judicial, purposes.

Before the victim is sacrificed the elder who is supervising the rite states aloud the main facts of the case. This recital is known as *adj*,[1] and is made to 'show the words'. It is made to both living and dead members of the lineage, to call their attention to the rite, to say that there is meat and beer and that the breach in kin relations is to be mended. It is said more to the living than to the dead, in so far as living members may be addressed personally whereas the dead are rarely addressed. I was told on one occasion that 'the ancestors died long ago. Who knows whether they hear or not?' My informant was immediately checked as being cynical and impious, but because he had spoken improperly rather than untruly. The saying of these 'words' marks the almost insensible formation of the congregation. Before there is merely an assembly of living elders and representatives, with the ghosts in the background. The ritual address gives all a common purpose and unites them as a single congregation with an interest in that particular sacrifice.

The second ritual address is made later, when the oblation has been placed in the ghost shrines but before it has been distributed among the living congregation. The first address is usually short. The actual purpose and circumstance of the rite are set forth at much greater length in the second address. This is said by both the supervising elder and other elders involved in the case. The elder states the facts of the case in full, sometimes with long and detailed genealogical discussion, and he may include the main genealogical history and relationships of the lineage segments represented in the congregation. At the telling of this address all the underlying animosities and quarrels are usually brought into the open; at least an opportunity is given for this to happen. It includes a public declaration as to the identity and motives of the agent responsible for the sickness. It is said that besides the living thus being able to thrash out their animosities and grudges, the ghosts will hear the 'words' of the case and will rejoice that they and the living are now in harmony and that the breach caused by the offender is mended. Then they are 'well in their hearts' and the sickness will not return. Ritual addresses are always much the same, although each clan and lineage has its own details, especially those of the doings and genealogies of the ancestors, which are

[1] I translate *adi* as 'ritual address'. Although I have been told that it consists of 'the words said to the ghosts' it is not a prayer. A prayer made to God is referred to as *Adroa a'j*, to 'beseech or beg God'. Prayers are made to God on rare occasions of famine, drought or other communal disaster; I describe them later in this chapter.

included and provide a focus for the solidarity of the assembled elders. Those I have heard stressed the same things, that there should be no discord within the kin-group, that the girls should bring in good bridewealth and not behave promiscuously and so destroy the lineage, and that their wives should bear good and obedient sons. Addresses end with these pladitudinous appeals, as a fit ending to the spate of listing of grudges and disputes within the group and between it and others. Addresses are long and involved and are usually almost unintelligible without some knowledge of the internal affairs of the group. They are important and their content includes the nearest approximation in Lugbara to knowledge that is secret and kept from members of other lineages. Lugbara are very averse to giving accounts of ritual addresses to an enquirer who has not attended the rite. Whereas the first address creates the congregation, the second marks the time when the congregation and especially its living members, shares the oblation as a communion. It may be said to mark the withdrawal of the ghosts from the congregation so that the living members enter into their own in order to share the sacrificial food. By the saying of genealogical and traditional lore in the second address, in a heightened ritual atmosphere, this lore becomes not a series of isolated details but a single coherent corpus of tradition and experience culminating in the present situation. I shall show later that sacrifice is usually associated with a change in the alignment of lineage segments. This culmination of tradition marks the re-alignment and so validates it. The address is not said merely so that members of the lineage should be reminded of their past history and of their present interrelationships that have come into being as a consequence of that history: rather it reformulates that past history.

While a man speaks a ritual address he holds a small bunch of sacred leaves in his 'ritual' hand, the one used for inserting the offering into the actual shrine. To hold these leaves is a sign that a man is acting in his formal ritual status, that he has left his individual prejudices and grudges and is thinking only of the good of his lineage. Lugbara emphasize that a ritual address must be 'true'; a man must not lie while telling it. To lie while holding these leaves amounts to perjury. It is said that even if other men do not, the ghosts do know it to be untrue. If a man speaks untruth in this situation then the entire rite is nullified, since the ghosts refuse to allow the patient to recover fully or send further sickness to his family. While making the address these leaves are used to punctuate the points made, when the teller may spit on them to emphasize that he is telling the truth. At the end of the address the leaves are spat on by all senior men present and placed upon the shrines. This is done to 'show their hearts are good'. Sometimes the leaves are also placed on the shrines the previous evening, to 'warn the ghosts'. Later they are used in other parts of the rite, and I shall discuss them later in this chapter.

The sacrificial animal is killed by being held on the ground and its throat cut with a knife. The blood is collected in a pot and the carcase scorched, skinned and cut up, and the contents of the stomach and intestines are squeezed out into a pot. This is the 'cutting' (*alʝ*) and is done in the same way as is the killing of an animal for any other purpose, ritual or otherwise. All this is done under the general direction of the elder, but the actual killing and dismembering are done by 'sisters' sons' of the lineage, if possible by those of the patient. It is said to be 'bad' if this work is done by a member of the lineage, but I have seen them doing so at small and unimportant sacrifices. It is 'bad' in the same way that it is 'bad' for a lineage member to dig a grave, which should also be done by sisters' sons. I was told that lineage members will become sick if they do these things, and that sisters' sons do the slaughtering because they are outside the lineage. They are not usually concerned in the lineage's tensions and quarrels; they do not, therefore, share in the sacrificial meat and have no interest in its distribution. To help at the rites of the lineage whence one's mother came, and of which one would have been a member had she only been born a man, is an act which expresses the essentially personal nature of the kinship tie, a tie with little formal jural content; ritual occasions are ideal for its expression.

The meat is divided into portions and distributed among the members of the congregation. I discuss the distribution in detail below. The meat distributed consists of the four limbs, which are not cut up, and part of the back and shoulders which are divided into small portions to be taken away by members of the congregation. Part is placed in the shrines for the ghosts. The rest of the meat, with the stomach and its contents, except for certain parts which go to the officiating elder and his family, is cooked with porridge and blood and is eaten by the members of the congregation in a sacrificial meal, with beer. The elder's portion consists of the chest (a man is an elder 'because he eats the chest of meat'), the tongue, liver, kidneys and other internal organs, the penis, testicles and part of the intestines. The rest of the intestines is distributed, eaten by the congregation, or even given to the children of the household, together with the chyme and chyle mixed with blood. The parts that go to the elder include those that are thought to contain the vitality of the beast. They are 'strong' and other men 'fear' to eat them and will refuse them if offered. The elder and his family eat them on the following day, with no special ceremony.

The offering of the oblation to the ghosts and the subsequent anointing and blessing of the patient form the climax of the whole rite of sacrifice. Details vary greatly from one part of Lugbara to another, and elders change details and order of the elements with what is at first disconcerting frequency. But this variation is not significant. Lugbara have no notion that precise words or actions have virtue in themselves; the rite is efficacious if the actors are sincere in their words, and if the ghosts and God have approved of the rite being performed. Without these prerequisities no elegance of performance or meticulous following of detail is of use.

The blood of the sacrificial victim is placed in a large pot and some is poured from it into a small calabash. The elder pours this blood over all the stones of the shrine, and not merely over that of the ghost which the oracles have named as being responsible for the sickness. It is poured by the officiating elder himself, and not by the head of the homestead. This is to 'pour the blood' and 'it is bad to give blood to one ghost only, for then the others are jealous.' This is done immediately after the slaughter. Later the rest of the blood is cooked with the meat, or boiled with chyme and chyle, and distributed among the congregation and consumed. If the offering is a cock, which has little blood, it is all poured over the shrines and none is consumed by the congregation. Blood is essentially the food of the ghosts, while that of the living is meat. In certain purificatory rites blood is used to sprinkle the homestead and to anoint the congregation—I mention these below. But in sacrificial rites it is a means of communion with the dead as well as one of purification.

Beer is placed in the shrines, in small calabashes used only for this purpose. It is unsqueezed beer, taken from the main supply of beer while that is being squeezed for human consumption. It is unsqueezed because the 'soul' of the beer is in the grains which are removed from the liquid by the squeezing: the grains are the 'strong' element of the beer.

The meat is then cooked. One or two small pieces together with cooked porridge are put in the shrines, or on them in those areas where the shrines are flat stones and not proper 'houses' of stone or mud. This is known as 'inserting the hand' (*drị tị*). It is the central act of the rite and its performance is said to be one of the marks of status of an elder. He uses right and left hand according to whether the ghosts are male or female. In northern Lugbara the right hand is for males and the left for females; this corresponds to the side on which they are buried. In some other areas the left hand is for males and the right for females, the opposite to the side on which they are buried. The 'male' hand is the 'ritual' hand.

The second ritual address is then said by both the elder of the minimal lineage and by the head of the compound in which the sacrifice is being made. The invoker follows with another address to show that his heart is now free of anger; then any of the elders assembled who may wish make short addresses in turn. A man is likely to speak if his segment is concerned in the case. These latter addresses are not essential to the success of the rite.

V. SACRIFICIAL ANIMALS

Before discussing the other elements of the rite, I wish to consider the oblation in more detail. The crucial questions are that of the purpose of offering a blood sacrifice and of the notion as to the relationship between the living, the dead and the sacrificial animal.

Two features of domestic animals that are significant in this context are that they are said to possess souls and that they belong to the lineage, in particular to the minimal lineage, as a corporate group. Only cattle, sheep and goats possess souls, not fowls, which are also used sacrificially, nor wild animals. The former (including fowls) are grouped as 'animals in the home', the latter as 'animals in the grass'. I was told that the ghosts 'eat' the souls of the animals sacrificed. This should not be taken as a literal belief, but as a metaphor to explain the mystery of ghostly eating.

The ghosts consume part of the oblation, its 'soul', the equivalent on a mystical plane of the meat eaten by the living members of the congregation; thus they enter the communion of sacrifice. Domestic animals are destined for sacrifice and are attributed souls for this reason.

Sacrificial animals need not be castrated, nor need they be of a single colour nor of any particular colour. The exception is the case of a scapegoat offered to God in times of drought, which must be a white ram. Beasts offered to the dead should not, however, be wretched skinny creatures and in an important sacrifice a man will offer the best beasts he can. Lugbara say that this is so that the ghosts and living members of the congregation may eat well. They do not say that the beast need be unblemished as far as the efficacy of the rite is concerned. I have seen sacrificial beasts that certainly were not unblemished either in colour or in condition.

Domestic livestock are ultimately the property of the lineage, more especially the minimal lineage. Livestock that a man acquires through his own efforts (by sale of crops, labour migration, working as a doctor or oracle operator, and so on) are his own property and used within the matrisegment, the set of full brothers of whom he is one; and livestock received as bridewealth are used within the same group. But, more important, since the continual cycle of development of the lineage makes it difficult to know what is the actual using group at a given time, within the minimal lineage livestock may be borrowed without the transaction being a 'debt' (*mari*). If borrowed from another minimal lineage, even if of the same minor lineage, it is a debt; repayment may in fact never be made or may be delayed for years or even generations, but the animal may be demanded as of right at any time. Repayment is then enforced by public opinion, approved force and fear of ghostly vengeance; and today the courts support the plaintiff in such cases.

Domestic livestock should not be killed merely for meat; a greedy elder is accused of sacrificing fat beasts merely to satisfy his desire for meat. Today men often sell livestock for money. But this is done only at the direction of government chiefs, who have to maintain regular markets and supplies of meat; usually they order homesteads to supply meat in turn. Lugbara accept this as a means of making cash but they do not regard it as being a proper thing to do; it is merely one of the many tiresome things that have to be done now that the Europeans have 'spoilt the land'. It is thus outside the sphere of traditional behaviour and so is hardly considered as a breach of it. By Lugbara notions livestock is meant for ultimate sacrifice. If asked why they sacrifice live-stock they reply: 'Because they are the beasts of the ancestors'; 'because they are the things of men' (that is, not things in nature outside the sphere and control of men); 'because our ancestors did so.' It is not clear whether Lugbara consider that their livestock belong as much to the ancestors as to the living. Certainly they do accept that the living are stewards for the ancestors, for the lineage is an everlasting group—the expected behaviour of an elder shows this. In this sense it can be said that the livestock are the property of the ancestors as much as of the living, so that a man sacrifices a beast to the dead who already have rights over it. He is not offering something that is uniquely his to offer, but something that is already a symbol of his link with them.

Sacrifice to the dead and to spirits may be of a living animal or of grain and dried meat. The former is associated with ghostly sickness, the latter with sickness sent by disease spirits and by the ancestors in non-ghostly roles. The former has the more to do with sin, as an offence against lineage unity. The actual offender may not be struck; it may be his wife, child or junior sibling. How-ever, it is the head of the offender's family segment who supplies the animal; if he cannot do so then he may obtain it from the elder. Evans-Pritchard has shown for the Nuer how the person who offers the sacrificial animal to God is aware that he is offering to God what is God's; it is not so much a gift as a recognition of God's power and rights. Something of the sort holds also for Lugbara. A man offers to the ghosts a beast from the family or the lineage herd. So far as I know Lugbara do not consider that an offender should supply an animal of his own acquisition, although he often does so. But it is clear that it is the family segment, even the minimal lineage, that may be considered to supply the beast, rather than the offender himself. It cannot be said that the offender himself yields up his own property, at any rate in the case of an animal needed for immolation. The situation is different in the case of non-animal sacrifices, which are provided by the offender himself—but in such cases the oblation is of comparatively little value and the lineage aspect of the rite is lacking.

In cases of immolation the offender's atonement is in the sickness, which 'shows him words'. Immolation is concerned with sin; non-animal oblations lack the moral content of the immolatory rites. By his sin not only the relationship between him and his lineage is breached but the lineage group as a whole suffers by this disruption: 'the lineage is destroyed, its words are lost and destroyed.' It is both the desire and the duty of the responsible members—heads of families and the elder himself—to mend this state of affairs and to resume orderly relationships with one another and with the ghosts. This is done by the sacrificial gift to the ghosts and the sharing of the meat among themselves and them. Once God has shown that he accepts the promised oblation, and once the sickness is removed by the ghosts, then the sacrifice and communion are made, not as a propitiation or bribe, or even as atonement by the patient, but as a recognition by the lineage that its ties are restored. The visible sacrifice is the sign of an invisible reality, lineage order. Oblation marks the return to lineage order, by the resolution of conflict within the lineage. Immolation marks the cleansing of sin; oblation that involves no immolation of animals is made at ancestral shrines, where sin is not significant as a factor in the total process.

Evans-Pritchard has suggested that for the Nuer the sacrificial animal is a surrogate for a man.[1] Lugbara have never suggested to me that the sacrificial victim is in any way a substitute for a man. But there is one rite in which substitution is implied. In Omugo, in east-central Lugbara, rainmaking rites are performed on a small hill called Ili, to the north-west of Mt. Eti, the mountain on which the hero-ancestor Dribidu is buried. Until the 1930s the rites on Ili involved human sacrifice. A stranger, taken from another tribe in war, and with umbilical hernia, was killed in time of drought by a rainmaker of Omugo, who still performs the rites of rainmaking. He told me a myth that tells that the stranger was himself a substitute for a child of the community; his blood, especially that from the hernia, was offered to the immanent aspect of God, who dwells in streams and on mountains. Since about 1930 they have feared the government and no victim has been killed. Instead the victim was first taken to Ili and his ear cut to provide blood. Today a ram is killed and its blood offered with prayers to God; there is apparently no shrine.

[1] E. E. Evans-Pritchard, *Nuer Religion*, Chapter X.

Unfortunately I was in Omugo for only a very short time and was unable to get further information, nor did I visit Ili. I was not told how the body of the victim was disposed of. It is likely that similar sacrifices have until recently been made for rain at the grave of Dribidu, on the top of Mt. Eti; today rams are offered but this would seem a recent innovation. It seems plain that at Ili the roles of human victim and ram are similar, the latter being a substitute (due to direct external intervention) for the former.

Although it is doubtful whether this rite should properly be called sacrifice, it is certainly made to God, as the controller of rain. And just as the animal offered to the ghosts is already something that is theirs, so is a stranger or client (*atįbo*) regarded as a man without kin ties who is already associated with God. But to suppose that, by analogy, offerings made to the ghosts are also surrogates for men would be a mistake. There is no kinship between man and God, as there is between living and dead. Lugbara say specifically that an oblation is made to the dead to say 'thank you' and to 'rejoice'. But an offering to God is made in order to ask for rain or other blessing; it is not a matter of 'thanking' or 'rejoicing'; and men do not sacrifice to their dead kin in order to ask for favours of this kind from them.

VI. RITES OF PURIFICATION

I now turn to the second element in the total rite of sacrifice, that of purification. Fully to analyse Lugbara notions as to ritual impurity and its removal would require far more space than I can devote to it here; here I present only an outline account. There is a vast number of rites and situations associated with some kind or degree of impurity; here I consider only the more common ones and those often mentioned by Lugbara even though the rites may not actually often be performed—as those made to remove drought, for example. Those I mention are those that throw some light on the significance of sin and sacrifice for the Lugbara.

Lugbara say that the purpose of ghost invocation is 'cleansing the territory' (*angu edezu*), that is, to purify the lineage home and to mend the breach in lineage relations that has been caused by the original offence. There is also, conjointly, the purpose of 'cleansing the body' (*rµa edezu*), which refers to the individual patient and the members of his immediate family.

The concepts of 'cleansing' and 'repairing' are both included in the Lugbara verb *ede*. It also means 'prepare' or 'make ready'. A person or territory (especially in the sense of a lineage home and so of the collectivity of lineage members) is cleansed of sin, and the network of social relations that compose a man's status or a group's position in its social system is repaired.

A sinner is in a state of sin which is removed by purification at the rite of sacrifice. This is quite distinct, of course, from a state of sickness, which ends before the sacrifice is made. The sinner breaks normal relations with his lineage and his community, which are shown to be repaired at the communion after the oblation. But God also enters into sacrifice. The relations of a sinner to God are not made explicit by Lugbara, just as those between any individual man and God cannot be made explicit. A man is one of God's creatures. God created him and his ancestors, and created, through the hero-ancestors, the orderly pattern of society. It is for man to maintain this pattern, and the dead watch their living kin to ensure that they do this. But God is behind the dead and is ultimately, though not directly or immediately, concerned. I was told that:

God stands behind the dead, as the District Commissioner stands behind the chiefs. Their power comes from him—are they not also men like us who are little and without power? . . . When we do wrong the chiefs punish us to show us that we do wrong, but it is the District Commissioner who tells the chiefs what they should tell us to do.

When I asked how God is concerned in sin, an offence primarily against the lineage, I was told:

To offer sacrifice is to give food to the dead. It is not to give food to God. We do not do that. But truly God is there. Does he not see the sacrifice? He sends the rain or holds it back. He is behind the ghosts, he stands there behind them and is pleased that we give food to our fathers.

Rites of purification are found both as part of sacrificial rites and in rites in which there is no oblation. Both are referred to as 'cleansing the body' when an individual is concerned, and as 'cleansing the territory' when a lineage group is concerned. Some rites may have both purposes, and in many cases the same rite may be referred to by either term, according to the situation of the moment. Purification is part of the purpose of sacrifice and so all sacrifices include certain actions which may be called rites that purify body or territory, or both.

In ghostly and ancestral sacrifices the rites that effect the purification of individual and lineage follow the placing of the meat and blood in or on the shrine. The second ritual addresses are made, and while reciting them each speaker holds sacred leaves in his 'ritual' hand and after each point made spits on them. They are then handed to the other elders who hold them in their hands and spit on them in turn. They then blow in turn into the patient's right ear, using their right hand, cupped, as a funnel. This is 'blowing breath' (*avįvį vų*). Its purpose is 'to cool the sickness' so that the patient's body will be well and not become sick again, and also to ensure that there is life in his body. The 'cooling' is a mystical one, since by the time the sacrifice is made overt symptoms of sickness have already disappeared. The invoker then anoints the patient's body with the leaves and spittle; he is followed by the officiating elder who does the same. The body is anointed on the sternum and insteps, and sometimes on other parts also. It is said that the sternum is the 'place of the heart', and anointment there will help bring coolness to the heart, as the seat of the emotions. The insteps are also anointed as the emotions that have prevented the heart's being cool are said to pass out of the body by moving downwards and out at the feet. Lugbara are not more explicit than this over the matter, and it is not possible to say more of what is considered to be in the heart to prevent its cooling.

The elder then places half the bunch of *larįgbį* leaves[1] in the roof thatch over the door of the senior wife's hut and the rest of the *larįgbį* leaves and all the *ajįgbį* leaves on the shrines, if the patient is a woman or a child; if he is a man all are placed on the shrines, where they are left to wither.

This is done in cases of ghost invocation; in those of ghostly vengeance there is no 'blowing breath'. In this case it is said that God will send a cool wind on behalf of the dead. It is the dead, not the living, who are responsible for the sickness and so only they can judge the matter fully.

In these actions to do with anointing and blessing there are three interconnected elements: spittle, breath and sacred leaves.

---

[1] I discuss the significance of these leaves below.

The anointing with spittle is called *adʒ co* (to 'drive out trouble') or *rʉa co* (to 'make the body well').

This is a part of sacrifice, but there are other rites called *rʉa co* which are not sacrifices, and which also have as purpose 'cleansing the body'. Perhaps the most common are the rite of blessing a girl at her marriage by the head of her minimal lineage so that she will become pregnant and not miscarry, and the rite of removing leprosy, or the threat of it, which has been sent by a woman, now dead, to a kinsman who offended her during her lifetime. In both of them spittle is used. In the former the elder spits on the bride's face and forehead, before either she or the elder has washed, on the morning that she leaves her natal home to go to her husband. In the latter the sisters of the dead woman take *ajʒgbʒ* and *amatrʒgbʒ* leaves and with them brush their spittle on the patient's chest and insteps. The leaves are then placed in the grass near the compound. If on the following morning there are traces of hyena excrement on them, this is a sign from God that the rite will be unsuccessful; but if there are none it will succeed. Again, neither patient nor anointers may wash that day before the performance of the rite.

These rites, and others which I need not describe, are not associated with sacrifice, shrines, or the sharing of ritual food. They are solely rites to remove a state of impurity which may follow a curse or an ill wish, even if only a covert one. It is not merely the result of the curse that is removed, but also the condition of being under a curse or in the state of danger that follows a curse. It may be an automatic curse called *o'yo*, which is made by a man's promising himself that he will use livestock or money for a certain purpose; if he uses it differently then he will be 'seized' by *o'yo*. *O'yo* is said to bring any type of sickness that leads to rapid death; the cases of which I know were all fatal fits or trances, or the man may be struck by meteors, lightning, fireflies or terrible snakes—all these things being manifestations of God's power. Thus *o'yo* is not the concern of the dead. If a man wishes to use his property differently, and especially if he wishes to give it away, he can break *o'yo* ('strike *o'yo*') by spitting on his own chest; in the case of a child his parent of the same sex does this for him. In the latter case the application of spittle is thus not even by the same person who set the *o'yo* in action. This is said to be because the spittle of a child, a socially incomplete being, does not contain the mystical quality, *talí*, found in adult spittle. There is here, however, one significant point: a man must have his father dead before he can come into contact by sacrifice with the dead, but this is not so in the context of *o'yo*. Here it is only that he must be adult. Lugbara say that whereas the dead contact only their own children, all adults are in relationship of equal status with God:[1] God is as it were outside the kinship and lineage systems of authority.

It is difficult to say clearly what is the notion behind this use of spittle. Lugbara say that a sorcerer may use a person's spittle, nail parings, excreta, semen and other body products in order to harm him, but in fact sorcerers are usually said to use other objects in their medicines. Spittle has an intimate connexion with the breath. In its ritual use it is expelled with a loud and breathy '*pa*' in quite a different manner to that in which it is expelled in other contexts. To spit in an ordinary manner is considered ill-mannered, even to imply a threat of witchcraft, if one has been eating and drinking as a guest; but in this case it is merely a sign of dissatisfaction and has no mystical content. When spat breathily in a ritual situation it is an anointment. It contains breath, in which is something of soul and life, the transfer of which may relieve a state of impurity. By spitting the placer of a curse may neutralize it, even when he spits on his own chest. The ritual anointment with spittle may be done only in the morning before the spitter has washed and cleaned his teeth and mouth. Spittle in this context has *talí*, a word which I have earlier translated as 'personality'. *Talí* refers essentially to some manifestation of the power of God, and it is divine power which effects the anointment.

It is said in some areas that the effects of witchcraft may be removed by the application of the witch's spittle. This may be done if the witch is a member of his victim's own family cluster. There is here the notion that spittle may contain something of the the essence of kinship. Witchcraft destroys and denies the bonds of kinship, which may be recognized again by the use of the destroyer's spittle.

The blowing of breath is similar. It contains mystical force, the transfer of which both blesses and re-creates a broken or weakened kinship tie: where the latter is not broken, as between patient and

[1] In this context: at other times it is said that only the very senior men and rainmakers are close to God.

living kin in cases of ghostly vengeance, then no breath is blown into the patient's ear.

I have already mentioned that holding special leaves a man takes on his formal ritual status, so that he is in close contact with the dead and cannot tell a lie without their knowing it. The leaves used are three, in most parts of Lugbara, *ajịgbị*, *larịgbị* and *amatrịgbị* or *olụgbị*. They are said to get their power, which is thus seen as being immutable, from God or from the hero-ancestors. *Ajịgbị* are used to cure the body of the patient: they make it 'good' and 'clean'. They are used for anointing in all rites known as 'cleansing the body'. *Larịgbị* (the leaves of the fig trees planted at graves) have a wider use and are connected specifically with fertility;[1] I have heard them compared to semen and the secretions of women. They are used in the blessing of a girl by her natal kin at her marriage, to promote her pregnancy. They are also used by a man who visits his sick sisters or daughters at their husbands' homes. He goes to 'see the sickness' and says a short ritual address, spits on *larịgbị* leaves while holding them in his 'ritual' hand and places them in the thatch just inside the doorway. They are called '*larịgbị* for the saying of the ritual address to do with sickness'. He performs this rite to show that he is not withholding the fertility of the women born of his lineage, and that whatever the cause of sickness it has nothing to do with him. I heard a man at a funeral of his sister's son say

My sister's son has died. . . . Your mother was married with our wealth (that is, the wealth that had been given to the speaker for his sister) now your son is dead. The pot is broken, we cannot mend it. I have eaten your wealth, I cannot eat here with you now.

He then placed *larịgbị* leaves, on which he had spat, in the thatch of the hut so that his sister could conceive another child immediately.

Larịgbị leaves cannot be used by women, who use other leaves, *amatrịgbị* or *olụgbị*, for blessing. This is because it is thought best that men should control the fertility of the women, rights over whom are vested in men, because women would misuse the powers the sacred leaves might give them. Fertility is connected with legal rights in the women of the lineage and so must be controlled by

---

[1] In Low Lugbara dialects the word is *lengbe*, which is used also for the High Lugbara *drịleba*, 'good fortune', used especially in connexion with fertility.

the men, the full lineage members. 'Women are useless; in the past they did not wage war; so we do not give them *larjgbj*.'

I have said earlier that when holding sacred leaves a man is acting with his full ritual and spiritual powers. It is not the leaves themselves that have the intrinsic significance—they are not magical objects that can be used by anyone and still be effective—but they have power only in conjunction with the ritual and spiritual power of a person of full adult status. This may be man or woman. Only a man may use *larjgbj* leaves, which are symbols of his ritual status and of his control of fertility; and he has power to bring sickness and cure it, through the medium of invocation of ghosts, and this is symbolized by *ajjgbj* leaves.

There is in most areas a fourth leaf, *edogbj*, used by elders when saying ritual addresses at death and certain other non-sacrificial occasions which are connected with God rather than with the dead. These are the 'leaves of the elder' used particularly to symbolize his status as possessor of mystical powers that come directly from God. No one else would pick these leaves, and women do not wear them as apparel.

However, all these leaves do have certain qualities that are independent of the elder who may hold them. I have been told that they are chosen for their appearance, texture and pleasant smell. They are said to be soft and beautiful and so pleasing to the dead and to God:

The ghosts see these leaves and are pleased. They think 'Truly our child loves us, he holds these leaves for us.' Then their hearts are good and they rejoice and love their children and forget their anger.

The grass called *etindi* is also used in place of *ajjgbj* leaves: it is soft and sweet-smelling.

The place of these elements may better be understood if seen as elements in sacrifice considered as a *rite de passage*. The patient, in a state of sin, is changed into a sinless person who is re-accepted as a lineage member. He is identified with the sacrificial animal by consecration. The animal becomes a completely sacred object by its slaughter, by which the patient is put into contact with the sphere of the dead and God. He is re-accepted into the lineage by the blessing and anointing by lineage representatives, whose spitting marks his re-identification with them as fellow lineage members. The making of ritual addresses, accompanied by the use of sacred leaves, occurs at his changes of ritual status. Also the non-washing of the actors' faces sets them apart from the every-day world; of them it is said:

A man sacrifices; he does not wash his face in the morning and he can then insert his hand (into the shrines). He does not fear the ghosts.

A man who does not fear (or respect, *rµ*) the ghosts is set apart from ordinary lineage obligations. The spittle of such a person has *talị*, a manifestation of divine power: he is thus 'outside' the sphere of the living and dead of the lineage. It is only God who can affect such marked changes in the patient's status, and it is for this reason that he enters into the rite of sacrifice at various points and in various ways.

There are also other purificatory rites that are not connected with the dead at all. In these, which are said to be the 'true' rites of *rµa edezu* and *angu edezu*, purification is from mystically-caused sickness, the consequence of breaking a taboo, certain curses and states of ritual danger caused by past quarrelling which has not been settled due to the death of one of the parties, and so on. They are usually performed in the presence of a congregation whose members share the ritual food; but there is no sacrifice. It would be tedious to list all those rites of which I have knowledge, and it would hardly be possible to list all the occasions on which they might be performed. The reason, which I discuss further in the following chapter, is that they are not performed in isolation, but as part of the ritual history of a given lineage. A state of impurity, which one lineage thinks must be removed by one of these rites, may be considered by another lineage to require a rite of sacrifice to a spirit or fertility shrine. Also the usage of the two terms is never very definite, many rites having elements of both and perhaps being referred to by either term, according to which element is predominant. A Lugbara who is asked to list these rites and their occasions merely gives those in the recent ritual history of his lineage: certainly the accounts of these rites in general that I have been given by Lugbara have varied considerably in content from one area to another, and even from one lineage to another within the same area. But there is, of course, general agreement as to their nature and details.

After a man has died the rite of 'contacting the soul', (*orindi tị zịzu*) is performed. Usually, but by no means invariably, a rite of 'cleansing the body' (*rμa edezu*) is performed at the same time. The former rite involves the offering of a goat, and when they are done together the same goat is used for them both. But a rite of 'cleansing the body' may be performed on behalf of a recently dead man quite independently of the rite of 'contacting the soul'. Its purpose is to cleanse the members of the compound from any possible trouble brought by the dead man who may bear a grudge against his living kin, no matter whether they or he were guilty of quarrelling at the time of his death. Guilt is thus not significant in this rite: its purpose is merely to purify from the general effects of a recent death. I was told,

Now a man has died. We do not know his thoughts. Later, perhaps a year later, or seven months, we will build a shrine for him. We call a diviner to contact him and to build a shrine. But perhaps his heart was bad when he died. Who can know the heart of a dying man? Perhaps he could not utter the words of his heart. So we may perform the rite of 'cleansing the body' so that the home will be well and clean. Then his children and his widows will be well, and there will not be 'words' or sickness.

When it is performed alone a sheep is used, not a goat. It is slaughtered, and the elder of the minimal lineage of the dead man uses the blood to anoint the members of the compound and close kin—including married daughters—on their chest and right instep, and it is also smeared on the thresholds of all the huts. Neither meat nor blood is placed on the shrines, and although the meat is shared and eaten it is not a formal ritual distribution but rather a ceremonial meal of kinsmen only. It is significant that members do not necessarily eat by generation, as they do invariably at a sacrifice to the dead. This rite is performed only for a dead man, not for a woman.

A case of 'cleansing the body' that is often given as a stock example of these rites is one that is performed if two brothers quarrel severely, especially if they are full brothers. Their elder slaughters a sheep and pours blood over their feet; he smears the chyle in a line down their chests. If this is not done it is said that they will both die 'of the words of God the creator'. In the case which I saw the brothers had quarrelled so long and so deeply that I doubt whether the dispute was settled in their hearts. The elder thought that after the rite they would be frightened and not open it again. In discussion with him it was clear that the form of the rite was thought sufficient, in marked contrast to the situation at an offering to the dead, where it is most important that men's hearts should be tranquil and free from dissension. The guilt of the brothers was not mentioned and did not seem to be considered important.

There are other rites which are called 'cleansing the body', of which the most common are that made for a girl who has become pregnant while unmarried and for a person who has committed incest. A ram and a cock are used in these rites. In none of them is there any offering made to the dead. The patient is smeared with blood, chyle or excrement by the minimal lineage elder. There is no anointing with spittle, blowing breath, nor use of sacred leaves. These last three elements are thought to do more with purification made as part of sacrifice to the dead. In the 'true' purificatory rites anointing is by blood, ideally that of a sheep. Where 'cleansing the body' is part of the rite of sacrifice, the animal is usually a bull or a goat, but if performed alone a sheep should be used. Its meat is consumed, but not in a formal ritual manner; it is not distributed into portions but is all eaten on the spot. The sheep is an animal distinct from others in that it is a 'thing of God' and its use brings the performers into contact with God rather than with the dead. The blood of the sheep is said to contain the soul of the sheep, and it is smeared upon those parts of the body associated with the man's soul and also upon the hut thresholds. The use of sheep's blood 'shows the words of God'. It is used to avoid the possible consequences of the anger of a dead man, who is not yet an ancestor but is thought to be with God[1]. It is used as a sign that brothers who have committed the sin of quarrelling have had the state of sin removed. It is used in case of illegitimate pregnancy to remove the sin from the girl and her family. Illegitimate pregnancy is a sin 'because God made her a woman to bear children for her husband', and so she has misused the power given her by God (the injury to her guardian is redeemed by the payment to him of the 'bull of fornication' by her lover). These latter two occasions have in common that they are not concerned with ties of kinship (for full brothers are too close to be mere kin, just as fratricide is more than a killing of a fellow-kinsman, heinous enough though that is). They are concerned rather with the misuse of the status given by God. I was told:

1 I discuss this further below; see page 201.

These people do deeds and forget the words of God. Did not God create us here on the earth? A person is a man or a person is a woman. He has his father and his mother and his brother. Each person has his work. These people are become like clients or strangers, and are bad.

Clients have no ties of kinship, and are 'things' rather than 'persons'. So are they who have sinned in ways so as to 'forget the words of God'.

Incest is, like fratricide, a denial of close kin ties. But it is also more than that and is an offence against God.

They forget that they are brother and sister . . . they are not like people of one lineage but like strangers.

Incest is associated with witches, and also with death dances, when 'we forget the words of the lineage' and much incest is said to be committed. I discuss witches and death later; both are associated in Lugbara thought with God. At the cleansing for incest a bull and beer may be given by the girl's close kin to those of her lover, or by his kin to hers. The rule is that they are given to the kin of whichever of the pair has become sick, the sign that culpable incest has occurred. They are consumed by the sick person's senior kin of the minimal lineage; these spit on his or her chest to show that their anger has gone. Here the kinship element is also shown to be important; both kin and God enter into the situation.

In the rites that I have so far mentioned it is the individual and his or her immediate family who are purified. There is no ritual congregation nor are there sacrifices. The sin is personal. But there are also rites that involve a congregation, and which are said to have as a purpose—not necessarily the only purpose—'to cleanse the territory'. Certain rites are always called by this term. They have in common that they are performed because of sickness, disaster or evil omens that are the consequence of the talk of men who are grumbling about the behaviour of the men of the affected group. The rite is performed to rid the group of the trouble. Reparation is not made to living people nor need the dead be concerned at all. A sign of trouble is that a hut or compound is infested with snakes, or that they are seen near it daily; or a jackal, hyena or wild cat defaecates near the huts at night. The head of the compound goes to the oracles and is told that it is because the members of his lineage want food and are grumbling at him behind his back. They have been saying that when his father was alive they often ate there sacrificial meat and beer. But for the last two or three years they have not been offered food. His wife then prepares beer and the compound head calls the elders of the inner lineage. They come one morning, before washing their faces. When beer has been drunk, the elder of the minimal lineage takes *ajigbi* and *larigbi* leaves and makes a ritual address, in which he relates the facts of the case. All then spit on the leaves, which are placed on the path outside the compound. Next morning the elder inspects them: if an hyena has defaecated on them, it is a sign that the evil omens are confirmed, that the rite is unsuccessful and that God wants to take a member of the compound in death, since the head has behaved in a way unfitting a kinsman; but if there is no excrement, then all will be well and the evil omens have been countered. In this rite there is no sacrifice, no killing of a ritual beast, no anointing or blessing It is a rite in which the home is purified by the elders cooling their hearts; God accepts, or refuses, by this sign. The elders say aloud that their hearts are cool as they spit upon the leaves. If the rite is successful, the elders assemble again, they all deliver a further ritual address, saying that they are joyful, and all spit on the leaves, which are then placed on the internal ghost shrines, 'to show the ghosts'. I was told that this is sometimes done also even if the rite is unsuccessful, but it seems that such rites very rarely fail.

I describe one of these rites in the following chapter. Here I need say only that the situations in which they are said to be performed are generally three. The first is when sickness strikes a lineage—when it actually appears, and is not merely shown likely to appear by omens, as in the case I have just mentioned—as the consequence of a group of kin blaming a man for wantonly causing feud and warfare which destroy or seriously weaken the lineage.

The mouths of men say those words. Then that man is sick, and the lineage members are few. Many brothers have died. These are the words of 'cleansing the territory'.

The second principal occasion is concerned with the killing of the 'girl beast' (*zamva ti*) that is given at marriage to mark the bestowal of the right of sexual access to the wife. This is the 'bull of fornication' that I have mentioned above, paid by the seducer of a girl

—married or unmarried, including the husband's deflowering of his wife—to her guardian. The last rite is that of 'striking the boundary' (*esele cozu*). If there is feud within the tribe, it is sooner or later stopped by the elders of the groups concerned. They cut a bull and distribute the meat, mark a dividing line on the ground and threaten to curse any member of either side who ventures to cross it bearing arms. The meat is eaten by all the representatives of the lineages of the tribe. It has not been performed for several years now—I know of a case as late as about 1935—and I have no detailed information about it. In the two former cases a bull is eaten by a wide congregation. Ritual addresses are made, but there is no blessing or anointing, and the ghosts are specifically said not to be concerned.

Some of these rites are made to avoid the condition known as *nyoka*. This is the persistent disaster that befalls an entire lineage, and which is said by Lugbara to be sent by God. God hears 'the words of men', who grumble about the behaviour of one of their kinsmen. The grumblers are those upon whom the disaster has fallen as a consequence of the original offence. God may act directly by sending disaster, but in his transcendent aspect he cannot be contacted directly by oblation but only through the 'hearts' and 'mouths' of living men, assembled as a single lineage entity. They show, by the sharing of the meat, that their hearts are now without anger. By their eating it outside the compound they show that the rite has no connexion with the ancestors.[1] There is a connexion between the bush land and the immanent aspect of God, and God is explicitly brought into these rites by the reference to the hyena, which he uses to show his intentions. But God's connexion with these rites is less than that with those of 'cleansing the body'. Sheep are not used, but cattle, 'the beasts of men'. The people concerned are not in a state of sin, nor of ritual impurity. The cleansing is of a potential state of *nyoka*, that is, of a state brought about by grumbling, that may lead finally to a condition of *nyoka*. Once this condition has appeared there is nothing that can be done; one cannot alter God's will. These rites are made not so much to prevent that condition

[1] I have been told this by Lugbara. When I replied that sacrifices are made to the dead at the external lineage shrines I was told that the rites are 'different', and also that the purificatory rites which I am here discussing do not occur at or near the ancestors' burial trees, as do those at the external shrines.

from maturing as to know whether or not it will do so. Hence if the omens are unpropitious afterwards, or if evil omens persist, the matter may be taken to the ghosts, in case they are responsible after all—and in any case the omens have shown that even if God is responsible, he refuses to alter his intention.

Rites of purification are not sacrifices or offerings; they are not called *owi* (oblations). Lugbara say that they do not give food to God. If it were necessary only to feed and to anoint, a goat or bull would be adequate. But sheep are used, and they are not common beasts like goats. They are associated with God. But they do not belong to him, as their 'owner', in the sense that other livestock belong to the dead members of the lineage equally with the living. It might be said that since God created everything, everything is his; but this logic is not followed by Lugbara. The sheep is not offered to God as a sacrifice. When men eat of sacrificial meat offered to the dead, they show that their hearts are pleased, and the dead are thought to know this. Likewise, there are certain rites, those of 'cleansing the territory', in which a bull is eaten by the members of a congregation, who by doing so are said to 'show' God that their hearts are free of anger and dissension. It would seem that men cannot 'show' either the dead or God by eating a sheep, only by eating a bull or goat. For anointing to remove sins sent by God the blood of a sheep should be used, although in fact that of another beast often suffices.

There are two other cases in which the connexion between sheep and God is shown. On occasions of persistent cerebro-spinal meningitis, which reaches epidemic proportions in many dry seasons, a ram is taken; blood from its ears is placed at points along the boundary of the tribe (sometimes of lesser units); a ring called *drungo* or *mele*[1] is placed in its right ear; and it is driven out of the tribal territory. This is done by the rainmaker, or the senior elder of the sub-clan in those areas where there are no rainmakers. The ram is called 'the sheep to drive away death'. I have not seen this rite, but am told there are no prayers made to God, who is said to have sent the meningitis.[2] The other occasion is during severe drought, when the rainmaker cannot make rain. He takes a ram from his own flock and places a single bead on a string round

---

[1] *Mele* is also used in some areas for the iron wristlet worn by older women.

[2] See Chapter V where the close connexion between God and this disease is discussed.

its neck. The bead is taken from the sacred *ngaliki* necklace which is part of the rainmaker's paraphernalia. The elders of the tribe, and even of neighbouring tribes, place their hands on the ram's back, prayers for rain are made to God by the rainmaker and the ram is driven out of the territory. I have not seen this rite either, but was told of it in great detail in Ole'ba, in northern Lugbara, where it is driven across the River Oro towards Mt. Liru, one of the two sacred mountains. There it is said to become a leopard and to become or in some way to produce lightning. Sometimes *edogbɨ* leaves, which are only used by rainmakers and senior elders and which are associated with God, are placed on its back.

In these two rites the connexion between God and sheep is clear. They are not concerned with sin. They might seem to be classic examples of scapegoats, although I have never heard it said explicitly that the sheep carries away the sin of the community, although in one case its blood is used to anoint the subclan territory. Lugbara say that the ram is 'a thing given to God to beseech him to send rain.' The word I translate 'beseech' is *a'ɨ*, which also means 'implore' or 'pray'. This is the only occasion in which prayer, whether to God or to any other agent, is mentioned by Lugbara. I was told that

> We Lugbara only pray to God when the land is destroyed, when there is no rain. We all pray together, all the people of Lugbara, all people pray there together.

The rite is not an individual matter, nor even that of a family or small lineage, but of the entire community, the tribe.

Details of these purificatory rites may be summarized:

'Cleansing the body'	Beast	Leaves	Spittle	Hyena excrement
Blessing bride:	none	used	used	none
Removing leprosy:	none	used	used	used
After death:	sheep	none	none	none
Brothers' quarrel:	sheep	none	none	none
Illegitimate pregnancy:	sheep	none	none	none
Incest:	sheep	none	none	none

'Cleansing the territory'	Beast	Leaves	Spittle	Hyena excrement
Grumbling at feud:	bull	used	used	used
Bull of fornication:	bull	none	none	none
Striking the boundary:	bull	used	used	used
Other rites				
O'yo:	none	none	used	none
Seeing the sickness:	none	used	used	none
Meningitis:	sheep	none	none	none
Drought:	sheep	none	none	none·

Certain conclusions may be drawn from this summary:

1. Sheep, associated with God, are used to remove a state of impurity arising from the denial of the basic ties of kinship in the case of individuals, and to remove disease or disaster in the case of tribal groups. There are no anointing and blessing in these cases.

2. Bulls are used to signify that lineage members, dead and living, are involved. These rites, those of 'cleansing the territory' are to remove the possibility of future *nyoka*. God is therefore not immediately involved, but in two of them his concern is shown in the use of hyena excrement.

3. Spittle and leaves are used when the interests of the lineage are involved. They are also used to remove curses in which lineage interests are, though less immediately, concerned (leprosy, in which the curse is by a senior kinswoman; and *o'yo*, in which lineage property is concerned).

There is the major distinction between rites involving lineage interests, in which God is not directly concerned and in which leaves and spittle are used, and those not involving lineage interests, in which God is involved and there is no use of leaves or spittle. I am here making a more rigid distinction than Lugbara would make themselves; for example, God is concerned indirectly in most of these rites, since he is associated with sacred leaves, which are said to have been given to men by God. But the main distinction is valid.

Granaries, with shrines set beneath them. The nearest granary has agnatic 'ghost-houses' beneath it, the farther one has a set of small shrines for the ghosts of the owner's mother's lineage. The granary covers are tilted up for access to their contents.

An external lineage shrine, set in the bush away from the homesteads. The nearer shrine is the 'house' for the lineage ghosts, the farther one is a fertility shrine; it consists of an old grinding stone worn through the centre.

VII. COMMUNION

People attend a sacrifice to 'eat meat', *za nya*. The ritual character of the event is shown by the use of the term *awi̧*. Besides bringing the ghosts into direct contact with the living, sacrifice brings together the living kin in a single congregation. It is this aspect that is stressed in the concept *awi̧*. *Awi̧*, or *awṷ* in some areas, is a verb meaning 'to remain', as in the compounds *awi̧ta*, *awṷ afa* (*afa*=thing) or *awṷrṷso*. These are the goods that remain after a man's death, when many of his intimate personal possessions are destroyed; those remaining are distributed among his close kin. The other and related use of the word is in the compounds *awi̧'bṷrṷ*, (*awi̧* (in) the home), and *awi̧amve* (*awi̧* outside (the home)). These words are used to refer to two differently composed ritual congregations, which I discuss below. Here it is the offering that 'remains' and is distributed among the members of the congregation. *'Bṷrṷ* is a term for homestead, usually in a figurative sense, and *awi'bṷrṷ* is that ritual distribution of the offering made inside the home, both literally as compound and figuratively as the home of a lineage. *Awi̧amve* is the distribution made outside, in the grass or bush. The range and composition of these congregations vary with the nature of the offering, and the identity of the shrine at which the offering is made. With differences in the congregation are associated differences in the purpose of the rite, due to differences in the nature of the kinship and lineage ties which exist between the component persons and groups concerned.

At a sacrifice at the internal ghost shrines the members of the segment of the minimal lineage act as hosts to representatives of other segments and lineages. Both hosts and guests play formal ritual roles, and do not behave merely as individual kinsmen. The members of the entire minimal lineage of the hosts may see themselves as a single group, as contrasted to their visitors. The host lineage includes several categories of members: the ancestors, the living elders, adult men, boys, pre-adolescent girls, adult unmarried girls, married daughters who now live elsewhere, old lineage daughters who are past child-bearing; and in this context it includes also its men's wives and widows if these are still living with their sons. At sacrifices at the ghost shrines wives do not take part in the main rites. They and their daughters cook the porridge to be eaten with the sacrificial meat, which is cooked by sisters' sons, and they also prepare the beer; but they do not take part in the sacrifice itself. They may sit in the background, in the doorways of the huts or in the shade of the compound fence, but they do not sit near the centre of activities nor share in the sacrificial meat. Small girls of the lineage may, however, take part. They and the small boys sit near the place where the rite is performed, they share in the meat and blood and are usually anointed. It is said that small girls belong to the lineage, but bigger girls sleep with their lovers and so no longer fully belong to it; their hearts are elsewhere. Legally, of course, rights in them are still vested in the lineage, but they have ties outside it; lovers and their respective families use affinal kinship terms and observe affinal behaviour, although somewhat informally, in preparation for marriage. Once they are married the girls do not take part in ghost sacrifices. They take part in ritual only indirectly through the participation of their guardians, fathers, brothers or husbands. Old women past child-bearing who have returned to their natal homes may take part: 'they are now like men and are big'. They may even make offerings at certain rites and 'put their hands' inside the shrines.

The representatives who attend from other lineages are known as *enyatị* (*enya*=food). This may be translated 'commensal partner' or 'commensal group'. It is used both for individual representatives who are summoned to eat meat together and for the group as a whole and its component segments which are so represented. It is said 'these people are our *enyatị*' and 'we here are a single *enyatị*'. The term is used properly only in a sacrificial context: people who share food on other occasions, at, for example, a funeral, are not properly called *enyatị*. Ritual commensality is an expression of the tie of ritual collaboration, and the relationship is coterminous with others that are operative in other situations. They are those in which the tie of agnatic kinship is significant. The word *enyatị* is often used for a small lineage, especially in contexts in which large lineage segments are significant: a man may say he lives in Ezuko major lineage, in which the *enyatị* are Anyanya, Adravu and the other small lineages which compose Ezuko. Thus its use is extended to non-ritual contexts. A man may say that a certain minor lineage is an *ori'ba*, 'because it dances alone, as one'; but that its minimal lineages are *enyatị*, 'because they dance together', that is, they join together as dancing teams at death dances and so express the same ties of kinship that are expressed in ritual commensality.

Commensal partners compose the congregation which attends the two kinds of rite in which ritual congregations are essential, those called *awį'burų* and *awįamve*. Sacrifices at the internal agnatic ghost shrines are *awį'burų*. Lugbara say that people attend them in order to 'rejoice with their kin'. Therefore they must not have anger in their hearts but must be cool so that the rite, with its anointing and blessing, may be efficacious. It is said

> When a man goes to *awį*, he must remain peaceful, without a hot heart. He must stay thus for at least a day. If he quarrels on that day or is hot in his heart he becomes sick and destroys the words of the lineage and of the sacrifice.

The lineage includes the dead. The *awį'burų* is said to be 'the affair of the *enyatį* only', and the exclusiveness of the local group and the agnatic ghosts of its associated core lineage is emphasized.

However, the *awį'burų* congregation also includes representatives of immediately contiguous lineages, whether agnatically related or not. As I have said earlier, both lines of descent are significant for Lugbara, although the agnatic line is formally emphasized. Ghost invocation is effective against both agnatic and extra-agnatic kin who are the dependants of a single elder and who form a cluster of cognates. The congregation of *awį'burų*, the rite associated with ghost invocation, reflects this pattern. It consists of those minimal lineages which form a close cluster round the minimal lineage making the sacrifice, and with accessory kin of at least the central lineages, those immediately concerned. In the congregation there are the host minimal lineages of the inner lineage, which are descended from common ancestors, and attached groups of different agnatic ancestry. When these are 'sisters' husbands', especially if assimilated as 'brothers', then they are accepted as kindred. If they are 'sisters' sons' then they are accepted as descendants of the same ancestors. A client lineage which is not yet assimilated by the rite of cutting a bull in two may not send its elder, but since it is nevertheless part of the community it is given a little of the meat received by its host group, 'because we like our clients'. Clients do not send their own head to the rite, but are given a share of their own host group's portion at a later distribution by lineage segments after their representatives have returned from the rite with their portions of uncooked meat. Potential assimilation is thus recognized by their own hosts but not by wider groupings. A remnant clan that is territorially adjacent is also usually invited. The congregation is thus composed of representatives of the community of which the sacrificing unit is the centre, socially and territorially. The importance of social distance may be better seen if the position of an accessory lineage is considered. Its commensal partners consist of its own host minimal lineage and that lineage's minor or even major lineage segments, and of its own parent lineage elsewhere. This latter tie is forgotten after a few generations, when only the parent minimal lineage (or their descendants) sends a representative—at first representatives may come from minor or major lineages. This tie is significant both in this way and in the reverse direction—an accessory group is called to its parent lineage's rites also. An accessory lineage may or may not call other accessory lineages attached to the same hosts, since the tie that links them is only an indirect one. It usually depends on whether they are territorially contiguous and on the degree of friendship between them. Since they are allowed to intermarry this may be used as a reason not to observe the indirect accessory link in a ritual context, since intermarriage and commensality are mutually exclusive.

The congregation thus consists of two parts. First, the true agnates who are members of the same lineage as are the ancestors, and secondly, the accessory kin and clients. Although all share the sacrificial food, only the former may eat with the ancestors; only they may sit near the shrines and consume meat and beer part of which is placed on the actual shrines. These consume the cooked meat. The uncooked meat is then distributed to the wider congregation, including the same agnates and the accessory kin and clients. These latter categories do not come into direct contact with the lineage dead. Their link is thus not primarily a mystical one. It is one of kinship expressed in the sharing of food, the fact that it is sacrificial food marking the occasion as a ritual one. The dead are said to approve of this tie being so expressed:

A sister's son will fear to eat the meat of the mother's brother's shrines, and to drink of that blood and beer. He fears to sit near those shrines because those ghosts would say 'Oh, who is this stranger? Why does he sit here? Was his mother a man, a man of our lineage? She was a woman and his clan is another, that which gave us cattle for that sister. Therefore we love him, since he is our child, but it is not good that he sit here, he will be with shame.' Therefore he may attend to cut the meat and to help his mother's brother, but he eats that meat later, perhaps the following day.

All the males of the minimal, and sometimes the inner, lineage attend and share in the offering. The legs of the beast are divided among them, a leg going to the head of each component segment. Distribution is according to lines of genealogical segmentation and not according to numerical strength. The actual division is not made to any fixed formula but depends largely on the judgment of the officiating elder and local opinion.

The remainder of the meat, including the stomach and certain other organs, is shared by the outside lineage representatives and by the 'men behind', the younger men and those who are not heads of families of the lineage itself. They take the legs to their own homes and there they are re-distributed by the heads of the segments themselves, but all eat the rest of the beast on the spot, with porridge and beer, except for the special portion for the officiating elder, which I have mentioned earlier. It is clear that often the portions allotted to outside representatives may be very small. In an important sacrifice, to which many people come, more than one beast may be killed. Only the originally consecrated beast is offered to the ghosts and only its meat is offered ritually with a ritual address, but another beast, often a goat even if the sacrificial beast is a bull, may be killed and its meat distributed and eaten by the members of the congregation. The actual distribution is directed by the officiating elder who gives orders to sisters' sons of the lineage; these dole out the pieces of meat, placing them on small sticks, one for each recipient. A man thus receives many small pieces of meat cut from different parts of the animal, care being taken to ensure that all portions are approximately equal.

The distribution of meat and beer reflects the distribution of agnatic and quasi-agnatic (host-client) kinship and lineage ties which define the distributing group's field of social relations. It also reflects the principles of segmentation and fusion on which the territorial organization of Lugbara is based. At a sacrifice meat is both cooked and eaten and distributed raw. The distributed meat is taken home by the representatives of lineages and family segments. There it is re-distributed, some eaten at a common meal and some taken home by the heads of the junior segments concerned. In each case the distribution of raw meat is according to lines of segmentation. The groups that give and receive raw meat are linked by one degree of lineage span in each case. The links are between a minimal lineage and its accessory lineages, the other agnatically related lineages of its minor lineage, and the other minor lineages of its major lineage. The links are seen in terms of the kinship ties between the apical ancestors of these groups, of which the genealogies are quoted and the legends recited in the ritual addresses. The one degree of kinship is thus a single degree from an agnatic descent line, from the lineage itself and not from the living members of the lineage group as it is composed at the present time.

The eating of cooked meat and the drinking of beer, on the other hand, is by generation. At ritual meals the partakers eat in groups, each group consisting of different generation-grades, in which seniority is by family status and not by age, although the two are assumed generally to be coterminous.

The representatives of the various commensal groups each receive one portion of raw meat, and they partake of the cooked meat and beer together, in this case grouping themselves by generation. In this way the tie of kinship is re-affirmed by the sharing of undivided cooked meat, as is the tie between any individual kinsman and another. The raw portions are then taken home and re-distributed among the smaller group's segments according to the same principles, the distribution also being accompanied by a meal, of meat, porridge and beer, at which eating groups are arranged by generation. There is rarely further distribution, the segment heads who receive the secondary portions eating with their families and inviting any attached individual non-agnatic kin.

At each stage, therefore, the distinctness of each segment, related by a single lineage link, is affirmed by its receiving a portion of raw meat; its unity with other segments is emphasized by commensality, the actual eating of cooked food and drinking of beer jointly with them. Here individual identity of segments is forgotten, and their unity is emphasized.

The distribution and sharing of sacrificial meat at *awȝ'bȝrȝ* rites is only the ideal pattern. In actuality the alignment of lineages to one another is always changing, with lineage segmentation and amalgamation and the movement of accessory segments. The constellations of lineage ties that provide the pattern for meat distribution are thus also fluid in respect of any given minimal lineage. It may be said that the distribution of meat may affirm these ties, but to say that it merely reflects a constellation of ties that are already in existence is a distortion. It is at these rites that changes in alignment are recognized, that, in fact, they actually take place. The alignment of lineages is relevant only in certain situations, of which the most important are fighting, marriage and ritual. Feud and warfare are now prohibited and marriage is the affair of sub-clans and major lineages rather than smaller lineages, in the sense that since it is the former groups that are the exogamous ones the small everyday segmentation of minimal lineages is rarely immediately relevant; and in Lugbara bridewealth is collected only by the minimal lineage and the mother's brother (a non-agnatic kinsman), other co-ordinate lineages not being involved. Realignment at the minimal lineage level is therefore significant mainly on ritual occasions. It is at and through ritual ties of commensality that lineage realignments, that is, 'political' relations, are conceived and expressed by Lugbara themselves.

In short, segmentation and amalgamation of lineages, which take place primarily at the minimal lineage level, occur and are primarily meaningful in ritual situations, at which realignment actually occurs. They are the only occasions at which all the members of the local community, or their representatives, living and dead, meet together. The reason for their meeting is the occurrence of sickness brought in response to certain anti-social actions, which have destroyed or weakened the kin ties which compose the social relations of a given group. They destroy the *status quo*. At the meeting together of all the kin concerned a new balance of authority comes into being. Lugbara usually conceive of the situation as being one in which the *status quo* is restored: they regard their society as being unchanging. But this is by no means so. The pattern of relations that composes the overall structure remains, but its actual organization changes over time. This reorganization is carried out and recognized—carried out by being recognized, in fact—in ritual. The giving of the ritual address is important in this context: it tells of the accepted pattern of organization and provides mythical and legendary validation for it.

I have mentioned earlier that lineage segmentation is a gradual process. There are both conditioning and precipitating factors. The stage at which it can be said that segmentation is complete is the moment when the head of the new segment is so recognized by his own dependants, by outside heads of co-ordinate and wider segments, and by the dead. A segment is defined as having a recognized head. His position is recognized internally by the acceptance of his domestic authority by his dependants: this is exercised in any critical situation by his invocation of the ghosts. Externally his position is recognized by his being asked to act as representative at sacrifices and other rites of outside groups. A new head who is asked to a rite is given a portion of meat as one of a set of representatives of co-ordinate segments, and is given food to eat in the company of his social equals—by social generation. In this way he is accepted in his new status. And lastly his position is accepted by the dead when they 'hear' the words of his invocation of them. It is in this sense that I speak of the realignment of segments actually taking place at rites. A new realignment may or may not be accepted earlier; for example, sexual relations between members of two groups may or may not be regarded as incestuous: if there is any doubt then there is soon set in motion ghostly sickness or some other process that leads to sacrifice or some other rite, the giving of ritual addresses and the recognition of any new alignment of relations between the groups concerned by the status allotted to their heads at the distribution of ritual meat. I do not wish to imply that there is a reorganization of segments every time a rite is performed. But rites are performed as a result of attempted change in segmentary organization. Most of these attempts are abortive, just as most revolts are abortive; only a few are successful. But a series of attempts usually ends in success and change is recognized. Lugbara do not see the whole situation in these terms. The system enables changes to be recognized while the belief in an unchanging order of society remains unshaken.

It may be asked why a sacrifice that is concerned with the effects of sin upon the internal unity of a family cluster should call for a congregation consisting largely of members of outside lineages. The actual offence is not their affair and is concerned with relations of authority between persons of whom they probably know comparatively little in any intimate sense. The composition of *enyati* that I have given is the ideal one: it is that given by Lugbara when discussing sacrifice in general. But in actuality the range of *enyatị* varies considerably from one occasion to another. In general the range is wide when the status of the patient or the invoker is a senior one, and narrow when junior. The elder is both the exerciser of lineage authority over his dependants in the family cluster and is also their ritual representative *vis-à-vis* co-ordinate lineages. Sacrifice in which he is involved as patient or invoker is, among other things, a sign that his status as representative is either being sustained by him in face of opposition to his authority by his dependants or that it has been changed in face of this opposition. The *enyatị* attend as part of the obligation to him to attend his rites, his right to expect attendance being part of his status as effective elder and showing recognition of it. He reciprocates by attending their rites, this mutual obligation being a central part of his status of lineage representative. When patient or invoker are persons of little importance, the *enyatị* may consist of only one or two individual kin who are in a particularly intimate relationship with the patient. The same applies to the attendance of members of the patient's own family cluster: only a few attend a rite performed for a woman or child.

Congregations at junior ghost shrines and ancestral shrines are small because senior men are not involved. They are not concerned with sickness sent as a consequence of ghost invocation, but only of ghostly vengeance. The status of an elder or a senior man is therefore not seen as being an issue in the total situation. The offence is usually one of misdemeanour by an individual *qua* individual rather than *qua* lineage member.

The congregation at the external shrines are also small in numbers, though not in range. Only elders may see these shrines, and the congregation consists of the elders of co-ordinate lineages whose lineage ancestors share in the shrine at which the sacrifice is made. The range of lineages so represented is thus determined by the process of lineage segmentation, as I have mentioned when describing these shrines above. These rites are usually called neither *awị'bụrụ* nor *awjamve*, but are known merely as 'sacrifice at the external shrines': they stand apart from the rites at internal shrines.

Awị'bụrụ rites are concerned with authority within the lineage and family cluster. *Awjamve* rites are not so concerned. They do not mark realignments of patterns of authority as do the former;

rather elders assemble to re-affirm already existing ties and the presence of ghosts is not required. In the case of 'cutting the boundary' the units concerned are in a state of feud and so by definition beyond the range of common effective ghostly ties, even though they are related agnatically as units of the same sub-clan.

Awi'buru congregations attend sacrifices to the internal ghosts. *Awiamve* congregations are different in composition. *Awiamve* (*awi* 'outside') offerings are made literally outside the compounds and there are no ghosts present. They are made in the grass between the settlements, which is a no-man's-land unoccupied by lineage ghosts. *Awiamve* refers to a rite in which an animal is killed and the meat distributed among the representatives of related lineages, but not offered to the dead. These lineages are not all the sacrificing group's *enyati*, strictly speaking, although. they may loosely be so called. But Lugbara stress that they are not 'the true *enyati*, who are near us'. The rites which are known as *awiamve* are those rites of purification which I have described, such as the rite to remove sickness due to grumbling brought by the 'mouths of men' against a man responsible for warfare and death, the rite of killing the 'bull of fornication', the rite of 'striking the boundary'. In all of them it is said that their purpose is to 'cleanse the territory'.

These rites are known as *awi so* or *awi li* ('to cut *awi*'); they involve 'cutting' a beast without offering it to the dead, who are not involved in the offence or event that has led to the rite. When the dead are involved it is the maintenance of community ties that is at stake; these are based upon the agnatic lineage at the core of the community, and this group is represented at *awi'buru*. At rites in this category agnatic lineage ties are used to integrate the local community. The *awiamve* congregation attend a more secular ceremony which is concerned with less moral and more purely political relations—those to do with feud, marriage and segmentation of lineages—although the concept of sin may be present also. This latter congregation consists of the agnatically related lineages within the entire sub-clan. Representatives are called to include all minimal lineages of the major lineage, and a representative of every other minor lineage of the sub-clan. Lineages which are accessory to the tribe usually send representatives, although they are often not specifically invited and when they do attend they may be accused of greed for meat rather than welcomed as observing ties of community and friendship. But this reflects a general sense of lineage exclusiveness, since the ceremonies are concerned, after all, with matters of mainly lineage interest. But whereas they would never come to an *awį'bụrụ* rite—their presense is said to cause fighting if they do try to force their way in—they do come to *awįamve* rites more or less as a matter of course. Smaller accessory lineages do not come, but are given portions of meat by the elders of their host lineages when the latter return home. Women do not attend—a sign that political rather than purely lineage interests are the main concern.

Each elder attends as a representative of a local section, based upon a lineage of certain span, depending on the lineage distance between him and the group carrying out the rite. Each elder is accompanied by the elders of the groups which he is representing. For example, a major section of three minor lineages is represented by the senior elder of the whole major lineage (A), accompanied by the senior elders of the two minor lineages to which he himself does not belong (B and C). It will be remembered that elders are ranked by genealogical seniority of their lineages up to the level of the major lineage. The representation of a minor lineage is analogous. These assistants are called *ondrụ*. Only the main representative may say a ritual address or anoint with blood`

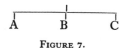

FIGURE 7.

and chyle, and it is he who is given the portion of meat to take home to distribute among the component segments of the group that he represents. His assistants eat of the meat that is cooked on the spot, and drink beer. They sit with him as a single group. Assistants must be taken to *awįamve* rites, of which the main overt function is the sharing of meat together by all the lineages of a group, without involving the ghosts and without curing sickness. Their hearts should be 'cool', but they are not attesting that they have forgiven a breach of kinship ties of the type that is the concern of ghostly sacrifice. In the latter case, the situation of *awį'bụrụ* rites, all people present must take part as full members of the congregation, which includes the dead. Mystical participation of this sort cannot devolve upon a representative in the way that participation in the non-ghostly rites of *awjamve* may do. In the latter it is the sharing of food among living kin and neighbours that is all-important —by it these ties are re-affirmed. In the ghostly rite an elder represents a lineage by virtue of his senior genealogical position—his lineage seniority is mystical, as it were, by 'blood'; but in the more secular ceremony of *awjamve* he is not thought to represent a local territorial section in the same way. He may, therefore, take assistants, the heads of component lineages of the section, both host and accessory, related or unrelated agnatically. The main 'supernatural' agent is God, who cannot be represented by living men.

This essential difference between *awj'bụrụ* and *awjamve* rites is more easily apparent in northern Lugbara where each tribe has its rainmaker-chief. He is the elder of the genealogically senior lineage and possesses rainmaking powers inherited from the founder of the sub-clan which provides the core of the tribe. He is not concerned, in that office, with the *awj'bụrụ* rites of lineages other than his own, since he has no special status *vis-à-vis* the ghosts of their lineages. But he is summoned to officiate at all *awjamve* rites, where he leads and generally supervises the entire proceedings. He is here the single representative of the entire tribe, and his presence signifies that the tribe is a single group with common values and a sense of unity. Besides his ritual powers he has certain rather rudimentary political authority, as I have described above. His role in *awjamve* rites, which settle the repercussions of former disputes and fights, is connected with the more overtly political aspects of his total role.

IV

THE FIELD OF RITUAL ACTION

I. RITUAL AND THE LINEAGE: THE ACTORS

I HAVE described Lugbara social structure and the cult of the dead. In Lugbara thought a mystical agent sends sickness to living people, usually as a consequence of an invocation made because of an offence. Oracles and diviners are consulted to discover the nature of the case and the identity of the responsible agent; oblation is promised and made, usually after the recovery of the patient. This is a logically consistent system and explains most sickness and provides a social and psychological response to it; it also provides sanctions against anti-social behaviour.

Lugbara accept that these agents do in fact send sickness. But I assume that the sequence of events accepted by them is without scientific foundation. Its significance is sociological.[1] In actuality the sequence of events is different, for the theoretically prior invocation and mystical sending of sickness are not usually known until after the sickness has been diagnosed. Its diagnosis can be sociological rather than medical, due to the notions of sickness held by Lugbara; and the agents are not known until after divination. Although Lugbara state that in theory each type of sickness, as known by its agent, has its own type of oracular consultation and confirmation, and its own type of oblation, purification and congregation, in actuality these variations are decided upon in the light of the social situation in which the actors find themselves at the time.

The significance of these beliefs may best be understood by an analysis of the rites associated with them. I here make such an analysis with regard to a particular family cluster, in which I lived

---

[1] I omit consideration of psycho-somatic conditions induced by threats of invocation. These may well occur, and I have seen cases of trembling and hysteria clearly induced by threats of sorcery. But in this account I am concerned with the sociological significance of Lugbara religious beliefs and actions.

for about a year. This particular group, Araka in Maraca,[1] is typical of those of north-central Lugbara. At the time of my stay it was about to segment, and the amount of invocation, sacrifice and dissension, expressed largely in ritual terms, was correspondingly greater than at other times in its history. But since all family clusters go through this stage periodically, this is no disadvantage. During my stay many rites were performed, most of which were part of the process of realignment of patterns of authority within the group. Here I describe these ritual cases as they occurred. Their occurrence was not haphazard, since the oracular definitions of responsible agents and ritual instruments were very largely determined by their place in this process. In general the members of the group discussed these cases in cultural terms, as though they were isolated events. But it soon became apparent that they were able to do this precisely because they took the whole framework of realignment for granted. They lived within it, among members of other kin-groups all of whom lived within a similar framework. At first I misunderstood the sociological significance of their explanations, by trying to understand them in isolation as referring to ideal patterns of behaviour. As I realized the great variation in behaviour associated with oblations at any particular shrine, so I realized that details of behaviour were largely agreed upon *ad hoc* according to the patterns of authority and the motives of the actors in any ritual situation.

The particular local group around which I build up this account of ritual is a family cluster called Araka, based upon a minimal lineage of the same name, in Maraca, in north-central Lugbara. Maraca is an area of high density of population, over two hundred persons to the square mile, and is a long-settled area. A generally accepted genealogy of Araka as it was in 1951 is given in Fig. 10. At the time of my study it was a single minimal lineage consisting of two large segments named by the lineage members Lari'ba and Nyaai, after the lineage names of the two ancestresses by whom they are differentiated. Their identity is not usually known, however, to members of neighbouring lineages, who refer to the whole group as a single one, Araka. Araka is a lineage that has expanded from three to nine households during the past sixty years, although its total membership has not tripled during that time. In 1951 it numbered 90, including one attached

---

[1] I have changed the names of lineages and actors in this account.

family of 'sister's sons'; Lari'ba had 46 and Nyaai 44 members.

In 1900 there were only three homesteads in Araka, then also a single family cluster, under the eldership of Dria. These were those of

> Dria, with whom lived Ondua, Oguda, Angura and their families.
>
> Abiria, with whom lived his own elementary family.
>
> Cakida, with whom lived Goloko, Avuye and their families.

The compounds of Dria and Cakida were both large, and all were within a hundred yards of each other, some two hundred yards from the burial tree of the lineage founder Ombasa. Their fields stretched eastwards for about a quarter of a mile, down to the stream that marked its boundary with its co-ordinate lineages Ambidro and Ombavu.

Goloko and Avuye were younger than Dria, and both died before him, about 1903-4. Angura was killed by the Belgians in 1901, and Dria died in 1906. His successor was his eldest son Ondua, who was then only twenty-two years old. Although he held the mystical power of eldership his authority was not accepted throughout the lineage. Secular authority was exercised by Cakida who inherited the only one of Dria's widows who was inherited. She bore a girl by him and then died. Cakida exercised tutelary eldership until his death in 1911, then Ondua was still only twenty-seven. Tutelary eldership was then exercised by Abiria until his death in 1927, when Ondua was forty-three and succeeded to full authority as lineage elder.

During Cakida's period of tutelage the men of Lari'ba resented his authority, and after his death those of Nyaai resented that of Abiria. There seem to have been no real efforts at segmentation for two reasons. There were no other senior men alive, except for Pokoni, whose antecedents are not clearly known. Although today he is said to have been a son of either Toba or of Avuye, he or his father were almost certainly clients attached to Nyaai. The second reason was that there was no land or population pressure; land seems to have been sufficient for Araka's needs until the 1930s.

About 1916-18 there were serious outbreaks of cerebrospinal meningitis, in which many members of the lineage died, including Angundru, Gala, Kanyi, an attached 'sister's son' Nyoka, and many of their young children. The remaining men therefore decided to move the cluster of homesteads from the site on which they had been since before 1900. During that time there had been only very slight movement of huts, new compounds being built literally next to old hut-sites, which were used as specially fertile gardens.

In 1919 the compounds were moved some hundreds of yards to the south-east, to the sites marked on Figure 8. Ondua was elder, under the tutelage of Abiria. There were now four homesteads, the additional one having been set up at Ondua's marriage, when he moved away from his brothers. In 1924-5 there was an outbreak of cattle disease, after which only three cattle out of a former total of some one hundred and twenty were left. Ondua, as head of Lari'ba segment, had owned forty-seven and was left with three, while Olimani, as head of Nyaai segment, had owned seventy-three of which every one died. It is said that after this catastrophe the men of Nyaai began to think of becoming a distinct lineage. It was about this time that the generation of Ondua and Olimani were marrying and having children, and land shortage began to be a problem. The members of Nyaai began to spread out over the flat land near the stream to the east of Araka. In recent years they have put three homesteads beyond it, in much poorer land that was traditionally part of Mjrjdrj, a neighbouring lineage. Many of the junior men of Nyaai have worked as labour migrants in the past twenty years, both because land has been scarce and because the cattle sickness had removed their wealth at a single stroke.

Lari'ba's land is in the heart of the lineage territory, for in it are the groves in which have been the lineage's external shrines, and the grave sites of the more famous ancestors. The soil is better, but there is more overcrowding than in Nyaai, and two of its younger men have lived continuously in Arua, the district township, for many years. Both say they would return if they could find land.

During my stay in Araka, the two segments Lari'ba and Nyaai were constituent segments of the lineage, under the eldership of Ondua. Ondua died in 1952. He was a gentle old man, greatly respected, with an immense amount of mythical, legendary and genealogical knowledge. He was assisted, informally, by his half-brother Oguda. Ondua's formal ritual assistant was Olimani,

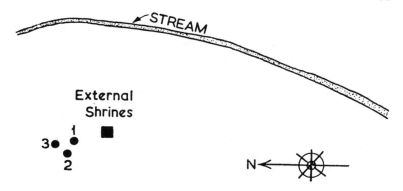

1900

1—Dria. 2—Cakida. 3—Abiria.

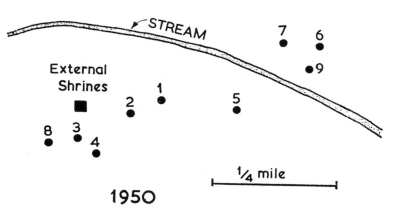

1950

1—Ondua. 2—Oguda. 3—Draai. 4—Benyu. 5—Olimani.
6—Okwaya. 7—Otoro and Obitre. 8—Edre and Siki. 9—Njima

FIGURE 8. Araka—hut sites.

the head of Nyaai. But there had always been considerable antagonism between them, and Ondua never asked for assistance from Olimani unless obliged to do so. On my second visit, in 1953, the two segments had become independent of each other. Olimani was elder of Nyaai; he is a rather bad-tempered old man, jealous of Ondua's successor in Lari'ba, Yekule, whom he thinks should accept his authority. Yekule, the elder of Lari'ba, is only thirty-six, and is under the tutelary care of Oguda; it is assumed that the latter will act in this way until his death—he is an old man.

I shall refer back to this lineage to provide examples of the operation of various parts of the Lugbara system of ritual.

II. RITUAL AND THE LINEAGE: THE CASES

I now give an account of the ritual history of this one lineage during the period I spent there. Of course, this short period cannot be isolated from the past, but I shall refer only to such events that took place before my arrival as are necessary to an understanding of the rites I describe. Altogether there were thirty-four rites performed. Most of them take their significance from the fact that they occurred during the final stages before segmentation into two lineages, a process that lasted in all about half a century. But in order to avoid unnecessary confusion I shall describe only the more important in the order in which they took place, and consider the less important at the end of the account.

Case *1*

Ondua cut a sheep at his senior ghost shrine on account of his own sickness. He had been unwell and weak for many months—he was then an old man—and the onset of the heavy rains in March brought on aches and pains. It is very cold on the Lugbara plateau at this time of year, and there is much sickness; most older people die during the months of July and August, which are the wettest and coldest, but Lugbara say that they 'get ready' to die when the heavy rains begin in March. Old men therefore feel apprehensive when they are sick at this time, and part of the reason for the offer of a sheep was that it is the beast considered particularly associated with God, who is the agent responsible for death. In fact Ondua died the following year, in April, but he was very sick on this occasion.

Ondua was confined to his compound, and the oracles were consulted by his half-brother Oguda. In any case a man should not consult the oracles on his own behalf, although an elder may do so. Frequently, perhaps usually, he consults his own rubbing-stick oracle to confirm the decision of the oracle that has been consulted on his behalf elsewhere, and Ondua did so on this occasion. Usually he trusted Oguda, since Oguda was his assistant and adviser in almost everything; but it so happened that they had quarrelled a few months before, a very rare event that had greatly disturbed Ondua. In fact his son, Yekule, told me that at the time that Ondua had told him that this was an evil omen, since it was the first time they had quarrelled since 1900 when Oguda had gone to work for the first Belgian administrator, who had set up a post at Ofude, a mile or two to the east of Araka. Ondua consulted his own oracles after Oguda had returned to tell him of the result of his oracular séance with Ayua of Kimiru, a well-known oracle-operator who lived about half a mile from Araka.

Oguda told Ondua that the sickness was the consequence of invocation by Olimani and Oguda himself together because Ondua had not made a sacrifice for some time but had eaten greedily of sacrificial meat at recent offerings made by Olimani and others in Nyaai. The sickness came from Dria, the father of Ondua and Oguda. Ondua consulted his own rubbing-stick, and told Oguda that it had disagreed with this statement, but that he had not been able to determine what was the cause. Oguda then returned to Ayua, who operated his oracle again. This time it decided that the sickness was the consequence of ghostly vengeance by Dria, for the same reasons: Dria had decided to 'show' Ondua, because he had eaten greedily of Olimani's meat but had rarely offered his own beasts. This time Ondua did not consult his own oracle. Oguda consulted his own chicken oracle which confirmed the oracular statement.

Immediately, this case was a response to two recent events. A few months before Ondua and Oguda had quarrelled. Ondua, who had been drinking at a death dance nearby for another elder, had suggested that Oguda was waiting for him to die so as to step into his place, and that Oguda had joined Olimani and Draai as an ally against Ondua. Ondua's successor in any case was his son

Yekule; being only a youngish man it was likely that Oguda would act as his adviser and in fact exercise all the authority of eldership except perform the actual rites of sacrifice, which only Yekule would be able to do. Thus his suggestion was an offensive one, since the wicked guardian of the young elder is one of the stock Lugbara figures in genealogical legend. Besides this suggestion following on Ondua's attendance at a brother elder's funeral it may well have been due partly to a recent suggestion by the local parish chief that Oguda should be made a headman. Oguda did not accept, mainly because he was in any case old himself and preferred traditional authority as Ondua's assistant. But Ondua was said to have remarked on that occasion that Oguda was becoming 'big', a remark that was said by others to have been due to his age and near senility. Ondua also claimed that Oguda had tried to speak a ritual address before he did at a recent sacrifice. This would have been a way of taking over Ondua's role.

The other antecedent event was a public statement made by Oguda about an ox of Ondua's. Oguda had said, at a beer-drink when the subject of conversation had been sacrificial meat eating, a frequent topic on these occasions, that Ondua possessed a fine ox but that although both Oguda and Olimani had frequently urged him to offer it at a sacrifice he had refused to do so. Oguda said that both of them were growing old and that they might die without eating of the ox, since if Ondua died it would probably be that ox which would be given to his mother's brother's successor as the *avuṭi* or 'corpse beast', a beast that should be as fine a one as can be obtained. Ondua had told Olimani that he (and by implication Oguda also) was prompted by greed rather than by piety, and there had been disputes. After Oguda's remarks at the beer-drink, which were relayed to Ondua by Yekule, his son, Ondua had treated Oguda with silence. 'A man should talk good words with his own brother, if brothers do not talk their hearts grow bad.'

Although Ondua and Oguda had been close for many years, and although it was generally stressed in Lari'ba that they had never previously quarrelled since 1900, there was considerable tension in this relationship. Both men were gentle and intelligent, and Oguda had created a reputation for himself by his attachment to the Belgian administrator. But the position of a junior brother is always difficult, since it is unlikely that he will become an elder in his own right. Typically these are the men who tend to become oracle workers or other ritual specialists, or who become attached to the missions or the administration in junior capacities. Oguda made frequent allusions to this situation; these were often phrased in terms of the superiority of his own son to the son of Ondua, and he often said that Ondua was 'strong' (*okporu*), a term that has the implication that the subject of it is inclined to witchcraft. An invoker of the ghosts is liable to be accused of witchcraft, and the same term, *ole ro*, is used for the two processes. A man speaking of an elder who is universally popular and to whom no suspicion of witchcraft attaches is more likely to use words like *onyiru* ('good'), or *yere* ('slow'). *Okporu* has this undertone when applied to important men in the traditional system, although it may be applied to chiefs and such-like people who are seen as outside the traditional sphere of everyday life. Oguda did not thereby openly accuse Ondua of being a witch, but the implication was clear enough.

I have already described the different oracles and the methods of consultation. Lugbara theory is that in cases of ghostly sickness, which are 'big', all the confirming oracles are used to confirm the statement of the rubbing-stick oracle. In fact, sickness from the ghosts at the external shrines is even 'bigger' than is that from the internal ghosts, but in that case only the rubbing-stick oracle is used. So that the 'bigness' is not really a reason. The decisions of the oracles are determined to a very large extent by the questions put to them by the consultant and also by the general feel of the situation that the oracle operator has at the time of consultation. The statement of the rubbing-stick oracle reflects the pattern of conflict of authority within the family group concerned; the more complex and deep-rooted this conflict the greater the degree of confirmation required.

I was not present at the oracle consultation in this particular case. Ayua, the operator, told me that Oguda had discussed Ondua's sickness, saying that he thought it likely that Olimani had had something to do with it. Olimani, as I have explained, wanted to become an independent elder and so took any chance he could to show that Ondua's authority was limited and that he did not have the full trust of the dead as their sole representative in Araka. Oguda had said that 'many people' thought Ondua was overbearing and might practise witchcraft. Oguda had placed certain sticks to represent suspects, including Olimani, Ondua's father Dria, the more remote ancestors Moro and Oraa, and Ondua's mother's brother's son, to represent Ondua's mother's lineage. Ayua said that after the rubbing-stick oracle had decreed that Olimani had invoked the dead against Ondua, Oguda had agreed that he also had thought angrily about Ondua some time before, in the company of Olimani. The reasons given for the invocation, Ondua's greed and selfishness, is a stock one in the case of an elder's being sick; he is under no authority save that of the dead, and refusal to offer sacrifice to them is the classical type of impiety.

Yekule, Ondua's son, told me later that Ondua had consulted his own rubbing-stick to confirm Ayua's oracle's statement because he was both very angry and sad that Olimani had invoked the ghosts against him, as elder of Araka. Yekule said:

> That Olimani of Nyaai is a good man, but his heart is bad. He is an old man, who fought the Belgians and knew the words of the *Yakan* cult. Now people say he is 'behind' and so his heart has grown bad towards us here in Lari'ba.

The reference to *Yakan* is to the anti-European *Yakan* cult which I discuss in the next chapter. Yekule's reference to a good man having a bad heart is one often made by Lugbara when referring to an ambitious man in Olimani's or Oguda's position, that of a senior man who because of genealogical chance cannot become an elder and who is known to chafe under this ritual subordination. On another occasion I was told, by Olimani's half-brother, Okwaya:

> Olimani is a good man. But sometimes his heart is bad and he has anger towards us. Perhaps his heart is just bad, but how can a man's heart be bad, for no account? These are the words of a man's *talị*, those words that come from the ancestors. Every man has a *talị*, which comes from his father and that father's father. If the dead are angry then their child will also be angry in his heart, as a child follows his father.

Although Lugbara theory as to the nature of a man's *talị* is vague the general sense is clear in this context. Olimani's anger against Ondua is due to his position as head of Nyaai and representative of the dead of Nyaai. Yekule's statement that Olimani's heart is bad 'towards us here in Lari'ba' bears this out: it is not bad against Ondua as an individual but against him as representative of all Lari'ba. Oguda told me that Ondua was sad, because his 'brother' Olimani had come to dislike him, but added that all men dislike elders and are jealous of their power, and so Ondua had to expect that.

Ondua had consulted his rubbing-stick with only Yekule present. His stick 'refused' the statement of Ayua's stick. Since Ondua would have to make his own sacrifice on his own behalf, this refusal was sufficient for the process of oracular consultation to have to be done again. Yekule was sent to Oguda and told him this, and Oguda, this time with Yekule, returned to Ayua a few days later. Ondua did not discuss the matter with Oguda, since he was also angry with him and was ashamed that his own brother had sided with Olimani.

At the second consultation the oracles decreed that Ondua had become sick as a consequence of ghostly vengeance sent by his father Dria. Ayua's rubbing-stick oracle decreed this, and it was confirmed by Oguda's consulting a chicken oracle which he constructed himself. This consultation was attended by Oguda, Yekule, Oguda's son Aribo, and by Olimani. There was quarrelling during the consultation over the interpretation of the chickens' fluttering and falling about, Oguda and Olimani saying that the rubbing-stick oracle's verdict was confirmed and Yekule denying this. But he was a generation junior and so his word carried relatively little weight. Usually this confirmation would have been following by confirmation by either the boiling-water oracle or the rat oracle, or by both; but on this occasion no further confirmation was made. Yekule told me that when he told his father of the chicken oracle's verdict, Ondua said that he knew that these verdicts were wrong but that he would accept them because a man could not argue against others all the time and because it was not suitable for an elder to argue in cases of this kind. Yekule also told me that Ondua said that perhaps witches had entered into the matter and so it might as well be closed as soon as possible by the necessary sacrifice. Ondua was behaving as an elder should behave, in order to prevent the increase of hostility within Araka and to bring himself, his brother Oguda and his rival Olimani together again at the sacrifice. Aribo said also that Ondua thought that there was witchcraft, or more accurately the motivation for witchcraft, the sentiment of envy (*ole*), in the case, and that it was Olimani who was responsible. He said

Olimani's heart is big. Perhaps he has said words, perhaps he has said to many people that Ondua is greedy. Who knows the words of old men? But Olimani is 'strong' and those people there of Nyaai they follow the words of Olimani. Perhaps Olimani is a witch, but I have not heard this said.

Aribo was not willing to accuse Olimani of witchcraft, but was willing to accuse him of the sentiment of *ole*; as I have said earlier, this sentiment motivates both witches and invokers of ghosts, but when it is used in the way Aribo used it then, it usually implies that witchcraft is involved. I wish to discuss witchcraft accusations in these situations more fully in a later case, so will leave this particular matter for the moment. But it may be said that on this occasion it is clear that Olimani was thought to have been the instigator of Ondua's sickness, due to Olimani's jealousy and his ambition to become an independent elder. But it was not until later cases of sickness in the year that Olimani's position was made more explicit and the dispute between the two segments of Araka was brought more into the open.

Ondua decided to accept the oracular verdict, and decided to sacrifice a sheep. This was not, as far as I know, decreed by the oracles, or if it was it was still given as Ondua's own decision. For a sheep to be chosen was a recognition of God's immediate interest in the affair. This recognition was Ondua's own, and in it two notions were implicit. One was that Ondua, being an old man, and sick during the first rains, might be going to die soon; death is the concern of God, and although Lugbara state firmly that a man cannot sway God's will by sacrifice, they also say that a man can call God's attention to his activities by offering a sheep so that God may have the chance to think again:

It is God who carries people away by death. Yet perhaps God forgets a man, and he may carry a man away by death when that man is not yet ready to die. If we offer a sheep then God may think and remember that man and he may live another year.

The notion here is not that God is persuaded but that God may have made a mistake and be caused to remedy it, or at least be reminded of the chance to remedy it if he so wishes. On another occasion, when discussing the same subject, I was told:

Is it good to make appeal to the Judge? A man kills another, and goes to the District Commissioner and he sends him to the Judge.

When that Judge sits there in red cloth, in the Diwan at Arua, then his family begin to wail and his widow throws ashes upon herself; his brothers decide that they must dance his death dance. Then that man is taken away to Luzira (the central Protectorate prison near Kampala) and later his little finger is sent back to his widow so that she knows he is dead. Yet there was that man of Oluko who went to Luzira and many years later he came back, even though his brothers thought he had been killed by the rope. Perhaps he had shown himself to that Judge again and the Judge had thought 'Perhaps it was not that man who had killed, I shall not kill him with rope'. Or perhaps it was the Governor. So it is with God. He wants to take a man by death, but if he sees the sheep he thinks 'Perhaps that man can live another year and I shall take him another year; his years are not yet cut.'

The other notion in Ondua's decision to offer a sheep was told me by Olimani's brother Okwaya. I think that Okwaya may not have understood his motives, but it was a generally accepted motive, both in this and in similar situations. God is above sectional interests, in a way that the dead are not. So that by offering him a sheep Ondua was showing that he considered God at least partially responsible for the sickness, and so showed that he denied the verdict of ghostly vengeance, even though he appeared to accept it for the general good and peace of his lineage. If God had sent sickness, he would not have done so for the reasons that had been stated by the oracles, but either because he wished to 'show' Ondua that he was soon to die, or for other reasons that neither Ondua nor any other man could know. 'A man does not know the words of God'.

Ondua led the sheep round his own compound in the usual way and the sacrifice was made on the following day, as he was no longer very sick and, it was said, wished to make the offering as soon as possible since he had accepted his sickness as a sign that he was soon to die. On the morning of the rite all the men of Araka, including the attached 'sister's son' Njima, were present, together with the unmarried daughters of the group. The lineage's commensal partners were also present, the elders of the co-ordinate lineages of the inner lineage. These component lineages are those called Ambidro and Ombavu. Also the small lineage Nyaai[1] sent representatives, as did Aivu, Mitika, Nyoro, Padruku and Bura. Their relationship is shown in Figure 4. Together these lineages

[1] A co-ordinate minimal lineage of Araka, and not the internal segment headed by Olimani.

compose the lineage Minyako, a group which has today almost ceased to act as a single entity owing to the unequal growth of its segments, but the relationship is remembered at rituals. Every lineage sent a representative, and Ambidro and Ombavu also sent the heads of their internal segments to sit with their elders. The complete attendance was due partly to the fact that it was Ondua's own sacrifice for his own sickness, and also perhaps to the importance of the rite in the internal struggle in Araka, which affects co-ordinate segments as the segmentation of this lineage might lead to re-organization of the entire cluster. The rite was also important in involving the offering of a sheep. A bull and sheep are the important oblations; those of other animals are liable to attract a smaller congregation.

The first ritual address was made by Ondua himself; it was very short, and in it he stated that he was to offer a sheep because God had sent sickness to 'show' him that he was now old. He added that his father Dria had also had a hand in sending the sickness, and that he would soon eat of the sheep, together with the other ghosts of the lineage. No mention was made of the specific charges against him which had been decreed by the oracles. After he had spoken there was silence for a moment or two and Ondua then started the business of cutting and preparing the sheep. It was now obvious that Ondua had decided to change the whole nature of the sacrifice from one of offering as a consequence of ghostly vengeance for his own supposed misdemeanours into one in which he showed his seniority and superior authority by his close relationship both with Dria and other ghosts and with God himself.

The second ritual address is always the more important, and on this occasion addresses were made by Ondua, then by Olimani, by the elders of Ambidro and Ombavu, and by Draai. Oguda did not speak, it was said later because of 'shame' for his brother. Ondua spoke for about thirty minutes, quietly and fast. There is not the space here to give his address in full, but the main points made were:

1. He had succeeded as elder to the lineage which had been maintained and strengthened by his father Dria, who watched over his descendants.

2. Dria, as representative of the totality of lineage ghosts, was distressed by the hostility within the lineage, and especially by the

frequency and amount of indignation (*ole*) displayed by its members.

3. Dria was distressed at this especially because of Ondua's age and nearness to death, which had been shown by his sickness and by God's acceptance of the sheep as an offering to him, which showed that he had sent the sickness or had caused the ghosts to send it.

4. The oracles had been much confused over this case, due perhaps to witchcraft and perhaps to the fact that God was concerned in the matter. But they had decided that the cause of the sickness was ghostly vengeance, and this was Dria's way of showing the living members of the lineage how serious the position was.

5. The hearts of the men of Araka should be cool, and also those of other lineages whose representatives were at the sacrifice. This would show the ghosts and also God that they had 'closed their hearts against evil words'.

6. That there were people of Araka, 'perhaps in those children of Licu', that is, in Nyaai, whose hearts were 'strong'. They should forget these words and together eat with their agnates so that the dead would be happy with their children.

I have given only the briefest outline of Ondua's address. It was filled with genealogical information and also with details of past quarrels and disputes within the lineage which had been resolved peacefully. His argument was greeted with approval by the members of the congregation, though there was some muttering from the men of Nyaai. Ondua succeeded in throwing off responsibility for misdemeanour from himself and placing it fairly clearly on to Olimani and his supporters.

Olimani then took sacred leaves in his hand and made his ritual address. He is a much less subtle man than Ondua, and had also been angered by Ondua's address. He spoke much more directly, and only for five minutes or so. His points were that Dria had sent this sickness, and so had God, because there was trouble and quarrelling within Araka, because sacrifices had not been made often enough and the dead were angry in their hearts at the greed and impiety of their descendants. He had often thought of these matters in his heart, and so had other senior men of the lineage. Now indeed God had entered into the case. He then made a long statement that Oraa, the apical ancestor of Lari'ba, Ondua's

segment, had fought with his brother Licu, the apical ancestor of
Nyaai, over land and had taken the heart of Araka territory as his
own; perhaps Dria and God were also angry at this. They should
together eat of this meat and resolve that their hearts should be
cool, as they were all brothers.

By his address Olimani brought the original dispute for lineage
authority into the open, and used Ondua's bringing of God into
the matter to support his statements. His reference to lineage land
referred to one of the basic disputes between the two segments.
At that moment, I was told later, this was much in his mind since
his wives had been quarrelling among themselves over their fields,
which were being hoed for sowing in the first rains at that very
moment. His segment did not have enough good land and he was
resentful of the long-farmed and fertile lands of Lari'ba. It is
significant that he left the dispute open, making no attempt to
bring it to a peaceful resolution; to have done so would have meant
his acceptance of Ondua's authority both in the eyes of Araka and
of the dead. He paid lip-service to Ondua's superior authority,
but it was little more.

The elders of Ambidro and Ombavu then made short addresses.
Both were formal and referred entirely to the past of Minyako, when
it was united and peaceful. By implication present disputes within
it were deplored, but there was no open reference to them. Draai
of Lari'ba then made an address, which was clearly unpopular
with the congregation, who ostentatiously talked among themselves and laughed at his words. He said that Dria had sent
ghostly vengeance, as a consequence of the 'words' of Olimani and
himself; he did not mention Oguda, despite the fact that he had
been included in the oracular verdicts. Now his own heart was
cool, because of the offering of the sheep.

Draai wanted to be regarded as an elder of his own small segment, independent of Ondua's authority, and was here trying to
show that he was equal to Olimani in generation and seniority,
and was also as important in the eyes of the ghosts, who listened
to him and so showed their approval of his aspirations to eldership. Okwaya, sitting next to me, said to me that Draai's words
were always 'big' and that I need not trouble to write them down
since they were 'just words'. Draai's effort to use this occasion for
his own ends met with no success.

Lugbara theory holds that at the saying of ritual addresses the hearts of all the members of the congregation become cool, that all speak in harmony and show this to the listening ghosts; it also holds that all words spoken at these addresses must be true, that the speakers must not let their personal feelings override what they know to be the truth. These two ideas about ritual addresses may be in conflict, as this case of Ondua's sacrifice shows clearly enough. In certain ways this case was atypical of cases of ghost invocation and ghostly vengeance, because of Ondua's introduction of God into it. This is implied, I think, by a statement made to me by Okwaya at the time, in response to a question about the obvious discrepancy of view between the speakers:

It is good that at this sacrifice all men should speak with one word. They should stop their anger and their envy. They must say true words. There in the shrines are the ghosts of our ancestors who hear our words. They know that words are in our hearts. God does not know these things. God is far away, in the sky, perhaps he does not hear our words. But the ghosts know them and know the truth.

Ondua's introduction of God into the affair to some extent placed it outside the ordinary run of ghostly sacrifices, and, since God is outside and above segmentary conflicts of interests, the at least superficial unity of the lineage became less important than it would have been had only the ghosts been involved.

After the ritual addresses there followed the offering itself at the ghost shrines, which was performed by Ondua. Then came the blessing and anointing with spittle. Ondua was anointed on his chest and insteps by Olimani, the heads of all guest lineages, and by Oguda, Draai and Otoro. No others anointed him. Okwaya told me that neither Draai nor Otoro had been expected to do this, but that there was no reason that they should not: 'it is good that all men do this, to show that they "fear" the ghosts'. None the less, the other men did not anoint, an action which is said properly to be done only by the heads of independent segments and those closely concerned in the sickness. There was clearly the feeling that these two junior men were here trying to show their importance, but that their action was not of great significance, and certainly not of equal importance to making a ritual address.

The sacrificial meat was then distributed, some for immediate cooking and consumption, some for carrying home by the guests. The rite was one of the category known as *awɨ'bɨrɨ*, in which most of the meat, including the four legs, is distributed among the host lineage, the remainder being cooked and eaten at the place of sacrifice. Ondua gave the left foreleg to Olimani, the right foreleg to Draai, the left hindleg to Oguda and Benyu, and the right hindleg he retained for his own segment. Small portions were given to the elders of all the lineages mentioned above on page 141, each receiving an equal share. The remainder was cooked and eaten on the spot, after much beer-drinking. At the meal people were grouped according to generation, the elders sitting in one place, the senior heads of segments in another, junior men in a third, boys and unmarried daughters in a fourth. The significant point was the position of Olimani and Oguda. Draai attempted, although half-heartedly, to sit with Ondua and the elders, but was ignored and then called by others to sit with the junior men. Both Olimani and Oguda sat with the elders. Benyu told me later that this was to avoid embarrassment and open quarrelling with Olimani; his sitting with Ondua gave him a higher position than that to which he was entitled, but the fact that Oguda was sat with them also immediately detracted from this position. By inviting them both to sit with him, Ondua as it were changed their statuses from those of heads of component segments of Araka to those of old men and close agnatic kin; and the exclusion of Draai (the head of a distinct matrisegment) emphasized this aspect of their situation. The juniority of Draai was perhaps still further shown by the fact that I was invited to sit as an elder, although Okwaya, with whom I had been sitting and discussing the scene, was excluded.

The pattern of invitation by Ondua was not primarily to show Draai his place, however, but to show that he regarded Olimani and Oguda as his close 'brothers' and coevals, and so to smooth over the cleavage within the lineage that had become so apparent during the course of this case of sickness. In spite of the fact that by Lugbara theory neither Olimani nor Oguda should have sat with the elders, there was general approval of Ondua's inviting them, since 'they are brothers of one father', the 'father' in this case being Ombasa, the father of Oraa and Licu and founder of Araka: again, the kinship aspect of their position was emphasized.

Case 2

A fortnight later, Oguda sacrificed a goat at his senior ghost shrine as the consequence of sickness of his own grandson, the son of Jobi. The boy had been sick for a considerable time, and it was clear that the choosing of this moment for the sacrifice was closely connected with the events of Case 1. Jobi is nominally a Christian, and it was not until his father Oguda insisted on consulting the oracles that anything was done about the sickness; in any case it was not serious but merely a prolonged series of low fevers. Oguda consulted the rubbing-stick oracle, again that operated by Ayua of Kimiru, the operator in Case 1. The séance was very short. Oguda maintained that he had invoked the ghost of his father Dria because Jobi had been insolent to him, and the sickness had affected Jobi's son. We returned to Oguda's compound, and Oguda said that he would not trouble to confirm the verdict at the chicken oracle, since it was obvious to him that this verdict was the correct one. He then told Ondua, and asked him for a goat for the sacrifice. Ondua said that he wished first to consult his own rubbing-stick oracle to confirm Ayua's verdict, even though such confirmation could be only an 'unofficial' one, not recognized by the living and dead members of the lineage. The following evening Ondua stated that his rubbing-stick had not confirmed the verdict, and said that he himself would go, with Oguda, to consult another rubbing-stick oracle. He claimed that Ayua's oracle had failed to give clear or confirmable verdicts in Case 1, and that they should try another oracle that could not be tainted with any witchcraft or 'words' that might be spoken in Araka, or in its neighbourhood. They consulted a famous rubbing-stick operator several miles away in Rubu, which was the section of Ondua's mother. It was said that the operator would take care not to deceive his 'sister's son'; nor, by implication, to allow his rubbing-stick to be deceived or affected by outside agents. Ondua put the names of suspected agents to the oracle operator, including himself, Oguda, Olimani, the sick boy's mother's brother, and the ghosts of Dria and Moro. The oracle gave the verdict that Ondua was the agent, and Ondua agreed that he had invoked the ghosts against Jobi (the boy had therefore become sick as a substitute for Jobi). The ghost who had sent the sickness was Ondua's father, Dria. At the séance Oguda denied this, saying that it was he who had invoked against Jobi, adding that even if Ondua had also done so it was certainly his, Oguda's, invocation that had brought this sickness.

We returned home, and three days later Ondua and Oguda

constructed a chicken oracle and gave the case to it for confirmation. The oracle 'refused' both names, and gave no consistent verdict at all. In theory, the consultations should have started all over again, but in this case it was decided that since the oracles had agreed that Dria was the ghost responsible, and that the cause of the whole process was Jobi's insolence to his seniors, and since in any case the patient was only a boy, it would be best to agree to offer a goat and to set the sacrificial process in motion. A goat was supplied by Ondua, as head both of Araka and of Lari'ba segment, and a few days later it was led round the compound to be 'shown' and consecrated for sacrifice if the boy recovered.

It was very clear that this case was the occasion, or rather the expression, of the new quarrel between the two half-brothers Ondua and Oguda. Since Oguda was not trying to be considered an independent elder, as was Olimani, lineage segmentation was not at issue and the dispute was primarily a domestic one between the two old men. The struggle for domestic authority had been waged far enough, and openly enough, for it not to be necessary to start oracular consultation over again.

None the less, Ondua, in his position, was forced by the situation to use this quarrel to sustain his higher lineage status. Perhaps it would be more accurate to say that other members of the lineage interpreted it in these terms. Both men had the right, and the duty, to invoke the ghosts against Jobi. He was regarded as a good-for-nothing, wearing smart clothes, seducing girls and getting drunk in the company of his seniors. He was always at loggerheads with his father and other senior men, especially his father's brother Ondua, who had both kin and lineage authority over him. Being a youth it would normally be expected that his own father would discipline him by any means open to him. And this is what Oguda did. For many years he had remonstrated with him and tried to control him, as I heard many times; finally he admitted, after the patient had become sick, that he had invoked the ghosts against him. Aribo, his elder son, told me at the time that Oguda's heart was 'sad' at having quarrelled with Ondua, that he thought that Lari'ba was becoming too full of quarrelling and that he should try to bring Jobi's son's case to an end in order to decrease the amount of hostility within the segment. Therefore he chose that moment to consult the oracles about the sickness. There was, however, more to it than that. When Ondua consulted the oracles and denied Oguda's part in it, he was doing so partly to show Oguda that he, Ondua, had over-all authority within the segment and partly to show other members, both living and dead, that he had over-all authority within the entire lineage as well. Yekule told me

> Now Ondua's heart is sad, since he has quarrelled with his brother Oguda. It is not good for a brother to quarrel with his brother who is the elder. A man should speak slowly and follow an elder, even when he is his own brother. It is like the wife of an elder: she is 'big', but she must follow his words. So now Ondua has shown Oguda that he is 'big' and that Oguda has brought trouble to Lari'ba.

The last sentence refers to Oguda's responsibility for Jobi's behaviour.

Later Oguda pointed out that he did not deny Ondua's verdict because they were brothers and Ondua was the elder: to deny Ondua's 'words' would have been shameful; it would also have laid him (Oguda) open to a charge of destroying the unity of the whole lineage, of the segment Lari'ba and also the smaller segment consisting of the descendants of Moro (this last would have weakened the front against Draai). So he accepted this verdict, and in fact a compromise was reached, as I have described. However, Oguda went on to complain about Ondua's overbearing attitude: Ondua had been an elder for so long that he had begun to assume that his personal authority and his authority as elder were synonymous, so that he took slights to himself in his personal role as being slights to himself as elder. This meant that instead of leaving Jobi's control to Oguda, as he should have done, he took it upon himself to exercise elder's authority over him. 'Ondua now sees us all as children, because he is so old.'

Case 3

Obitre of Nyaai sacrificed a goat at his senior ghost shrine on behalf of his son. The rubbing-stick oracle was consulted by Olimani, who went to an operator in Mjrjdrj, just to the south of Maraca tribal area and about a mile from Araka.

About six years before four members of Olimani's segment, Otoro, Obitre, Okwaya and Njima, moved their compounds away from the immediate neighbourhood of Olimani's homestead to empty land across the small stream that formerly marked the boundary of Araka. Olimani's compound now stands alone, and from it the three other compounds (of Otoro and Obitre together, of Okwaya and of Njima) can be seen on the opposite slope, a permanent reminder of their partial secession. Okwaya is considered still to be loyal to Olimani, as his half-brother, but Otoro is thought by Olimani to be the ringleader in a movement to secede from his authority and to set up an independent segment, under the authority of Otoro. Okwaya told me that

Olimani sits here in his compound and remembers the words of long ago, when all of us lived in his compound, which was large like that of Oburu (the rainmaker of Maraca, who has a homestead of some ten huts). His heart is bad towards us who have moved across the water. But there there is no land, only stones, so we came here to Miridri and built our huts here, I and my brothers Otoro and Obitre and our sister's son Njima. First we hoed our fields and then slowly we built our huts. . . . Olimani remembers the days of long ago, when he moved from his father's compound so that he could hoe fields for his wife, the mother of Omba. Now he sees Omba go south (as a labour migrant) and Omba forgets the words of his father. He thinks: 'Are not Otoro and Obitre and Njima also my children? Perhaps they also forget my words.'

Clearly, the factors of individual personality and of structural role are complex and intimately related, and it is difficult to decide all the grounds for Olimani's ambition; more accurately, it is difficult to decide the grounds for his kin regarding him as being a man of great ambition. It is generally accepted by Lugbara that an elder's ritual assistant himself wishes to become an elder; it is said that an elder 'shows' his assistant the 'words of the ancestors', so that when the elder dies his assistant will know how to act as an elder. However, an elder is ideally succeeded by his son, since the mystical power, the *tali*, is inherited in a single agnatic line of descent. It was known that Ondua would be succeeded ritually by his son Yekule. But part of Lugbara theory is that a lineage segments in three generations, the precipitating event being the death of an elder. The ritual assistant may therefore become a new elder. By generation a junior segment is equal, in theory at any rate, to the senior segment. The senior line is that in which the mystical power of eldership is said to run—until segmentation— but neither line is senior to the other by generation. As in any

segmentary lineage system, the balance between line of descent
and generation is ever-present, emphasis on the one tending to
exaggerate segmentary opposition, on the other tending to stress
the unity of the total unit. The ritual assistant finds himself in a
dilemma between these two tendencies, and an analysis of his
behaviour shows that it may be regarded as segmentary or unifying
at different stages in the cycle of development of the minimal
lineage. Lugbara see these differences in emphasis in his behaviour
mainly in terms of personal ambition, in much the same way as
they see the structurally significant behaviour of an elder in terms
of his ambitions to build up his authority and then to sustain it
against his rivals. In brief, the assistant's behaviour is such as to
support the authority of the lineage elder in the earlier phase of
the lineage development cycle, but such as to lead to segmentation
during the later stages. In terms of ambition, he grows more
ambitious during the later stages (and as he grows older). This
had been the pattern followed by Olimani since Ondua succeeded
to the complete eldership of Araka in 1927, at the death of Abiria.
Okwaya told me that 'long ago', Olimani had assisted Ondua and
that they had been 'true brothers'. But that 'slowly slowly' Oguda
had largely ousted Olimani as Ondua's adviser, although he had
always acted as his formal ritual assistant. Okwaya said that the
breach between them was a result of land shortage and disputes,
since the land of Nyaai, Olimani's segment, was poorer than that
of Lari'ba and was also more crowded; Ondua had refused to allow
the men of Nyaai to open new fields in Lari'ba, a refusal which
had shown the men of Nyaai that Ondua was biased in favour of
his own segment, since properly speaking all the men of Araka
had equal rights in its land. These disputes had become serious just
before the war, in 1939.

The dispute with Ondua had become open and accepted by
Araka about five years before my visit, when Ondua and Olimani
had begun to carry on the dispute in ritual terms. About 1945
Ondua had maintained that he had invoked the ghosts against
Ngoro, Olimani's brother; Olimani had argued that if he had done
so he was abusing his position of authority, since it was he,
Olimani, who should invoke against his own brother, and not
Ondua, although he was the accepted elder of the whole lineage.
Since then, Okwaya told me, there had been many occasions on
which this had occurred. Olimani's insistence on being ritually

responsible for his own segment was, of course, the final stage in the dispute between the two senior men; this was the most effective way in which Olimani could question Ondua's authority, since if he could show that the ghosts accepted his own invocation rather than that of Ondua, then he was near to being accepted as an independent elder. The ghosts would both accept his authority and deny that of Ondua.

Elders and would-be elders sooner or later find themselves in a dilemma. In order to show that they have ghostly support for their authority, they must show that they invoke successfully. Yet their repeated invocation is liable to lose them the support of their close kin. Ondua had this problem to face, and so had Olimani. After 1945 or so Olimani invoked against his dependants on many occasions, and Ondua also invoked against several members of Nyaai, in order to show that his authority was still superior to that of Olimani. This had led Olimani to increase his invoking, and by the time of my stay in Araka he had become extremely unpopular among his own dependants. The apparent defection of three households by moving across the stream on Nyaai's boundary was to some extent a protest against Olimani's over-frequent invocation, and it had also placed Olimani in the position of having still further to exert his authority over the members of these households. Their leader was regarded as being Otoro. It is significant that he was so regarded, since as far as I could understand this defection of the three families was not such a highly organized affair as Olimani and others liked to regard it. But it had strongly marked structural repercussions. Without the continued dependence of these three households Olimani's claim for Nyaai to become an independent minimal lineage could not be accepted by either the ancestors, the members of Araka or the members of other related lineages. As I have mentioned earlier, an elder is finally accepted as such when he is invited to attend sacrifices as representative of his lineage; and it would be unusual for this to happen unless he had a segment at least large enough to maintain its rights to its stretch of land by force of arms. Olimani was therefore dependent upon these families' support, yet had to demonstrate that they were under his authority and not under that of Ondua; the only way he could do this was by the oracles' decreeing that the ghosts had 'heard' his invocation rather than that of Ondua.

The immediate action taken by Olimani was to consult the oracles on behalf of anyone sick within his segment. He hastened to do this, without first informing Ondua, because this showed his responsibility for his dependents, and if his doing so was generally accepted by the members of the lineage then his senior and largely independent status would be admitted. As I have tried to show, the verdicts of oracles depend upon the suggestions put to them by consultants. If, as occasionally happens, a consultant does obviously 'deceive' the oracle in this way then the verdict may be ignored; an example was given in Case 2, where, although Ondua never accused Oguda of manipulating the oracular diagnosis, he certainly did not accept Oguda's consultation.

In this case the oracle diagnosed ghost invocation by Olimani. The verdict was confirmed by the chicken oracle, consulted by Olimani, Okwaya and Obitre. Obitre supplied a goat, which was led round his compound and consecrated. Olimani maintained that the reason for his invocation was that Obitre had refused to accept his authority in that he had not helped him with meat and beer at several rites which he had performed during the previous year; Olimani stated that as Nyaai was a single segment under his authority he had the right to demand economic and other assistance from all its members when he performed rites for their joint well-being. Obitre had refused on the ground that he was distant from Olimani, since within Nyaai their descent lines had been distinct for several generations. Thus he was using his genealogical relationship *vis-à-vis* Olimani to assert his independence in the same way as Olimani was doing *vis-à-vis* Ondua.

Okwaya told me that Olimani's invocation was a consequence of the move across the river, and added that a year or two before Olimani had invoked against a member of his (Okwaya's) family, even though they were brothers by the same father, and had also invoked against Njima.

Obitre and Otoro claimed that Olimani was using witchcraft against them. Young men who resent invocation by their seniors commonly accuse them of witchcraft, but usually, as in this case, their accusations are not accepted. I discuss this point later at greater length.

The sacrifice was attended only by the members of Nyaai; Ondua did not attend. Although this gave some support to Olimani's claims to senior status, he could hardly do otherwise unless he challenged the entire oracular proceedings: to have attended without doing so would have been to give in completely to Olimani. Later Olimani complained at this, saying sourly that Ondua treated them all like children.

Case 4

Otoro cut a goat at his senior ghost shrine on behalf of his daughter, an adolescent girl who was suffering from severe menstrual bleeding, a complaint that would usually be considered the result of invocation or curses by maternal kin. But her mother's brother had visited her compound and had shown great affection for the girl, so that Otoro said that it could not come from that lineage. Okwaya told me that even so it might usually be expected that the mother's brother would be called to deny any evil intent in public before other possible agents would be considered; but that in this case

> Otoro does not have to remember the words of the territory where he gave his cattle (in bridewealth). Here in Araka there are many words, and Olimani, our brother, has spoken many words in his heart against Otoro.

That is to say, Otoro considered the most likely agent to be the person with whom he was at that time in the most strained relationship, and that was Olimani, despite Lugbara theories as to the mystical aetiology of sickness.

The oracles were consulted by Olimani, who went immediately to an operator in Nyoro, a mile or two north of Araka. As in Case 3, he did this very quickly, part of the reason certainly being that by so doing he hoped to show his ritual independence of Ondua. This case occurred about a month after Case 3, and Ondua had criticized this behaviour by Olimani; saying that even if he, Ondua, did not consult the oracles himself, it was improper for Olimani to behave so independently. Olimani's doing so again at the first opportunity was a clear indication of his aims, and of the depth of his dispute with Ondua. At the consultation Olimani made only the most perfunctory suggestions for the oracle operator to consider. He stated at the beginning of the consultation that he himself had 'thought thoughts' in his heart because Otoro had led the members of his segment across the river (the move that was behind Case 3), and that 'perhaps' Otoro's brother-in-law had caused this but that he himself doubted it, because the hearts of the men of Mjrjdrj, the lineage of Otoro's wife, were good, and because all the bridewealth had been transferred. He added that he had supplied some of the bridewealth, even though Otoro had gone to southern Uganda as a labour migrant, had earned much money, and had refused to share it with his own kin on his return. Thus Otoro's move across the stream was a sign of his ingratitude. The oracular consultation was, in fact, little more than a listing of Otoro's gracelessness. The verdict given was that the sickness was the consequence of Olimani's invocation, the ghost concerned being Licu, who had sent Avuye as his 'policeman'. That is, the two senior ghosts of Otoro's descent line had shown their displeasure at his behaviour and their trust in Olimani's exercising authority over him, even though Olimani's line of descent was from Avuye's half-brother Toba. For good measure, Olimani added, after the verdict, that Otoro was impious and selfish in that he had not sacrificed to the ghosts for a long time, so that the ghosts wished to 'show' him his guilt in this respect also. Okwaya told me later that this latter outburst referred to the fact that Otoro is the senior of the direct descendants of Licu's second wife, and so head of the matri-segment of Nyaai that is segmentarily opposed to that of Olimani. Otoro is therefore considered likely to become an elder one day—and his move across the stream and so away from Olimani's immediate everyday authority is a factor in this assumption. Thus Olimani's anxiety and hostility was justified, or at least understandable.

Ondua then entered the scene. He chose a day or two after Olimani's consultation of the rubbing-stick oracle, when most of the senior men of Araka and many neighbouring groups were sitting under a meeting-tree. There he mentioned that he had recently invoked the ghosts against Otoro, because Otoro had been presumptuous at a sacrifice some months before by claiming a separate share of sacrificial meat for his segment (known as Nyaria, the clan-name of its ancestress). It was known generally that when this had happened Ondua had refused to treat Otoro as the head of a distinct segment, saying that Nyaria was merely a part of Nyaai. But clearly Ondua's mention of it again at this time was a counter-attack on Olimani. If Ondua's invocation were shown to have been the cause of Otoro's daughter's sickness then Olimani would have been shown to have been presumptuous and unworthy of ancestral trust. Oguda told me that Ondua was an elder who was 'slow', but that at last he had decided that Olimani was destroying Araka; this was, presumably, his way of expressing this decision. Ondua did not, however, consult oracles himself; to have done so would have been possible, but it would have brought the dispute into the open. As it was, Olimani was given the chance to withdraw and to admit that Ondua had at least the right—and in theory the duty also—to invoke against Otoro in this way.

Olimani's response was to say, a few days later, at a mortuary rite held in Ambidro, Araka's co-ordinate minimal lineage, that there was witchcraft in Araka, and that Ondua was a witch. The same evening he pointedly refused to drink at the same beer-drink as Ondua. The following day he told me outright that Ondua was 'perhaps' a witch—he was 'strong' and had acquired much power as an elder, and witches were powerful men. In Lugbara such actions and remarks are the strongest that can be made: a witch is not accused openly unless he is an unimportant man, as far as his lineage position is concerned. But a man is accused of witchcraft behind his back, directly or by implication. Olimani said the same to other people, as well as to myself.

Both invokers of the ghosts and witches are motivated by the sentiment of *ole*. This is both the indignation felt by a responsible man as behaviour that 'destroys' the orderly relations of authority within the lineage, and that felt by a witch at behaviour that insults or injures him individually, as an individual and not as a holder of authority.[1] It is right for man to invoke against a person who destroys lineage authority; it is not right—although perhaps understandable—for a man to bewitch another because of insults or injuries to him personally. The response to personal injury should be, in Lugbara theory, to ask the offender's elder or guardian to exercise his authority over him, either directly in words or indirectly by ghost invocation. Often, in fact, it is by fighting, which may be expected if the parties are both young. It is clear that the position of a young or junior man is simple enough in this respect: if he uses witchcraft, he shows himself to be presumptuous and arrogant, and also bad-tempered and evil in intention. The more junior, the less reason to act as a witch. But for a senior man, and especially for an elder, the position is often not so clear. His lineage status is not easy to distinguish from his personal

---

[1] I discuss this at greater length in Chapter V.

status, and an insult to the latter is difficult to distinguish from an insult to him as an elder. In this case Ondua claimed that he had invoked the ghosts against Otoro, as his duty as elder. He admitted to the sentiment of *ole*, as he had every right to do. Olimani's accusation was that his indignation was that of a selfish man who mistook his personal pride and position for those of eldership, and who abused his mystical powers to pay off personal scores. His sentiment of indignation was thus a perverted one. Olimani said that that the oracle had indicated that the cause of the sickness was invocation by himself and that therefore Ondua, by admitting to the sentiment of *ole*, was in fact showing himself to be a witch. He said:

That 'brother' there in Lari'ba is truly a 'strong' man. We all fear his words and also those people of Nyoro and Bura and Ambidro also fear him. He is old. Perhaps now he forgets the words of his father Dria, who loved us all his 'children' here in Araka. A 'strong' man forgets the words of his father. . . . Perhaps now Ondua's heart is bad towards us of Nyaai here, because we are many. He has eaten our cattle and our land, the cattle of my father Cakida, and we fear him. Do you not fear a man who is 'strong' and who eats your cattle like a chief eats a man's shillings? . . . Perhaps Ondua eats our things at night, perhaps we do not know his words, his thoughts are hidden, his words are not true . . . You are a stranger here, perhaps soon you will understand the words of *ole*. Witches are 'strong' men, perhaps the father of Yekule (Ondua) is also a witch, who can know these things?

The reference to neighbouring sections implies that they fear Ondua as a witch, since they would have no reason to fear him as an elder, because he could not invoke his ghosts against them; the reference to a man forgetting the example of his father implies that Ondua's behaviour is contradictory to the norms of kinship, as is a witch's; the reference to Ondua's acting at night also implies witchcraft; and the reference to his words and thoughts being hidden and unknown to his agnatic kin has a similar implication. Except for one reference there is no direct accusation of witchcraft, since the terms for to invoke and to bewitch are the same (*ro, ole ro*). The tenor of Olimani's remarks was that Ondua was perverting his authority and power for his own ends.

There are two important implications in this accusation. The first is that by bewitching Ondua was abusing the trust placed in him by the ancestors as guardian of his lineage. The second is that by bewitching his kin Ondua had denied the obligations of kinship and by so doing had shown that the kin relations of which these obligations were a part needed no longer to be observed. In Lugbara theory a typical witch is a man who bewitches unrelated neighbours. This is both a way of saying that a witch denies kinship and that he destroys kinship. So that by bewitching a man of Nyaai Ondua had shown that Lari'ba and Nyaai should no longer be within a single minimal lineage. If he had invoked justifiably he would have been behaving as the elder of all Araka should; by using his powers to bewitch he had shown that he no longer recognized the members of Nyaai as agnatic kin so close that he should protect their interests at all costs. He had shown that he was greedy for power which was more important to him than the well-being of all members of his lineage.

There was nothing that could be done about the accusation, which soon reached Ondua's ears. Its primary purpose was, however, to reach the ears of the men of Araka. Since usually the accusation can only be made obliquely, its effect is made only if the words are interpreted by its hearers as referring to witchcraft; they may be accepted only as referring to the proper activities of an elder, the invocation of the ghosts. There was no notion of making any sort of reparation to Ondua, nor of Ondua publicly affirming that he was not a witch. Lugbara have no institutionalized ways of withdrawing an accusation of witchcraft. In this case, either the men of Araka would agree with Olimani's accusations and so Ondua would be discredited; or they would ignore them and nothing further would be said openly on this particular occasion.

In fact the people of Nyaai, led by Otoro himself, accepted the finding of the oracle consulted by Olimani; Obitre told me that his brother Otoro had not 'heard' the words of Ondua in the matter. Otoro provided a goat, and led it round his compound to consecrate it. His daughter seemed to recover in a few days, which was a sign that the oracle had been correct. Otoro thus accepted Olimani's ritual authority rather than that of Ondua. This did not mean that he thereby accepted that Ondua was a witch, in so many words, but it did mean that he accepted the fact that Ondua's sentiment of indignation at his actions was unjustified; if it had not been then his daughter would not have recovered. Since Ondua had made his original remark only in passing, at an informal meeting of men outside Araka territory, the whole question could be left open. Ondua did not argue the matter, partly because he was old and near death, and partly because to have done so would have brought shame to Araka in the eyes of other lineages. Later he told me that these 'words' were 'finished', and he was soon to die and that then Araka would segment. He was willing to fight against the efforts of Draai to divide Lari'ba but was prepared to accept that Nyaai should soon become a new lineage. But in fact when dying a few months later he gave as his wish that there should be no segmentation (Case 33).

Case 5

Draai cut a goat at his senior ghost shrine for his own son, Kalfan, an idle youth. Draai consulted an oracle operator in Kimiru, a neighbouring section, who was known as a close crony of his. The oracles said that he had invoked against Kalfan, and that the ghost concerned was his father Abiria. Kalfan had been rude to his father and also to Benyu when they were at a beer drink. Kalfan had tried to enter to drink, but Draai had ordered him to leave, saying that it was not fitting for a young man who did no useful work and spent his time seducing girls to sit with his father and spend money on beer. There is no taboo in Lugbara against a son sitting with his father on such an occasion, although it would be usual for each to share his calabash of beer with his coevals rather than with one another. There was a sharp quarrel, in which Kalfan threatened to leave to live with his mother's brother, whereupon Draai stated that if he did so, going to his mother's brother who had already 'eaten' the wealth of Draai's family in exacting heavy bridewealth, then he need never return to inherit livestock. Draai then threatened to invoke the ghosts and Kalfan left. Draai sat muttering for several hours, growing more and more drunk and quarrelsome. He said that although Ondua tried to treat him as a child he would maintain order in his own family and that no child of his would insult his 'brother' Benyu. Draai was ambitious to be regarded as an elder in his own right, as I have mentioned, and this outburst was directed mainly against Ondua, to show that he, Draai, was also a responsible man and could act as protector not only to his own small family but also to Benyu, who was more closely related to Ondua than he was to Draai. Having publicly threatened to invoke the ghosts he had to admit to invocation when later Kalfan complained of sickness.

Draai said continually that he had invoked and it was pointless to consult the oracles. He was here trying to show his ritual power was independent of that of Ondua. Ondua, however, said that the oracles should be consulted and that he would ask Oguda, as his close assistant, to do so; whereupon Draai did so himself.

Draai immediately 'showed' a goat by leading it round the compound, and only a day or so later sacrificed it himself. He did not summon Ondua to officiate at the rite, as he should have done. This was a clear attempt to show his independence from Ondua, who was extremely angry, sending Oguda to Draai to tell him that only he, as elder, could perform the rite. He added—and certainly he told other people—that it was he who had invoked against Kalfan, when he had heard of his behaviour at the beer drink, and that only he could therefore make the sacrifice, and if he did not it would fail and Kalfan would become sick again. This was believed by all, since a sacrifice to the ghosts cannot be efficacious unless all the elders of the minimal lineage at least are present, and all agree in their hearts that the matter is closed. Nevertheless Draai persisted and himself made the offering. The only people who attended were Benyu and Kalfan's mother's brother, a sure sign that public opinion was with Ondua on this matter and that Draai's claim to independence was not supported by the lineage members in general.

After the rite Kalfan told his coevals and friends that Draai was a witch, and that Ondua was another. Little notice was taken of this except that Oguda and other senior men pointed to it as an example of the evil ways young labour migrants learn in southern Uganda.

It might have been expected that Ondua would do more than merely make an angry protest. He did not do so for two reasons: one was that he was 'slow' and preferred to wait for a suitable occasion to show his authority over Draai, and the other was that almost immediately the wife of Yekule became seriously sick and his attention was thereby diverted. She was the wife of his ritual successor and the mother of the future lineage elder and so of greater immediate importance than Draai.

Case 6

Yekule sacrificed a goat at his *andesia* shrine on behalf of his wife. She had been sick and weak for about a year, ever since the birth of her third child. She was now suddenly more seriously sick and Yekule hastened to act for her recovery.

Usually a man does not set up ghost shrines until his father is dead; then the senior of a set of full brothers places a senior ghost shrine while the senior half-brother places a junior shrine (*andesia*). But the first son of an elder or head of a large segment may set up *andesia* shrines while his father is alive.

Yekule's position was a delicate one. He was his father's successor as lineage elder, but it was very clear that when his father died there would probably be segmentation. It was likely that Olimani would become independent head of Nyaai, and also possible that Draai would try to become independent himself. When Yekule succeeded it was expected that Oguda would act as secular head, although only Yekule would be able to act as ritual head; he would take over the full role on Oguda's death. His present position was that of confidant of his father. There is no very obvious or institutionalized tension or hostility between father and eldest son in Lugbara, but it is none the less usually present.[1] But there are no customary avoidances between them. The high rate of mobility of young men, involving movement to their mothers' brothers' and wives' homes, and today the migration to seek work in southern Uganda are to a large extent a concomitant of opposition to paternal control. It is significant in this context that most labour migrants who send money home send it to their mothers' brothers for safe keeping, and the father who drinks away his son's labour earnings is a stock character.

The position of the eldest son of an elder is rather different, in that he is much less likely to move away from home, either to settle elsewhere or to go on labour migration, and there is therefore likely to be a greater ambivalence in the father-son relationship in these cases.

After the birth of his second son, Yekule's wife had been sick, apparently with the same sickness as she had at this time. Ondua had then said that he had invoked the ghosts against her, on account of Yekule's failure to hand over money he had earned from growing tobacco. Ondua had offered the sacrifice. On this occasion, however, although the sickness was said to be the same, Yekule himself consulted the oracles—admittedly his father was

---

[1] Among other occasions, it is expressed in the fear a son has of the ghost of his recently dead father. See page 206.

then sick himself and so this is not very significant in itself—and made the offering himself at his *andesia* shrine. Offering made at this shrine is always as a consequence of ghostly vengeance, and cannot be that of ghost invocation. So that by this it was clear that Ondua had had no direct hand in the affair. The oracular consultation was of the rubbing-stick oracle only, with no confirmatory oracle. Had Ondua been responsible then Yekule would be 'with shame', since it would have implied, and have been understood to mean, that Ondua did not consider him a fitting man to be his successor. On the previous occasion Ondua had not felt that his days as an elder were numbered, and so had been able to assert his paternal authority without any such implication. It was said that these days Ondua 'loved' his son very much, as an aid to him against the wiles and ambitions of Olimani and Draai; and it might be assumed that this might have been even more important to Ondua since his recent open quarrels with Oguda, normally his closest adviser, and with Draai. On a later occasion I was told that an elder who feels he will soon die begins to love his successor,

like a man who is fighting against many enemies; he closes his heart with those brothers and sons who are near him and they stand there together, and they close their hearts to kill many of those enemies.

This is part of the expected pattern of behaviour of an elder who feels his authority becoming weaker: he invokes more and more, to show that he still has ancestral support, but he does not as a rule invoke against his nearest kin. Or, if he does, it is a sign of despair.

Yekule made the sacrifice, at which only a few men attended: Ondua, Oguda, and also his wife's brother, since it was her sickness. *Andesia* is said to mean 'I refuse it', because the meat is not distributed to a wide circle of kin; the oblation is 'small', in this sense, a domestic affair between the immediate kin and their immediate ancestral ghosts.

Case 7

Olimani cut a goat at his senior ghost shrine for the sickness of his son Okavu. Olimani consulted a rubbing-stick oracle operator in Nyoro, a neighbouring family cluster. He had threatened Okavu with invocation some months before, with the words 'We shall see', after an open argument between them in Olimani's compound. Okavu had returned from labour migration but had refused to share his earnings with his brother Omba, saying that he wanted it for bridewealth for his own marriage. Olimani maintained that he should decide how it should be used, and wanted it to pay his brother Ngoro's tax. This was a straightforward case of ghost invocation by a man's own father, according to Okwaya, who said

That Okavu is bad. He stays away for many months. Then one day he returns home. His heart has become bad there, perhaps he has learnt the words of *elojua*.[1] Now he does not respect his father or his 'father' Ngoro. He comes to his father's compound and there refuses his words. He refuses those words 'in the mouth of the ghost shrine'. Truly then Olimani thinks 'My son is now lost to me', and he says 'The words are finished; we shall see.'

Having made this threat, when Okavu did fall sick, Olimani could feel sure that the ghosts had listened to his thoughts. The oracle operator was told this story, and the consultation was a short and perfunctory one.

I was told a few days later that Ondua had been given 'shame', by this case, since he was the elder and the elder has the right to allocate the wealth of the lineage. It is the elder who usually plans the course of labour migration for the lineage's younger men, so as to arrange for money to be available for taxes and to buy cattle for bridewealth. For Olimani to have ignored his will and opinions in this respect was a blow to his authority as elder. But he soon admitted, so as to bring the situation to an end, that 'perhaps' it was good for Olimani to invoke against his own son for having insulted him near his own ghost shrine, in his own compound. If this were the substance of the offence then Ondua conceded that Olimani was acting within his rights as a head of a large family segment: he had thus changed his views on this matter since Otoro's case (Case 4).

Case 8

Benyu cut a bull at his senior ghost shrine for his wife, who was seriously sick. The oracles were consulted by Ondua and revealed that the sickness was the consequence of invocation by Ondua,

---

[1] See below, page 246. *Elojua* is a new type of sorcery that young men obtain from Congo labour migrants while in southern Uganda. The implication is that a sorcerer no longer recognizes ties of kinship.

Oguda and Olimani jointly because Benyu had not sacrificed for a long time and had been recalcitrant in attending sacrifices at Ondua's homestead. The sickness was sent by Oraa, using Angura as his 'policeman'. A bull was an important beast to be sacrificed for a woman's sickness, and so the gravity of the offence, a serious breach of ideal kinship piety, was stressed. And although it was for a woman, the rite was attended by representatives of a wide lineage span, so marking the occasion as one on which it was necessary to secure agreement and close kinship relations within the lineage.

Benyu is in some ways a key person in the struggle between Ondua and Draai. I have mentioned above, in Case 5, that Draai had tried to impress Benyu with his authority. The fact that about 1947 Benyu moved his compound well away from Ondua's, where he had formerly lived, to near Draai's and especially because he moved his hut but not his fields, added weight to Ondua's suspicions of Draai's attempts to gain authority. This case took place about six weeks after Case 5, and in it Ondua was clearly trying to show Draai that he was a junior, and that both he and Benyu were under the authority of himself. The oracles indicated Olimani as co-invoker with Ondua and Oguda, and this stressed that all responsible senior men (carefully omitting Draai) were worried about Benyu's behaviour.

The sacrifice was attended by all the men of Araka, and the elders of its co-ordinate lineages (as in Case 1). The senior men who ate together included Ondua, Oguda (as a close 'father' of Benyu), Olimani and the elders of the co-ordinate lineages; Draai and Otoro were delegated to the position of 'men behind'. Ondua and Olimani both made ritual addresses, but when Draai tried to follow them he was told to sit down and let the elders of the other lineages speak first. Neither did so, and before Draai could do anything further Ondua continued with the sacrifice. On this occasion, at any rate, the breach between Ondua and Olimani was closed and a united front presented to Draai.

Case 9

Olimani became suddenly and seriously sick, with signs of fever and sharp pains in his stomach. This was obviously a serious case, and action had to be taken quickly. Okwaya and Ondua consulted the oracles of Ayua of Kimiru, an operator whom I have mentioned before. After the consultation had started we were joined by Otoro.

Ondua, as head of all Araka, first gave Ayua a long account of the disputes between the two segments. He related all of them as far back as genealogical knowledge was known, stressing land disputes, occasions when the head of one segment had been able to use livestock of the other without it being a debt (*mari*)—thus implying they were of a single close segment, whereas recently there had been many disputes over the repayment of these livestock—and disputes that had arisen over the inheritance of widows between the segments. In recent years the two segments had become further apart and dissension had increased. Ondua blamed this largely on the ambitions and greed of younger men, who had worked as labour migrants and had then refused to use their earnings for the common good and had denied the authority of their seniors. He also stated that 'mothers' brothers' had tried to enter into these domestic disputes by taking the sides of their individual sisters' sons. In general, Araka had become torn with dissension which he feared might be a consequence of *nyoka*, the repeated troubles that beset a lineage that is dying or near to dissolution. He said that this sickness was the sign of more troubles. He then said that Olimani himself had brought trouble and dispute into the lineage. He had quarrelled with Otoro and Okwaya, his own 'brothers', because they had moved away from his compound, which he emphasized was a thing to be expected as people married and wanted more land; to take it as a personal affront was unwise. He said that Olimani had tried to repudiate Ondua's own authority —'If brothers fight, how can they share one dish of relish?'—and had 'forgotten' the words of their ancestors Dria, Cakida and their forebears.

Otoro then spoke about the move away from Olimani's compound, and related the cases that resulted from it. He told how Olimani had often been thought to be using witchcraft for his own ends, and how he was known as quarrelsome and unjust.

Okwaya then spoke saying that he also had been grieved at Olimani's behaviour in quarrelling with him, his own brother, because he had moved away.

Ayua then asked questions. He asked when had Olimani last offered a large sacrifice to the ghosts, when had he last performed an offering of the kind called 'cleansing the territory', at which a large number of kin are called to partake of meat, and also whether Olimani had ever been sent sickness by his own dead father, Cakida. He asked also whether 'those people of Ole'ba', the clan to the north-west of Maraca whence Olimani's mother had come, had ever sent trouble to Olimani, and whether Cakida had ever owed bridewealth to Ole'ba for his wife. He then asked whether Ondua had known that Olimani had said that he was a witch, and whether his heart had been angry at this. These questions touched all the obvious and important matters of dispute in which Olimani had been involved.

Ayua then consulted his rubbing-stick, having placed straws on the ground in front of him to represent certain ghosts—Cakida, Toba, Moro and Ombasa, the lineage founder—and certain living men—Ondua, Otoro, and Olimani's mother's brother. There was also a straw for witchcraft. The rubbing-stick pointed out Toba, and then gave unsatisfactory replies, as far as Ayua was concerned. Finally he told us that it pointed out both Ondua and Otoro. Okwaya explained to me that it was understood by all present that the oracle said that Ondua and Otoro had caused Toba to send this sickness. Ondua then said that a year or so before he and Otoro had sat together and discussed Olimani's actions in not sacrificing sufficiently often. They had quarrelled about the matter, Otoro saying that Ondua was greedy for meat, and Ondua saying that he feared only for the good temper and support of the ghosts if they were not offered food by the senior men of the lineage. Ayua agreed that Toba must have heard these words and sent sickness to Olimani, the delay of a year or two being in order to see whether or not Olimani did in fact offer sacrifice. Toba had then finally sent this sickness to 'show' Olimani, by the process of ghostly vengeance. The oracles, said Ayua, decreed that Olimani should offer a bull, a large offering, to the ghosts at his senior ghost shrine.

Okwaya told me that for Ondua to have invoked the ghosts against Olimani would have been shameful, but that it was not shameful for the ghosts to send sickness by ghostly vengeance.[1] Oguda, however, told me that this ghostly vengeance showed that the ghosts did not approve of Olimani's arrogance in trying

---

[1] Two months later this oracle indicated that a new sickness of Olimani was the consequence of ghost invocation by Ondua (Case 13).

to deny the authority of Ondua, who was their representative to the living in Araka. Oguda said

That day Ondua showed that he is truly a big man. When Ombasa (the lineage founder) begot those sons Oraa and Licu (the founders of Lari'ba and Nyaai) it was the mother of Oraa who bore her child first; she was the first married. So now Ondua is elder of all the children of Oraa and Licu and he consults the oracles for sickness. Now the ghosts have showed that they hear his words alone.

Olimani's reaction was to show great anger that he had not been allowed to recover to consult the oracles himself, because he was not a child for Ondua to consult them on his behalf. He said much the same as in Case 4 about Ondua being 'perhaps' a witch, to 'throw him low'. But he accepted the verdict in that he obtained a bull and Okwaya led it round Olimani's compound to consecrate it. Olimani then lay sick for several weeks, and the bull was not sacrificed, but finally his sickness grew worse again for a few days, then cleared up completely, and he made the sacrifice. I think that there was considerable pressure brought upon him to do this by the oracle operator concerned, Ayua. Okwaya told me that Ayua had visited Olimani and that they had drunk much beer together, and added that 'it is good for a stranger to speak words'. Ayua, not being personally involved in the internal Araka disputes, could use his influence, which was considerable, to help solve them. Certainly after the visit Olimani became more amenable.

The rite was attended by the same commensal partners that had come to Benyu's sacrifice (Case 8). The ritual address was made by Ondua only, who spoke shortly. This was because the case was mainly the concern of the ghosts, who 'know these words already; have they not discussed the sickness among themselves?' It was added that Olimani would have been ashamed if too much notice had been taken of this sickness. He was anointed by all the elders present; others did not anoint, as by abstaining Olimani's seniority was not called into doubt. Behind all this was the forcing hand of Ondua, who wished to heal the breach rather than stress his own sole authority.

Case 10

Olimani cut a sheep at his senior ghost shrine for his second wife. She had quarrelled with her senior co-wife and so Olimani invoked the ghosts against her. He was 'heard' by his father Cakida. Olimani is old and cannot do heavy field work, and this work for his wives had devolved upon his sons and other close kin. But since four of them had moved away across the stream, there was little labour easily available for Olimani's fields. His second son, Okavu, had been away as a labour migrant and had only just returned, and Omba, the eldest son, by the first wife, helped his own mother and then refused to work on the second wife's fields. The latter's fields had therefore been left almost unhoed at the beginning of the farming year, and now, near harvest, were a mass of weeds, so that she knew that she must open new fields the following year. She had quarrelled continually with her co-wife and with Omba (her husband's successor and so probably her future pro-husband). This had reached a head when she claimed that the co-wife would have to support her with food, since she had not enough for her own household. She had brought serious discord into the home, a stock reason for the head of the household to invoke against her.

The rite was attended only by members of Nyaai; Ondua did not come. This was because she was a woman, and in any case the offence was not one of great structural importance for the lineage. The choice of a sheep was made because she had once been a diviner, possessed by God, although she had rarely practised. Sheep and diviners are both closely associated with God in Lugbara thought, and Okwaya told me that it was hoped that God, who had once interested himself in her, might thus be made to notice her and to cause her to behave better in the future. Okwaya also said that the fact that the oracles had decreed a sheep showed that Olimani was not so responsible for her actions—the husband of a wife who brings discord into the lineage is always considered partly to blame for not disciplining her properly. This was a consideration as far as her paternal kin were concerned, who might have blamed Olimani for being harsh with her. She was in fact a quiet and rather pathetic woman, who had long suffered under the authority of her husband and his senior wife. At the oracular consultation the operator decreed that a sheep should be offered without any prompting from Olimani, but Olimani had emphasized in his account of the case that she had been a diviner; the operator had taken this into account.

Case 11

Benyu sacrificed a goat at his *andesia* shrine. It was on account of his own sickness, 'growing thin', which had affected him for several years. Benyu had become worried about his sickness after that of his wife (Case 8), a month previously. He had wished to consult the oracles on his own, but had agreed that it should be done by Ondua, who had impressed him with his authority so very recently. At the consultation Ondua made it plain that he had not invoked against Benyu. Aribo said

Perhaps this is because Ondua has heard the words that men have said (i.e., that he was a witch). Ondua is a good man, and does not wish to bring trouble to his 'children'. This sickness is from the ghosts. Perhaps they have watched the deeds of Benyu, perhaps he has not sacrificed to them (see Case 8). The ghosts and his father (Angura) have shown their child that they guard him.

The decision of the oracle was that Benyu had offended the dead by his impiety, and that they wished a goat to be offered for them at his *andesia* shrine.

The effect of this decree was that Ondua showed that he was not harsh to his dependants, that the dead themselves agreed with his actions in the former case, and that also Benyu was a fairly senior man in his own right who could be 'shown' by the dead. The fact that the offering was in Benyu's junior shrine implied that the case was not one of great importance, and so neither was Benyu. Later Draai talked about the case to me and said that Ondua had 'spoken' to the ghosts to say that Benyu was only a child (he is a man of about forty), and that Benyu was 'with shame'. Benyu is a man without great strength of character, not highly regarded in lineage counsels.

Case 12

Draai offered a goat at his senior ghost shrine on behalf of his second wife, a woman from Oluvu-Otravu.

Draai at first wanted to consult the rubbing-stick oracle of his crony in Kimiru, whom he had consulted in Case 5. But his wife's brother came to visit his sister as soon as he heard of her sickness, as her ritual guardian (a brother has final ritual authority over his sister, and not her husband). The brother insisted that the elder of

Araka, Ondua, should consult the oracles. Ondua, Draai, the brother, Okwaya and I went to Ayua of Kimiru. The case was first explained to him by Ondua, saying that the same woman had been seriously ill a year or two before. On that occasion, she herself thought she had become sick as a consequence of ghost invocation by her own father in Olu̟vu̟, and her father's oracles had supported her in this; but Draai had consulted an oracle in Ombavu which had decreed that Draai had invoked the ghosts against her because her children had been rude to him and because her brother had accused Draai of owing goats from the bridewealth. Ondua said that she was now ill again, and had been 'thrown' a week or two before. She was now unable to leave her sleeping mat except to crawl about. Her senior co-wife, a woman from Biliefe, some twenty miles away beyond Mount Eti to the south-east, was helping her: they were both 'strangers' in Maraca.

Ayua asked the woman's brother if there were 'words' about the matter in Olu̟vu̟. He replied that it was true that two of the goats given by Draai had died soon after they had been received, and should be replaced; he had asked for this on many occasions. There was clearly a strong hostility between the brothers-in-law. His father had recently died and his successor, his father's brother, was not concerned in the matter.

But perhaps these are the words of my father, since often he sat with me there and we spoke of this livestock, because now our children have no wealth and cannot get girls. Perhaps these are his words. When our sister came to visit she brought us food and we rejoiced because she is a good sister.

The point here is that they were concerned for her interests, and might well send sickness in order to bring Draai to his senses.

Draai said nothing during this time. Ayua asked for details of the bridewealth and of those that had died. He then asked Ondua whether he knew her late father and whether they had drunk beer together (that is, whether they had quarrelled or not). Ondua said that they had often done so, both in Araka and in Olu̟vu̟. Ayua asked whether the woman had siblings and whether she had children—these questions were addressed to her brother, not to her husband. He said that she had two brothers, and one boy and one girl child. Ayua was then told by Ondua the details of the sacrifice made on the occasion of her former sickness, in great detail, relating the members of the congregation and the ritual addresses that had been spoken.

Ondua then placed eight short sticks on the ground in front of Ayua. They were in two piles. Ayua knew that five of them in one pile represented suspects in Araka and that the three in the other pile represented people of Oluvu, but he did not know their actual identity. Later Ondua said that they were for

> Araka: Draai
> Ondua
> Olimani
> Draai's mother's brother
> witchcraft
> Oluvu: the woman's dead father
> her mother's brother
> her father's brother, the present elder.

Ayua then began to operate the stick, and the verdict was that the agent was the woman's dead father. Ayua did the same operation again to make sure, then said

These words are spoken by Otravu, by that dead man there. His heart is bad because he called for food last year and it was denied (that is, the former sacrifice was performed wrongly). He remembers his daughter brought him food, and now he wails to be fed. Now he wants a goat, to stand for that goat that was given him to eat (that is, was put into his herd but died). These are the words. The words are finished.

Beer was brought and we drank. We then consulted Ayua's boiling medicine oracle, to confirm this verdict. This was done in near silence. I need not describe the working of the oracle, except to say that all the suspects, except witchcraft, were presented to it, and that the answers given were quite haphazard. None of five attempts showed the same response as that of the rubbing-stick oracle.

Ayua then rubbed his stick again, without further discussion, except to ask Ondua whether he had any further suspects; Ondua said that he had not, but perhaps witchcraft was involved to destroy the efficacy of the oracle. Sticks were placed on the ground:

> the woman's father
> her mother's brother
> Draai

Ondua
Abiria and the ghosts of Draai's agnatic line (in case of
    ghostly vengeance)
Dria and the ghosts of Ondua's agnatic line
witchcraft.

He rubbed the stick, which pointed out the sticks representing
Dria and Ondua's descent line and witchcraft. He then consulted the boiling medicine oracle, placing four cups, for Dria,
witchcraft, Olu̞vu̞ in general and Abiria. The pots all boiled over,
instead of one not doing so, and so the confirmation was again
invalid.

Ayua then said that there might be 'words of witchcraft', and
that the oracles had not heard correctly. It was decided to consult
the same oracle again the following morning. We returned home,
Draai maintaining that it would be better to consult another
oracle, particularly the one he had at first suggested. But Ondua
insisted that they should return to Ayua, whose oracle was a
reliable one.

The next morning the same people assembled, this time including Aribo, who spoke at length during the preliminary enquiries.
Ondua repeated briefly what he had said the day before as did
the woman's brother. Draai said that he had beaten her because
she was quarrelsome: 'she has brought those evil hearts of those
people there in Otravu̞.' The brother then stated that she had been
badly treated and that he had tried to make her leave Draai on her
last visit home, to wait until the goats had been repaid; she had
refused because she had crops which she could not leave and had
also beer in the process of being brewed which she would later sell
at a beer-drink. Aribo then said that she had quarrelled with his
wife; her brother laughed at this, saying that Aribo's wife was
merely a whore whom he had had to send back to her home in
Kakwa. Aribo repeated that she was quarrelsome and had insulted the wives and daughters of Araka and had brought discord
to them. She had taunted them by saying that she, a 'stranger',
now lived near the ancestral tree, while they of Araka lived 'in the
grass' outside, and that her children would multiply and form a
new lineage, while the rest of Araka would decline. This referred
to the dispute between Draai and the other senior men of Araka.
Draai had placed his compound in the traditional heart of Araka,
near the ancestral *a'bi̞* tree. She had also taunted them by saying

that her own fields were more fertile than theirs because they were on the original hut sites of the early ancestors of Araka. Also she had taunted one of the wives with having a miscarriage, implying that the ancestors favoured Draai's segment as being closer to them.

Draai then spoke again, saying that this was true, and that his other wife was also a 'stranger' but had made no trouble. 'Let her take her children there to Otravụ, and we shall see'. There followed a string of threats and abuse against her brother, who replied in kind. Ayua intervenẹd to calm them down, and Ondua said that truly she was a troublesome woman and had been seen taking firewood from the ancestral tree of Araka, a thing completely forbidden. This was also a hit at Draai, who thereupon changed his tune and denied this: 'perhaps, but I did not see these things'. Ondua then said

Truly, that woman has brought trouble and warfare to us here. Truly long long ago our fathers Oraa and Moro and Biya, and my father Dria, and also her father-in-law Abiria, did not like these things. . . . If I say these words in my heart, they will hear them, they will listen to me, Abiria, my 'father', will listen to my words. He was a good man, once we fought together against those people of Yịvụ and those people there of Mt. Eti and against the Belgians. We drank together, we were chiefs (of the Yakani cult—see below, page 259). Now Abiria sees my daughter-in-law bring these words, he will be with shame, he will be with sorrow. Truly our territory is being destroyed.

This speech was to show that Ondua had invoked Abiria to send sickness, and that Abiria had accepted his invocation even though it was against Abiria's own son's wife. Ondua appealed to cross-segment age-grade ties, which make for lineage unity. He had also stressed that Abiria had not listened to Draai, who was trying to segment the lineage. His reference to the woman as his daughter-in-law emphasized this, since genealogically he and Draai are 'brothers'; but in terms of authority within the lineage Ondua regarded Draai as junior.

During this time Ayua had been twisting his rubbing-stick about so that it could 'hear the words'. He then started to rub it, having himself placed six sticks before him, for

> the woman's father
> her mother's brother
> Ondua

Olimani (he gave no explanation for this, although
         Olimani had not been mentioned)
Abiria
Draai's mother's brother.

His omission of Draai seemed a little ostentatious, and Draai got
up and went to urinate, not coming back for ten minutes or so.
Ayua then announced:

This is ghost invocation. Not from her husband there, nor from his
father, nor from those people of Mịdrịa, nor from those people of
Anguruku, but from those brothers, those people of Lari'ba. That man
of Anguruku has heard their words beneath the granaries, and his
father and his father's father have heard those words and have sent him.
The people of the borassus-palm have come to Maraca and have
destroyed those compounds there; women have fought there, because
livestock bring trouble there.'

Mịdrịa is the lineage of Draai's mother, Anguruku of Oraa's
second wife, the mother of Biya; it therefore stands for Draai's
segment. Lari'ba is the lineage of Oraa's first wife, mother of
Moro; used here it refers to Ondua and Oguda, who had invoked
the ghosts against her for bringing discord. The 'man of Anguruku'
is the ghost of Abiria, who had been invoked by Ondua, a man of
a different descent line. His 'father' and 'father's father' are the
ghosts Oraa and Biya. The borassus-palm refers to Olụvụ, which
has one sole borassus known for miles as a landmark. The reference to 'livestock' is a euphemism for vagina; it is often so used to
refer to trouble-making women.

Ayua then said a goat should be sacrificed, and consulted his
boiling medicine oracle to confirm the verdict. He put only two
cups this time, one for Olụvụ and one for Araka. The latter was
'shown' and this was regarded as being sufficient confirmation.
Since the patient was a woman, it was said that further confirmation from other oracles would be unnecessary.

This consultation showed very clearly the way in which the
operator felt his way into the tensions inherent in the total situation, starting with the obvious one of hostility between affines but
later allowing the main protagonists of the dispute within Lari'ba
to bring this fundamental dispute into the open. This consultation
could not be denied by Draai, precisely because he had been
present and had been able to speak freely.

Case 13

Olimani cut a bull at his senior ghost thrine for his own sickness. The oracles were consulted by Ondua and by Olimani's half-brother Okwaya; Olimani himself was very sick and could not attend. The oracles decreed that the ghosts (led by Licu and Toba) had been invoked by Ondua and Otoro, who had sat in Ondua's compound and discussed Cakida, Olimani's father. Cakida had been a generous man and had always given food to his dependants by making sacrifices, but Ondua and Otoro had said that Olimani had not offered sacrifices with good fat beasts for many years, and had not offered to his dead father for a long time. Cakida 'heard their words and threw Olimani low'. This discussion had taken place about a year before. It had followed a sharp dispute between Olimani and Otoro over the latter's moving across the stream. When I said that it was unusual for Otoro to find himself alone with Ondua in the latter's compound, Okwaya said that Otoro had 'feared' Olimani and had gone to discuss the matter with Ondua, and a further quarrel had therefore ensued. Olimani had said that Otoro was trying to destroy the lineage by making complaints about him behind his back—certainly it was an unusual thing to do.

Olimani was extremely annoyed at the oracular verdict, told to him by Okwaya, his trusted half-brother. Before he went Okwaya told me that he feared to tell this to Olimani, thinking that the latter might make accusations similar to those he had made against Otoro. At first Olimani refused to accept the verdict, and shouted that Ondua was a witch and that he knew this because this sickness was serious and had struck him down suddenly, as does witchcraft sickness. These open accusations embarrassed Okwaya and Ngoro, who was also present, and they said that clearly Olimani was raving (also a sign of witchcraft or sorcery). Ngoro said that he did not know what to think, and Okwaya said that he was a Christian and so did not concern himself with the question: these were the affairs of old men. Both were clearly torn between loyalty to their own brother and a realization of his unpopularity and the popularity and sincerity of Ondua. On the following morning, however, I heard that Olimani had accepted the verdict. He was very worried by the sickness, and thought that perhaps after all Ondua's mystical powers of eldership were behind it.

The bull was provided by Ondua and was consecrated, to be sacrificed if Olimani showed signs of recovery. He did so, and the beast was sacrificed. Ondua made a short ritual address, in which no direct reference was made to Olimani's accusations and hostility towards him. Instead he stressed that Olimani had been his ritual assistant and that 'the ghosts had struck him down'. No reference was made to invocation. However, at the anointing, he and the elders of the co-ordinate lineages Ambidro and Ombavu all 'blew breath' into Olimani's ear, a sign that the process involved was invocation and not ghostly vengeance. No other men, such as Draai, nor Otoro himself, even though he had been involved in the invocation, 'blew breath'; nor did they make ritual addresses. At the sharing of the meat Ondua sat next to Olimani, while Otoro was placed with the 'men behind'. I was with the elders and Olimani, and after considerable drinking Olimani began to mutter against Otoro as being the man who was destroying the lineage. His resentment against Ondua was deflected into Otoro, who was said to 'fear' Olimani. However, the main rivalry was quite clearly understood by everyone, and Okwaya told me afterwards

'This day Ondua shows that he is truly a big man. When Ombasa (the founder of Araka) begot his sons Oraa and Licu (the founders of Lari'ba and Nyaai respectively) it was the mother of Lari'ba who bore her child the first, because she was the first married. So now Ondua is elder of all the children of Oraa and of Licu also and so he consults the oracles for this sickness, and he has cut and distributed the meat.'

Case 14

Olimani made an offering of a goat at his fertility shrine (*eralengbo*) and also at the shrine called *rogbo* (or *rįdį*). This took place about six weeks after his sacrifice for his own sickness (Case 13), and the two rites were closely connected. He decided to make the offering because there had been no babies born to wives of men of Nyaai for over a year, and also because they had few calves or kids. Also the harvest had not been good this year. This had been a matter for conversation for several months, and it was his own sickness that finally convinced him that an offering should be made. He and Otoro, representing the two main segments of Nyaai, consulted the rubbing-stick oracle of an operator in Mjdrja, two miles to the south of Araka, who was renowned as the operator of an oracle which 'knew the words' of sterility of women and cattle. That is, he had decided before the consultation what type of offering was necessary and went really to confirm his own suspicions.

Olimani called the senior men of Nyaai, Ondua, Oguda and Draai of Lari'ba, and the elders of the co-ordinate lineages of Araka within the same minor lineage. In addition the wives and some of the daughters of Nyaai, including those married elsewhere, attended. Usually a cock is sacrificed, but the matter was thought serious enough to offer a goat. Olimani made a short ritual address, saying that for a long time no offering had been made at these shrines, and perhaps 'they' were angry because they saw and smelt the food at the ghost shrines, but had been told by the ghosts

No, get your own food. This food is our food. Go and ask our child yourselves.

Then the fertility shrines had sent sickness,[1] the process known as *eralengbo ka* and *rogbo ka*, *ka* being the verb used for the process of ghostly vengeance. Meat and the leaves *ajịgbị* and *larịgbị*, which symbolize fertility, were placed on both the shrines in Olimani's compound and cattle kraal, and the women present were anointed with spittle by the elders. Ondua made no ritual address, which was remarked upon by several people with whom I discussed the rite later.

Ondua was said to have anger in his heart, but agreed to take part in the rite so as not to give shame to his 'brother'. But clearly Olimani's taking all upon himself was an implied rejection of Ondua's authority. This was particularly obvious in that these shrines are 'big', although all senior men own them. They are closely connected with the external lineage shrines, possessed only by elders; and so Olimani's statement that the fertility agents were hungry implied that Ondua had not fulfilled his elder's duties adequately. He should have made more sacrifices at the external shrines. In fact Ondua had offered at the external lineage shrines the year before, but he had not offered at the lineage ancestress shrine (*dede*) since 1913, when as a young elder he had made one of his first big sacrifices. The fertility shrines are more closely linked with the *dede* ancestresses than with the ancestors in the other external shrines, and the affair also had to do with a

---

[1] The agent inside the shrines is never clearly known, and the shrines themselves are spoken of as sending the sterility.

long-standing grievance of Nyaai, that at that time their head, Cakida, had just died. Ondua was the new ritual elder but was helped in secular matters by Abiria, also of Lari'ba; and the men of Nyaai were disgruntled to find that both ritual and secular authority had thus passed from their segment. I was told this by Oguda, who said that this resentment had never ceased to burn in the hearts of the members of Nyaai. He said

Now Olimani remembers those words of long ago, that our *dede* are not fed by Lari'ba. These are bad words, but who knows what is in the heart of a man?

Okwaya told me that Olimani had said that the fertility shrines had in fact caused his recent sickness, and had tried then to show him that they wanted an offering. This also meant that he was rejecting Ondua's authority, which had been demonstrated to him on that occasion.

Case 15

This was an example of the rite of which the only purpose is 'to cleanse the territory'. Whereas this rite may be performed after the appearance of omens only, it is also performed in response to actual sickness, and is then a matter of much greater importance. In this case Draai, his wife and some of his children were all sick with some minor stomach infection. At the time Draai was talking of witchcraft and sorcery, especially the latter, since sorcery sickness is likely to affect the victim's stomach and also to be sudden and fairly severe. But Ondua thought that this was unlikely, and said to me that we might expect Draai to be a witch himself, and 'a witch knows other witches'.

He then told me that Draai feared to consult the oracles, since he feared 'the words of our ancestors'. Ondua therefore consulted his own rubbing-stick oracle, in the company of Oguda only. Later he called Olimani, and together they went to Draai and told him of their findings. This was an unusual action, and done partly because by this time Draai was confined to his compound. Okwaya commented on it by saying

Now Ondua is like a man who hunts a leopard, or perhaps a buffalo. He goes slowly, slowly, then quickly he throws the spear. He waits for that beast to drink or to shelter in the grass, then he kills quickly.

A day or two later Oguda said about the case:

Ondua then spoke to Draai in these words: 'These are the words of your father (Abiria). Long ago, at the time of Ejerekedi (Weatherhead, the District Commissioner in 1914), your father went slowly to entice that girl of Mịdrịa over there. Then he gave three cattle and five lumps of iron ore and two spears and many arrows. She came here with him and stayed here for three years. Then she ran back to her father there, with her grain baskets. . . . Then Abiria thought of those cattle. . . . But they refused to return them, saying that he had beaten their daughter and that he could come to see them (that is, they would drive him away empty-handed). . . . Then Abiria, with his brothers (actually, he went with Oguda) went there slowly and he killed a man there, that man whose mother came from Tara, far away near Mt. Liru. Then those men there wailed, saying 'Ah, who has killed our man?' They danced his death dances, but Abiria refused to go there, so that they began to think. He told us here 'I went slowly at night and I followed that man of Tara to the place where are my cattle.' Then we here rejoiced. . . . Then those men of Mịdrịa there they came here, and sat silent and did not drink beer, and said 'Our sister's husband has killed our man.' Then we waited here for them (to come at night to avenge the death). They come, many of them, calling their calls. We said to them 'You ate our livestock and now you refuse to return it, so if you want then we are ready'. They began war with arrows . . . (a long account of consulting omens). . . . Then their arrows hit us, four or five or six, and those men chose to die, four or five; they there rejoiced and mocked us when our sisters went to fetch the corpses of their brothers. We fought and fought, and many died, both here and there in Mịdrịa, many days and many months. And then we left fighting. We said 'Now many of us have died, there are many orphans, we shall die of hunger because we wage war. Let us return to till the fields, for our orphans, then later they will grow big in the place of their fathers and we shall again be many.' But until this day we remember those words of Abiria. He destroyed our lineage because of his anger and animosity. Today we think 'Oh, there were once our brothers and our fathers, Angura, and Cakida and Kanyi. If that girl of Mịdrịa had not married then Abiria would not have started warfare. The fighting came from him, a man of quarrelling. We wail thus, everyday. And also those men of Mịdrịa wail, and remember the quarrelsomeness of our father Abiria. Now sickness has come to strike you, and your homestead. It comes because of the mouths of men, because of those words of Abiria. Truly Abiria was a quarrelsome man. He destroyed the peace of his 'father' Oraa.'

Sickness by 'the mouths of men' is brought upon a man who by his quarrelling or personal killing of an enemy started inter-group fighting. Those who suffered, or whose parents or lineage suffered, as a result of the fighting, bring this sickness by repeated 'wailing'. Their cries are said to 'go' to God the Creator, who sends sickness to the offender, or to his dependants, including, as in this case, his children. God is brought into the matter, rather than the ancestors, because the fighting was such as to destroy kinship entirely. In another case, which was recounted to me, I was told that a man 'wailing' would say

Your father did wrong, and now his words return to you. If my brother had been alive he would have tilled our fields and would have helped me in my fields. Our wives would have worked together and our children eaten together. But now I am alone. I am like a client. If a man kills his brother, he is alone. Now I am like that man.

The reference here to clients is significant, since clients, being without kin, are associated in Lugbara thought with evil, moral inversion and God.

A question that arises is why Ondua chose to say that this was the process that had affected Draai and his family. In historical fact, the three 'brothers' of Abiria mentioned, Angura, Cakida and Kanyi, all died at different times, and none of them in fighting started by Abiria. It seemed that it was true that Abiria had initiated a period of fighting with Mjdrja, but the details given, and the importance attached to it by Ondua after the event, were greatly exaggerated. Also this accusation was long after the event, since the fighting in question in fact occurred about 1923 (after all three of the 'brothers' had died). Like myth and genealogy, what we should call 'history' is used by Lugbara to explain and validate present-day relationships, and temporal historical events are seen as independently related to the present rather than to one another as events in a single scale of time; the precise order of their occurrence is therefore irrelevant.

Draai based his ambitions and claims largely upon the fact that his father, Abiria, had been an important man and an elder. Draai had stepped into much of his status, and should so have been regarded as an elder in his own right. By this accusation, Ondua showed that in fact Abiria's behaviour had been such that far from strengthening his lineage he had almost destroyed it; and by destroying Abiria's reputation Ondua destroyed much of Draai's claim. This case also showed that God himself supported Ondua's accusation. Although God is not normally invoked in support of claims to higher status, he is said to show his opinions and wishes in ways such as this.

The case was also referred by the members of the lineage to a spate of evil omens which had been experienced at various times over the past few years. Jackals had been seen at night near the external lineage shrine; several doves had nested in trees near the centre of the lineage territory (doves on a hut roof are an omen of impending death); some large snakes had been disturbed while fields were being hoed; and it had been said that the small male and female figures called *adro* had been heard near the external lineage shrine (they live in rain groves, and for them to appear elsewhere is an evil omen that God is to send disaster). I am not sure that all these phenomena had in fact been accepted as omens until this case brought their occurrence into sharper focus, but in any case they became linked with Draai's sickness, and so gave Ondua's interpretation greater validity.

The sickness was removed by a bull being taken from Draai's own herd, and killed in the bush, some way from the homesteads, and also away from the external lineage shrine: this rite was concerned with God rather than with the dead of the lineage. I was told that Ondua would have given a beast if he had had one and Draai had had none. The meat was consumed by the elders of all the inner lineage. This rite is an important one, and the dead are not concerned. Elders of different ritual fields as far as the internal ghosts are concerned are summoned, to show that they will no longer feel anger or 'wail' to God. The elder of Mjdrja was also invited, since his 'wailing' was said to have affected the case. Each elder gave a short ritual address, using sacred leaves. Draai was not present, because he was sick but also, and more important, as a sign that his claims to elderhood were not accepted by any member of the major lineage. There was no anointing or blessing, as the ghosts were not involved. By the way in which the case was discussed, Ondua here showed very conclusively that he alone was the elder of Araka and that Draai was a junior, that being the son of Abiria was no reason for claims to higher status, and that God supported Ondua's position. This was significant in that it is God who is concerned with radical realignments in authority and status, and here he had shown that he did not consider any realignment necessary or due.

Case 16

Olimani cut a goat at his senior ghost shrine for the wife of
Edre. Olimani consulted the oracles, which revealed that he had
invoked the ghost of Pokoni against her. Edre had returned from
labour migration and had refused to share his earnings, saying
that he wanted to acquire livestock so as to marry a second wife.
Olimani had been extremely annoyed at Edre's having moved outside Nyaai to place his homestead in Lari'ba, near Draai's compound. The confirming oracle was operated by Ondua, who was
asked to do so by Olimani, apparently to remove Ondua's anger
at his having first consulted the oracles, both because it is
the duty of the elder to do so, especially if the sick person is an
adult man, and also because Edre now lived inside the territory
of Ondua's segment. Edre's genealogical position was open to
doubt, as I have mentioned, and so he was by now often considered a dependant of Ondua, since he farmed on Ondua's land.
However, Ondua agreed to operate the oracle.

The sacrifice was made by Ondua, Olimani having thought
better of trying to be an independent elder in this situation. Being
for a woman, only men of Araka attended, and there were ritual
addresses by Ondua and Olimani only, both referring only to
Edre's refusal to share his earnings.

Case 17

Two months after the rite of 'cleansing the territory', Ondua
announced that he was to make a sacrifice at the external lineage
shrine of Araka. He had consulted the rubbing-stick oracle of a
renowned oracle operator who was a Kakwa living on the far side
of Yivu to the east of Araka and not far from both Kakwa and
the eastern Lugbara of Omugo. These latter speak a different
dialect from Maraca and are regarded with awe as being filled
with witchcraft, rainmaking and other miraculous powers. To
consult this operator was difficult for an old man like Ondua, since
he had to walk ten miles in each direction. He went quietly one
day without warning to anyone, accompanied only by his son
Yekule. He told me later that he had gone to this operator because
he had gone twice before when lineage matters gave him serious
cause for worry, once at the time of the cattle sickness of 1924-5,
when most of the livestock of Araka died, and once just before

1939, when his wives had 'refused' to become pregnant for several years. Oguda told me also that Ondua had consulted several local operators about the disputes in Araka, and had decided to go to Yịvụ only after three local operators had given him confused and contradictory verdicts.

Ondua was worried because of the general hostility in Araka between himself and Olimani, himself and Draai, Olimani and Otoro, and between many of the senior men and their sons who had been south as labour migrants and so, it was thought, had learnt bad ways and denied their seniors' authority. This was expressed usually in refusing to give their fathers their earnings, but spending them on cloth and presents for girls whom they seduced and made pregnant, with consequent law-cases and purification rites which cost livestock. In two cases they stayed away permanently in the south or in Arua, the local township, so becoming 'lost' to their lineage. Oguda told me

Ondua fears that God has sent *nyoka* to our territory, so that our wives will not bear nor our cattle, and we shall become few men. Our children will go 'to the other side' (of Lake Albert, as labour migrants), and our land will be destroyed. But perhaps these are the words of our ancestors, to show us that our hearts are evil. Perhaps it is the work of the (government) chiefs, who eat our wealth in fines and tax. Now Ondua is *oroo* (the last surviving senior man), his heart is closed to die. But can a man die with trouble in his heart?

Ondua returned and said that the oracle had disclosed that his recent sickness and those of Olimani were partially the consequences of ghostly vengeance sent by Onzima, the founder of the minor lineage, together with Ombasa the founder of Araka, and his son Oraa, the apical ancestor of Lari'ba segment. Sacrifice of a goat at the external lineage shrine would have to be made. The reason was the continual hostility within Araka, expressed in the disputes I have mentioned and in the fact that 'the mouths of men' had spoken recently of witches within the lineage, a sign that the cleavages within it were serious indeed. In short, the pattern of authority within the lineage had been changing radically during the past few years, and this verdict supported Ondua's claim to be the sole lineage authority and to maintain that authority as it had been ideally for many years.

The sacrifice took place within a few days of Ondua's return.

The goat was killed at the external shrine, which is shared by the three lineages Araka, Ambidro and Ombavu. In this shrine there were then said to be Onzima, the three founder-ancestors of these three lineages, and the eldest son of each of them. As far as Araka was concerned, only Onzima, Ombasa and Oraa were concerned, and only they would 'hear' the sacrifice, the other incumbents sharing in the oblation but not being concerned in any more direct way.

The congregation was a small one, since these shrines are 'big' and only elders and their ritual assistants may enter the grove where the shrine is kept. From Araka Ondua went with Olimani and Yekule only; not even Oguda went. And elders and their assistants came from the other two co-ordinate lineages. Yekule should not have gone, but Ondua said that he was old and would never make another offering at this shrine, so that it was good that his successor attend to learn the ritual; Yekule in fact sat with me and was given only beer and a small piece of meat; he played no part in the rite itself.

Ondua made a long ritual address, in which he stressed certain points at length. Those which were particularly relevant to the patterns of authority and dissension inside Araka were:

1. Ombasa's two sons were Oraa and Licu, but Oraa was born of the first wife and also born before Licu, and so he inherited the mystical power of eldership. Licu succeeded him.

2. On Licu's death, Moro had inherited the eldership, and had passed it on his death to his first son Dria, Ondua's own father.

3. While relating the genealogy of the lineage, Ondua stressed that of Lari'ba; that of Nyaai was telescoped so that Licu's son Toba and grandson Cakida were given as brothers. Later I discussed this with Yekule and pointed out that this would mean that Olimani was a generation senior to Ondua, which was hardly what Ondua wished to emphasize, but I was told by Yekule that

It is not like that. Those men of Nyaai are as our children. We stand before them. They are few, and they have many 'strangers' among them. It is we here who are the children of Oraa.

That is to say, mystical inheritance in a direct line of descent is more significant than length of genealogy as far as lineage seniority and authority are concerned.

4. Angura, Dria's full brother who had died without becoming elder since he died before Dria, had once tried to bring witchcraft accusations into Lari'ba. 'When Angura died his heart was troubled and he was seen by his son (Angundru) as a spectre. Perhaps his heart was bad.' This was a clear warning to Olimani. For once, on this important occasion, Ondua was speaking directly and personally without indirect references and circumlocution to avoid giving 'shame'. Yekule told me later that this was because 'only the ghosts there and the big men hear those words'; they were not later made public.

5. He referred to recent omens as a sign that perhaps God was angry with the people of northern Lugbara; he also mentioned the famine of 1942-3, when many people had died, and other earlier disasters, especially the 1924-5 cattle epidemic which had destroyed Araka's herds. He said that now the ghosts were showing Araka in time that they should not quarrel and that their young men should obey their seniors and their daughters not sleep wantonly with everybody and become pregnant.

Olimani then made a very short address, as ritual assistant, in which he mentioned only that God might have wished to bring *nyoka* to Araka, but that now the ghosts would eat and their stomachs would be filled and they would be content, so that these 'words' would be finished.

The elders of the other two lineages also spoke, but mentioned only the relationships between the three apical ancestors of the lineages, each of whom had inherited the mystical powers of eldership from Onzima, and through him from Sambala, Cereki and finally Jaki, one of the hero-ancestors of Lugbara, himself.

The oblation was then made, meat and blood were placed on the shrine, and some taken also to the ancestral burial tree, near the grove in which we were. The members of the congregation then ate part of the meat, the three elders together and the three ritual assistants together, and Yekule and myself together. Most of the meat was taken home by the three elders, to be eaten by themselves and their own wives at leisure.

The effect of this rite was considerable, since by it Ondua had largely re-established his waning authority. True, the cleavages within Araka had by this time become so great that they could be resolved only by segmentation, which took place after Ondua's death in the following year. Ondua had shown that only he was the elder of Araka. The distant ghosts who had founded the lineage, and even Onzima, who had founded the minor lineage, had shown their support of Ondua's authority by oracular consultation.

The composition of the congregation was important in this respect. Olimani had to assist as ritual assistant, not as an elder in his own right. Whatever disputes as to authority may be fought in terms of performing sacrifice at internal ghost shrines, it is the sacrifice at the external shrines that is ultimately important as showing the status of the elder. A man who sacrifices at these shrines, or who is called as lineage representative to them, is an elder; this is the final test as far as the opinion of living members of the lineage are concerned. Ondua showed publicly that Olimani was junior to him, as head of a segment of Araka, not of an independent lineage. He also showed publicly that Draai was only a 'man behind', neither head of a lineage nor of a named segment of the status of Nyaai. The same applied of course to Otoro, but Otoro's ambitions had not been so obvious as had those of Draai.

In his ritual address Ondua tried to show that the pattern of distribution of authority within Araka was then as it had been ever since he first became elder in 1906. Although clearly the distribution of effective domestic authority had changed many years before, Ondua had denied this. The genealogy of a lineage reflects the distribution of authority within it; conversely, the genealogy is seen also as validating an existing distribution, so that so long as the genealogy is accepted so is that distribution. The eating of the sacrificial meat by generation, as Lugbara see it, also confirmed Olimani's subordinate status and confirmed the genealogy that Ondua had given as the 'true' one of Araka.

Finally, Ondua had shown that Olimani's sacrifice at his fertility shrines had been presumptuous and wrong. Both the offerings were made as a consequence of the same events. But whereas Ondua's was made in recognition of the fact that the ghosts had sent these disasters as a warning to their living kin, Olimani's had been made to mystical powers that have very little direct connexion with the ancestors. The power within the fertility shrines may ultimately come from the ancestors, in Lugbara theory, but it does not come from the agnatic ancestors of the lineage, but from those of other lineages. Thus Olimani had implied that these disasters were not sent primarily as a warning to him and others that they were weakening the system of authority within the lineage, and he implied also that the ancestors of the lineage called Nyaai, by which his segment was differentiated, supported him in his efforts to attain independence for his segment. Ondua showed that Olimani was, if not mistaken in his judgement and his support, at least supported by powers that were distant and ineffectual. In short, Olimani had tried to disown his own guilt for much of the trouble in the lineage, by calling on powers not morally concerned in the affair, only to be told by Ondua, his ritual superior, that in fact the trouble was after all sent by the ghosts who wished to show Olimani his faults and to stress his ritual subordination to Ondua.

Cases *18*, *19*, *20*

In order not to make this account more confusing than it need be, I have so far left out the cases of offerings made to the internal ancestral shrines (*a'bįva* and *anguvua*), and shall now consider them together. They are structurally not of such importance as the cases I have so far described, so that to consider them out of their temporal context is not misleading. It must be remembered that Lugbara do become physically sick: although much of the sickness thought to come from the ghosts is relatively slight and becomes accepted as sickness very largely because of the structural position of the patient at a given time, sickness is none the less a common occurrence and its physical effects cause worry and unhappiness. And, of course, since Lugbara believe that most sickness is mystically caused, they cannot include the structural aspect of sickness in their consideration of the matter. They well understand that structural considerations enter into the consultation of the oracles, but this does not change their beliefs as to the causes of sickness.

There were three offerings at the *a'bįva* shrines during this period. Otoro offered dried meat for his wife, Njima gave beer only for his small daughter, and Edre gruel for his son. In none of these cases was it thought that the sick person had committed any offence towards the living, such as being disobedient to father or husband. Otoro is extremely fond of and gentle towards his second wife, who is regarded generally as being a good wife. Her sickness, a marked swelling of the leg, was generally taken to come from the *a'bįva*, who are said usually to send sickness in the form of swelling, before Otoro consulted the oracle and diviner at all. The same is true of the other cases, both of which involved swellings of the leg.

Cases 21, 22

There were also two offerings made to the *anguvua*. There is no shrine, the offerings merely being placed on the floor of the hut. Although it is said that any adult man may do this, I have never heard of anyone but the heads of family-segments making these offerings. The sickness from *anguvua* is also swelling of the body, usually of the leg. Usually senior men place offerings to *anguvua* while their juniors do so for *a'biva*. These two offerings were made by Ondua, who gave dried meat and porridge for his own sickness, and by Olimani, who offered the same oblation on behalf of his wife. Their doing so was partly the consequence of the explicit nature of the sickness, and also, I think, partly due to the positions they were in as far as their struggle for authority was concerned. Ondua made his offering immediately after a swelling from which he had suffered for many years re-appeared on his knee. He did not consult oracles or diviners, but merely made the offering with only his senior wife present. There were no comments made about this and it was accepted generally as being a case that needed no further explanation. Olimani's wife also had swellings on her shins, the result of yaws. But Okwaya said that Olimani was worried about the hints dropped by his dependants that he was invoking the ghosts too much, and so wished to show that he did not do so all the time. This remark is significant, but his deciding it was *anguvua* sickness was due to internal dissensions within his own domestic family: he did not wish to cause any exacerbation of the tension that already existed between his wives. He could not be held responsible for ancestral sickness, which comes only by ancestral vengeance. It is true that it is generally held that the patient has been guilty of some small offence, usually impiety towards the dead, but in neither of these cases, nor in those of offerings to the *a'biva* that I have just mentioned, were details of any supposed impiety ever mentioned to me. Okwaya told me later that in fact Olimani had gone by himself to consult a diviner on the matter, which would mean that he tried to contact the ancestors to discover the details of any impiety committed by his wife.

Cases 23, 24, 25

These were three rites performed at the *talį* shrines, by Ondua for his own sickness, by Olimani on account of the sickness of his son Omba's child, and by Draai for his son's sickness.

Ondua offered a cock, as a consequence of consulting his own rubbing-stick oracle. The sickness consisted of sharp pains in the chest. He made the offering himself, calling only Yekule and Oguda. Little notice was taken of the matter. It was said that the sickness had been sent because Ondua had not made an offering at this shrine for a long time. As I have said earlier, in fact Lugbara do not make offerings at shrines without prior sickness, but none the less this reason is one given for sickness which is not concerned with any obvious offence against the patient's living kin.

The case of Olimani was similar. He consulted the oracle of Ayua of Kimiru, which decreed that the *talį* sent the sickness as a warning that no offering had been made for a long time. Omba was concerned in this specifically; as Olimani's ritual successor he was also held partly to blame (even though he could not make a *talį* offering in his present status).

Draai's case was more significant. The incumbents in the *talį* shrines of both Ondua and Olimani were the *talį* of their agnatic ancestors. But those in the *talį* shrines of lesser men are those of their mother's lines. Draai consulted the oracle of a man in Yįvų, a mile or so away. He claimed that the sickness came from the agnatic *talį* of his descent line, then went to consult the oracle operator. While he was gone it was decided by both Ondua and Oguda that this could not be, since Draai was only a 'man behind', and so those ancestors could not be in his *talį* shrine. They discussed this with him after his return, and found that the oracle had not disclosed the actual identity of the *talį* ancestors, but had merely stated that an offering should be made since they were 'hungry'. Draai agreed with Ondua and Oguda, and offered a cock at the shrine within his own compound, attended only by his wife. The whole affair was not of great importance except as an indication of Draai's claims to independence and higher status.. This occurred shortly after his wife had been sick as a consequence of invocation by Ondua (Case 12), and so. Draai did not press his belief as to the identity of the *talį* ancestors concerned.

Cases 26, 27, 28, 29, 30

These were all cases of sacrifice at various shrines for matrilateral
ghosts and ancestors. Benyu sacrificed a goat for his wife's barrenness at his *lucugo* shrine; Obitre made an offering at his *lucugo*
shrine; for the same reason; Okwaya sacrificed at his *adro-ori*
shrine and Olimani at his *oku-ori* shrine; Oguda sacrificed at his
rogbo shrine.

In both the cases of Benyu and Obitre, the barrenness of their
wives was said by the oracles to 'come from' their mother's
brothers. In both cases the men had been quarrelling with their
'brothers' of closely related segments, and these quarrels would
seem to have decided them to consult the oracles about their wives'
barrenness. Barrenness is not a complaint that suddenly becomes
noticeable, and a second factor is usually needed before oracular
consultation is sought. It is safe to say that both these men are
somewhat ignored by their own agnates; Benyu is the least important of his generation in Lari'ba, and Obitre is overshadowed
by his 'brother' Otoro, with whom he shares a compound.
Oguda told me

A man is not angry when the oracle tells him to offer at his *lucugo*
shrine. Does not a man love his sister's son? Then a man knows that his
mother's brother remembers him, and he makes an offering with his
mother's brother at his *lucugo* shrine. Is a man not his mother's brother's
child?

To be sent this 'sickness' is not regarded as an affront or an
unkindness by the mother's brother's people, but rather as a
recognition of the tie, as a sign that they will stand by him as
against the rest of his agnatic lineage and will protect him against
them. I was told on another occasion that a man depends upon his
own lineage for land and wealth, but upon his mother's brother
and his lineage for the fertility of his wives. A man can emphasize
his importance as an individual by stressing this tie with his
mother's lineage. This is a commonplace in agnatic descent
systems, and needs no stressing. What is significant in these cases
is that these two men were told by the oracles that their mother's
brothers had sent barrenness and that the cause was not the agent
in the *rogbo* shrine. It is young and structurally unimportant men
who tend to sacrifice at the *lucugo* shrine, and this is partly a

recognition by their mothers' brothers that they are now heads of small segments in their own right. More senior men sacrifice at the *rogbo* shrines, as did Oguda some nine months after the other two rites. Oguda told me that he did so because

> Now my wives have no more children, and my penis is no longer erect. So I cut an offering at this shrine, that I may become strong.

Oguda had no need to emphasize his position by reference to his maternal kin; even though he was the junior half-brother of an elder his status has been accepted for many years. There is also another aspect: his offering was primarily in respect of his own failing powers, whereas those of Benyu and Obitre were in respect of those of their wives. Offerings at these shrines are made in cases of barrenness, a serious sickness for Lugbara and one likely to be associated with severe crises in their lives; they tend to select the shrine according to their lineage status.

Okwaya discussed his offering at his *adro-ori* shrine:

> Sickness has seized me from the ghosts of over there, in Erivu. My father (Cakida) married a daughter of Erivu, and gave iron and hoes for her, and a bull. Yet always we here (in Araka) have quarrelled. When my father died that wife was old, she was not inherited by Olimani, but lived in that homestead there where I used to live. Then she came here with me (across the stream) and she died here. Then there were words (i.e. accusations) of witchcraft from those there in Erivu. . . . Perhaps these words came from Olimani; I do not know. Or perhaps they came from Ngoro. . . . Sickness has struck me and Olimani went there (to Kimiru) to consult the rubbing-stick oracle, and its words were those of Erivu. . . . Olimani is my brother, he has not invoked the ghosts against me.

Okwaya was referring to a long-standing quarrel between Cakida and Okwaya's mother's people which culminated in a dispute over her treatment as a widow. Okwaya looked after her for many years, and is a kindly and considerate man often riled by Olimani's overbearing ways. Okwaya agreed with the oracular diagnosis.

> Yes, it is right that sickness has come from those at Erivu. Do they not love me, as their child? They watch over me. They are my people there. Olimani has his people there, far off in Ole'ba.

It was thus accepted that his mother's brother's ghosts were protecting him against his half-brother Olimani. Olimani did not invoke the ghosts against him, presumably because of Okwaya's obvious loyalty to him and his lack of personal ambition that might separate him from Olimani, even though he had moved his compound across the stream. That move and this rite both show the nature of the relationship between the two men, on both the levels of secular and ritual authority.

Olimani's offering at his *oku-ori* shrine was a small and unimportant matter, and was the consequence of his own sickness. It took place early in the period covered by these cases, at the first signs of a sickness that later assumed serious proportions and led to the cases which I have already described. He told me that he consulted the oracles merely to confirm a dream that he had had of his long dead mother's sister. But he clearly did not think much of the matter and little was ever said about it. The offering was made by his first wife (he has no sister still alive), and attended by him and Ngoro only.

Cases 31, 32

These were offerings at two spirit shrines. Ondua made an offering at his *ajualįrį* shrine, and later made another at his *Yakani* shrine. Both were in response to sicknesses of the chest that had affected several members of the lineage, the first during the rains in August and September, the second during the dry season, from December to March. The sickness in both cases is said to come from God, 'in the wind', and the offerings are of grain food only, placed upon *inzu* sticks (a wood especially associated with God) and then placed either in the thatch, for *ajualįrį*, or on the shrine (*Yakani*). These offerings are often made at these times of year, as a protection against epidemic sicknesses which come from God, and affect people over a wide area. They are not concerned with lineage morality.

Case 33

This case is really a complex of rites and ceremonies that occurred at and after the death of Ondua, the elder of Araka.

It is clear from what has gone before in this account that the death of an elder is structurally a most important event. It is at the climax of a long process of segmentation, and it is also at the beginning of another similar process. The entire process is one of the gradual change in the distribution of authority within a lineage and the section clustered round it; the elder's death typically marks a radical and final change in this pattern. Lineage segmentation is one means, and the most usual, by which conflict of interests within the lineage is resolved; and it typically occurs at the time of an elder's death.

In this brief account I do not wish to present all the ethnographic evidence, but only to discuss Ondua's death as a phase in the ritual history of Araka minimal lineage. An account of these rites and ceremonies may be written in many ways, depending on the frame of reference chosen. Ondua's death affected many people: his wives, his sons and daughters, the members of his immediate family, his uterine and affinal kin, the members of his joint family, the members of Lari'ba segment as a corporate entity, the members of Araka, of Nyaai, of the other minimal lineages of Kimiru, of the other lineages of Maraca, other elders of the neighbourhood, and, of course, himself and the dead. An account could be written from the point of view of the interests of any of these people. And it could be written from either a psychological or a sociological viewpoint. Here I am concerned only with the latter, and I try to consider it from the point of view of all these persons whom I have listed: their statuses co-exist and interact, and it is this co-existence and interaction that compose the field of social relations with which I am dealing in this account. Ondua was a husband, a father, an elder, a kinsman and a neighbour, and his status as any one of these cannot be understood in isolation, any more than he could see himself in any one of these roles in isolation from the others.

Death is said by Lugbara to be caused by God, in his transcendent aspect as *Adroa 'ba o'dupiri*, 'God the taker away of men.' Other agents may send sickness that leads to death—a witch, a sorcerer or the maker of a curse—either directly or indirectly by the sending of a spear, a buffalo or other instrument of death. But they are said to bring the man concerned to the notice of God, who causes him to die. This is not a very clearly conceived or expressed notion, but rather one thought out to be consistent with the axiomatic belief that it is only God who can cause death, just as it is only he, as *Adroa 'ba o'bapiri* ('God the creator of men'), who can create living beings. God is not concerned to punish by death. A man does not die because he has offended God by the commission of sins, although there are cases in which a man, for example

a fratricide, may die 'on account of blood'. In these cases Lugbara
say 'God has willed the death', but then this is said also of any
other death, whether due to old age or violence. What is important
is that God is not thought deliberately to kill people as a punishment for their sins: other agents send such punishment in the
form of sickness.

Death should be regarded, if we wish to understand Lugbara
notions, as one part of a long process of the development of a
lineage, Its members are born and die and then become dead
members; they leave the 'world outside' but they are not then lost
to the living. They merely change their status. I have remarked
that there is no idea of heaven or hell, and when a corpse is buried
there is no idea of a journey of the soul, even though objects are
buried with it.

At death there is a change in a person's social personality.
Certain attributes are extinguished, those to do with his physical
body. Those attributes to do with his soul, with his person as a
conscious and responsible kinsman, become part of his new status
as a ghost. Those attributes that are to do with him as a kinsman,
but which are not concerned with responsibility towards other
kinsmen, become part of the status as an ancestor, as distinct from
that of a ghost. Ancestors are to a large extent collectivized, whereas ghosts are regarded as individuals. And finally certain attributes
that are not part of the status of ghost or ancestor are as it were
depersonalized and become part of a collectivity: these are those
of *adro* and *talį*, that I have mentioned earlier.

The rites and ceremonies that are performed at and after the
death of a person, may be classified according to Van Gennep's
classic division of *rites de passage*. We cannot properly do this
either from the point of view of the dead man, nor from that of the
living kin concerned. It can be done only from the point of view
of the total constellation of cognatic kin that cluster round the
agnatic lineage as an everlasting group that is undergoing a
continual process of change in its internal organization and in its
relations with other like groups. The rites at death do not take
place in isolation, but within this wider frame.

The first phase of these *rites de passage*, that of separation, is
marked by the death and the burial. In these the dead person leaves
the world of the living and his social personality is divided into its
component elements.

The second phase, that of seclusion, is marked by the rites and ceremonies of mourning, death dances and exchange of arrows between kin. The living are here re-organizing themselves after the death of a member who was at the centre of a particular cluster of social relations; these must be changed and a new pattern affirmed. During this time the living most closely related to the dead person are in mourning, and the dead person is in the sky with God. He may revisit the living, as a spectre or dream personage, but he lives neither on the surface of the earth nor in the ground beneath.

The third phase, that of the rites of aggregation, is marked by changing the dead man into a ghost and recognizing him as such, by his soul being contacted by the living and by shrines being erected for him.

At death the soul leaves the body and thenceforth is able to bring sickness upon its living kin. The dead man is connected with his agnatic lineage, to the exclusion of most other ties, especially those not conceived in terms of kinship. As a man, he is dead; only his soul remains as an individual entity, and that has ties only with his kin, primarily his agnatic kin. Part of the role of a ghost is to bring sickness to living kin who behave in a way likely to harm the lineage and the kin clustered round it. Efforts are made before a man dies to ensure that he dies peacefully and contentedly, so that his soul will not prove troublesome after death. Unless it becomes a ghost peacefully it is thought to be bad-tempered and spiteful. It will then bring sickness haphazardly, instead of only a response to behaviour that deserves it. One of the most important aspects of the cult of the dead is to provide a means of social control within the kin-group, by the bringing of deserved sickness upon evil-doers. If the ghosts send sickness haphazardly and spitefully the working of the system is upset—even though Lugbara often claim the ghosts are spiteful in this way it is none the less axiomatic that generally they are not, but that they are calm in their hearts and exercise their powers responsibly. This is particularly important in the case of an elder, who is especially likely to bring sickness if dissatisfied at the time of dying. Lesser people are not the objects of such care.

When an elder or a senior man knows he is about to die he calls the men of his minimal lineage and any senior kin with whom he has been especially intimate—although it is rare for anyone but an agnate to be called. He then 'speaks words to his brothers'. If he dies without speaking, then he dies 'with a bad heart' and will later bring malicious sickness. After he has spoken the senior members of his family may consult the oracles to confirm that the sickness is now from God, so that there is nothing to be done and no hope of recovery. Then they leave him to die. His kin assemble to wail, often before the actual death, while his wives watch over him to soothe him and to arrange his bed and limbs.

On this occasion, one at which new ties and alignments are being created, any specific or latent hostilities within the group should be resolved, and the lineage values that are maintained by the ghosts are reaffirmed. A man who is about to become a ghost affirms the values by which he will in future judge the actions of his living kin. He thus defines his future relationship to the lineage; later, when he becomes a ghost, this relationship will be realized. Men who die childless do not become ghosts, even if they are old men, and they do not say words of this kind when dying— or at least anything they may say has little importance. The only women who say these words are the wives of elders, who may later become ancestresses of matrisegments of the lineage; but they are attended by their sons and husbands only.

Since lineage segmentation is especially likely to occur after the death of the elder, when the cleavages which have been more or less latent during his lifetime may be expressed openly, the question of his successor is particularly important. Much of the struggle for headship of the lineage is played out during the dying elder's last hours. His 'words to his brothers' have the force of a command, since if they are disobeyed it is thought that he will send sickness and will probably appear as a spectre. The fact that only his agnatic kin are present is significant in this respect, since the struggle for headship is the internal concern of the lineage only, and its entire future prosperity may depend upon it.

Ondua had been prepared to die for some time, and did so in April, in the rains, with little warning. He was sick, and on the second day called Oguda, his brother, and told him to summon his kin, to hear his last words. They came during the morning and he spoke to them during the afternoon. From Araka came Oguda, Yekule, Benyu, Draai, Olimani, Okwaya and Otoro; from beyond Araka came Ega, the elder of Ambidro, and Onyako, elder of Ombavu. During the afternoon Cakida, the elder of Kimiru and rainmaker of Maraca, also came, towards the very end of Ondua's words. This was not normal but he and Ondua had been elders of neighbouring lineages (though not closely related) for many years, and Ondua asked for him to come, Being rainmaker he was said to be above all sectional interests. I, of course, could not be present, but was given a reasonably full account by Okwaya.

Ondua said

Now God has finished my days. Now I go. I leave you, my children. Later you must follow my words, to live quietly with people without quarrelling. Do not destroy our home, live in peace.

He then spoke for two or three hours, with long pauses between statements. I give only the main points that he made to his kinsmen. They were:

1. Yekule was to be his successor as elder. He was to be helped by Oguda, who would 'show him to put his hand into the shrines.' Olimani would be his ritual assistant. Oguda, that is, would have most of the secular authority of elder, but only Yekule could act as ritual head of the lineage. Oguda knew the ways of Europeans and so could guard the interests of the lineage against the chiefs and their policemen. When Oguda died his son Aribo should return from Arua and become assistant to Yekule; they must become 'brothers' as had himself and Oguda for so many years, since first the Belgians came to take away Oguda (as their servant) and brought trouble to the land.

2. God had given good fortune and Araka had become big and wealthy. Let them all be as 'brothers' and 'follow the words' of Yekule. Then their ancestor Ombasa would rejoice. Let them not destroy the lineage by being 'strong'; they should sit together under a meeting tree as 'brothers'.

3. Let God prevent their girls from becoming pregnant and so destroying the wealth of the lineage (because unmarried girls who become pregnant may find it difficult to marry except for low bridewealth).

4. Let the men of the lineage be generous to visitors, and give them food and beer, and feed the lineage daughters and their children when they come visiting.

5. Two goats should be repaid to Ondiko of Nyoro; they had been won recently at a court case, but Ondua thought that this was not right, and that Ombasa might die also with

a bad heart and then bring trouble to the people of Araka.

6. He said that witchcraft had appeared in Araka, but that people should hide those 'words' and live in amity.

7. All the men of Lari'ba were 'sons' of Oraa. Let them not quarrel. Now only Oguda would be left as *oroo* (the surviving elder of his generation) and all others were his children. They must obey him, and he, with Yekule, should live near the external lineage shrines. (This was directed at Draai, who was in fact of Oguda's generation and wished to become independent of Yekule and Oguda; he had set his hut close to the shrines in the heart of the lineage territory).

8. Their sons should not go south and come back with sorcery medicines, since these evil things of the Congo would destroy the lineage.

9. His widows should go to Yekule, since 'the penis of his brother Oguda was finished'. Yekule's own mother was old and should be looked after by her son, who could not, of course, inherit her as a wife.

10. A goat should be taken from his herd to be given to Obitre, as repayment of a loan incurred by Ondua's father Dria, who had been given a goat by Obitre's father, Kanyi. This loan must have dated from before 1906, the date of Dria's death.

11. His heart had been 'bad' against Olimani, who had said that he had used witchcraft to bring sickness. But it was not good for senior 'brothers' to quarrel, and those 'words were finished'. Also his heart had been bad against the elder of Ombavu, since an occasion when they had quarrelled over the distribution of sacrificial meat at a rite held in Mitika.

In theory a man will return as a spectre to haunt his kin if they do not obey his last words. But none the less they are not always obeyed. I was told, both on this and on many other occasions, that during the telling of the last words the dying man's 'brothers' speak with him and among themselves, and 'they try to help him to say the words that he wishes to say'. Often the last words of a dying man are not clear or easily intelligible, and it is clear that during this ceremony the 'brothers' do not in fact merely sit quietly to hear the dying man's wishes so as to carry them out to the last letter. It is on this occasion that the future distribution of authority within the lineage or segment is determined. Okwaya told me that on this occasion Oguda and Olimani, as brother and ritual assistant, sat near Ondua and talked with him; others, and he specifically mentioned Draai, were pushed away and had to stand at the edge of the group. Although for obvious reasons the situation was not all that clear, it would seem from what Okwaya was able to tell me that the seven men of Araka who were present tended to stand or sit by segment, or, perhaps more accurately, by their temporary alliances of interest. What was clear was that they did not stand by generation, as they would at a sacrifice or other rite in which the order of sitting is formalized. When men sit by segment affiliation, it may be assumed that the occasion is one on which inter-segment rivalries are at least not hidden.

I have been told that a dying man is aware of cleavages within the lineage, and that if he has the true well-being of the group at heart then he will say those words which will lead to the least conflict later; he will conceal his own personal likes and dislikes. But in general it is clear that his words are taken by his hearers to mean whatever they like them to mean. Often the successor is not named. In theory, however, the successor to the dead man's status calls the personal call of the dead man, his *cere*.[1] This is done to 'show the words of that man, to show that his father is dead and that his heart is troubled. Now he is "big" and calls his *cere*.' It is thus largely by this calling of the *cere* that formal notice is given of his succession. In this case Yekule called Ondua's *cere*. This did not mean that segmentation would not occur, but only that for the moment the struggle between Lari'ba and Nyaai was stilled.

In Ondua's last words certain wishes seemed to be clear. The structurally important ones were that neither Olimani nor Draai should become independent elders, but should both acknowledge the authority of Yekule and, at least in the case of Draai, of Oguda also. The men argued about the meaning of these words for many hours that evening, and on later days. It was argued especially by Olimani's and Draai's parties that Ondua did not know the

---

[1] This is the personal call possessed by every man and woman. It is a long falsetto whooping cry, the melody of which corresponds to the tonal pattern of a word phrase associated with the possessor. It is made in times of danger, in fighting, and on formal occasions to show the caller's identity. Men also call their *cere* when returning home drunk, lest they be mistaken for strangers and shot with arrows, and to show pride in themselves. It is always made only by the possessor except on the one occasion of death; at other times to call another man's *cere* is to insult and belittle him.

significance of what he was saying. I was struck by the fact that Okwaya said immediately that they would probably 'forget' the words to do with repayment of two goats to the head of Nyoro— and in fact they were not repaid; that to Obitre was, however.

This is not an ethnographic account of Lugbara death cere- monies, so I shall not describe actual details of burial. The corpse is buried with various objects—Ondua was buried with his quiver, his favourite drinking gourd, his stool, and his rubbing-stick and boiling medicine oracles (which he had rarely used on behalf of consultants for many years). These objects symbolized his age-grade status, and not that in the lineage. The quiver is an object associ- ated with the young man who is warrior and hunter, the drinking gourd with the mature man who drinks with his kin and neigh- bours, and the stool with the elder. Although the elder's status is an important one in the lineage system, it was said that

> Ondua was an elder, therefore his stool was placed in the grave with his corpse. All elders are 'brothers', and when his stool is placed down there all the elders of Maraca and Ole'ba and Oluvu and Yivu and Miridri and Kijomoru (the neighbouring tribes) knew that their 'brother' had died and they came to bewail their 'brother'.

The oracle objects are associated with his status as operator. Again, the stress is on status in age and generation and in the community, rather than on status within the minimal lineage only.[1]

Ondua's corpse was buried in a grave dug in the floor of his compound, 'because an elder is "big"; we fear to bury him within his hut', and a small bark-cloth tree was planted at the head of the grave. As I have mentioned earlier, all elders' graves are marked with burial trees, and later offerings will be made at them. The corpse was buried by six sisters' sons, and his widows and close kin went into mourning.

Once his corpse was buried, there began the process of changing his status from that of a living to a dead kinsman. It has already become apparent how ambiguous is the position of an elder, or of any senior man: there is a very slight difference only between his being regarded as an ideal elder, exercising his authority for the well-being of his lineage, and his being accused of being a witch,

---

[1] Similarly, a woman is buried with her beads, the three firestones of her hearth and the smaller of her two grinding stones (symbolizing her statuses as girl, as wife and as mother—the larger grinding stone goes to her daughter, and her crops are destroyed by her brother).

abusing his mystical powers for his own selfish ends. This ambiguity is found also in the attitude to the dead. On the whole they are regarded as being beneficent, but people also fear them. This is true especially of the recently dead, since it is not known what grudges they may hold towards their living kin at the time they die. They are not yet full ancestors or ghosts, and it is at this period that any overt resentment of them arising from quarrels while they were alive may be expressed openly. After death, the soul of the dead man is said to go to, or at least to be in some way closely associated with, God in the sky. Here they are not directly concerned with the doings of their living kin, unless they bear serious grudges against them, when they may appear as spectres. They are contacted by diviners, a rite I describe below, and shrines are erected for them. Once they have thus become ghosts any resentment towards them is neither ideally permitted nor is it, in my experience, actually felt, since it should by then have been dispersed at the time of contacting the soul by a diviner. The ambivalent attitude towards a senior kinsman is very largely an aspect of the relationship with him as a known individual, which lessons after his death as memory of him fades and he becomes part of a collectivity—although as a ghost he is still an individual. Resentment and even hatred towards the dead man may be expressed openly at his death, when many of the overt ideals of kinship behaviour temporarily cease to be observed.

At the burial, immediately after the body has been placed in the grave, and while the death dances are beginning outside the compound, the successor and other elders of the inner lineage speak of the dead man and recount the 'words of the ancestors' in ritual addresses. They bring *edogbi* leaves (the use of which implies that God is involved), dip them in water and place them on the ground while speaking, 'so that they are near the grave'. At Ondua's burial the chief statements were made by Oguda and Olimani. The former made a long and confused speech (he was beginning to grow very senile) about the past glories of Araka and Maraca, listing ancestors and their exploits. Olimani's address was much shorter, and in it he said:

Now you, Ondua my brother, the child of that ancestress Lari'ba (the clan name being used as name for the wife of the lineage founder), you are dead. Your corpse rots in that grave. You are now nothing. Now you have gone and now you fear. It is good that you fear, truly these words are good. You have begotten children and have done many things. All of us here knew your words and heard you and the words of your heart. Now you are dead, as a pot that is broken. Perhaps your heart was good, perhaps it was bad. Your father Dria was indeed a good man and we all heard his words and knew his thoughts. He cared for us his children and his personality was big. All those people of Yivu there and Terego there and Oluvu there knew his words. . . . Now you are dead, and it is good that you fear. If your heart is bad, then tomorrow we shall see. If it is good, then tomorrow we shall see. Then we shall know your heart. Now you are dead and your words are little. You are little. Tomorrow we shall know these things.

This was a usual speech of the kind made on this occasion by the dead elder's ritual assistant, and was no more hostile than other addresses at burials elsewhere.

That night the leaves are left on the ground, near the new grave. If an hyena or other night animal defaecates on the leaves it is known that the dead man dies with a bad heart, but if there is no excrement on them the next morning it is known that he died content, and by the will of God. This is done for all men who die and who will become ghosts; it is not done for those who will become ancestors only (childless men) nor for those killed by lightning, a direct sign of God's will; it is also done for old and respected women who will later become ancestresses from whom new lineage segments will spring, but not for younger women or children. In Ondua's case, no excrement was found, a sign that his last words were 'true' and that he had died content. Draai said that he had seen jackals about during that night, but since they left no sign his statement was ignored.

After the burial there are the death dances. These are highly elaborated. There are variations, but always two main dances or sets of dances, the 'wailing dance', and the 'leaping dance', each consisting of several distinct dances each with its own song, the words telling of events to do with the dead man's life and way of dying, with much bitter and sarcastic allusion to the failings of other lineages.

Death dances are the occasions for the greatest coming together of kinsfolk and are of great importance. There is very little ceremonial or ritual at birth and marriage; there is no initiation. There are said formerly to have been large dances held at the first harvesting in the year, but today they are smaller than death dances and confined to members of at most the same major section. The death dances proper, *ongo*, performed immediately after the death of a big man, may continue for a week, and there are later dances at various periods after the death, called *a'bị*, all of which may last for several days.

The dances are danced by both men and women, separately, although the main dances in the centre of the arena are mostly by men only, those of the women being on the periphery. Much beer is drunk, and since men carry spears and arrows, there is almost always an outbreak of fighting. In the dance men stand by genera- tion, not by genealogical segment. The team may be of a lineage of any span, depending on the lineage distance between it and the lineage of the dead man. Fighting arises from co-ordinate lineages trying to dance first, according to seniority. The seniority of segments depends on the birth order of their apical ancestors, and the same order is rarely accepted by all segments; this is true especially after a death, when genealogical re-alignment is going on. The teams of dancers stand ready to enter the arena as the previous lineage's dances come to an end, and if one does not give way immediately there is fighting. In addition there may be fighting between segments within the dancing lineage itself. Men of the same generation, but of different segments, dance side by side, leaping up and down. To jolt one's neighbour is accepted as a reason for brawling and even for fighting with weapons, although the latter is sinful if between members of the same minor lineage.

Death dances are not solemn occasions. There is much flirting and seducing of girls, and it is recognized as an occasion for this. Since dances may continue for days and nights at a stretch, with the drums never stopping, many of the participants are in a trance-like condition. Normally expected behaviour, except for formal giving of hospitality, may be completely relaxed. Lubgara recognize this:

Death has destroyed the words, a big man is dead and we are like children with no one to help us. Our territory is destroyed.

I have often been told by young men that it is at these dances that they can meet and seduce clan sisters whom they cannot marry; it is considered rather dashing to do this. I have also been told that it is here that 'young men are shown who are their clan sisters', and that it is because people are 'like children' who do not recognize ties of kinship that fighting may occur between close agnates.

Death dances are the occasion for the recognition of the realignment of ties within a constellation of kin after the death of a person at its centre. In them the ties that are formally stressed are those that cut across lineage affiliation. Although groups come to dance as lineages, it is their kinship relationships that are stressed. People say 'here are our mother's brother's people come to dance', and not 'here are the people of such and such a lineage come to dance'. Men of the same generation dance together and generations should succeed each other. The almost expected clan incest and fighting between agnates are part of the same emphasis. Lineage relationships are being realigned and incest is one of the most frequent reasons given for fission or segmentation of distantly related lineages. Out of seven cases of segmentation at the sub-clan level of which I have information, in four incest was given as the reason—or rationalization—for segmentation; of these three were said to have taken place at death dances. In many other cases when it was known that such incest had been committed, but when there was no subsequent segmentation, the incest was not thought significant and soon forgotten.

In brief, realignment is decided inside the dying man's hut during his last words, and later at the dances when it is formally stressed that lineage differences should be forgotten and generation unity emphasized. The lineage alignment that has been accepted hitherto, and has been maintained by the dead man's authority, may no longer be accepted and lineages struggle to claim seniority over their fellow-lineages at this time of uncertainty. Death dances provide both a climax as well as a beginning to competition waged during the lifetime of a senior man.

After the burial and the death dances the soul has to be brought into a permanent relationship with the living. This relationship has its physical focus at the shrine erected for it, according to its status (ghost, ancestor, and so on). The bringing of the soul into this relationship with the living consists of three main parts: contacting the soul, settling any anger it may still feel towards the living, and erecting the shrine. Sometimes these are all done on a single occasion, sometimes they are done separately with days, weeks or months between them. In theory, much depends on whether sickness worries the deceased's immediate kin after his death. It also depends upon the energy of the family concerned, on whether they have the necessary livestock, food and beer, and also on the time needed—much therefore depends on the time of death in the farming cycle. In addition, the rites are more usually done together in the case of a junior man, who is not likely to contact his living kin because he bears grudges against them, than in the case of a senior, whom people fear and who is expected to show his anger to them in some way fairly soon after his death.

The soul is contacted when the dead man's successor dreams of him or if sickness comes upon his homestead and seems to come from him. It is, in fact, assumed to do so unless there is any other obvious cause of sickness, such as a recent curse. In the case of sickness the successor consults the rubbing-stick oracle and is told that the soul of the dead man should be contacted; in the case of a dream no oracle is consulted, as the reason is self-evident. Contact can be made only by a diviner, a woman who may contact the souls of the dead by means of a divining gourd. This is done at the rite known as *orindi ti zizu*, 'contacting the mouth of the soul', that is, contacting its 'words',[1] or 'contacting the soul in the house' (or shrine) *orindi jo alia zizu*. It is also known as 'raising the man who has died', *agu drapi 'bori engazu*.

If there is no sickness the diviner merely contacts the soul, ensures that it has no grudges against the living, and the simple rite of 'putting the ghost hut' (*orijo 'bazu*) is performed. But if contact is the result of sickness the ritual is more complicated, since the sickness must be cured and the soul put at ease before anything can be done about placing a shrine for it. What is done in this case is in fact often done even if there is no sickness but if the dead man's kin quarrelled with him before his death and the quarrel was not resolved by the time he died—usually by his last words. The rite is performed in order to prevent later sickness— one of the very few rites of propitiation in Lugbara. Sickness in this case is typically a sudden sickness that takes his successor or one of his family, or it may take the next child of one of his widows—it is thus usually a year or so after his death.

In the case of Ondua he had made up the quarrel between himself and Olimani at his last words. Oguda told me that there were still outstanding quarrels with Draai and with Yekule, in spite of

---

[1] This refers to its speaking through the diviner as a medium.

the latter being the successor (this is common; of fourteen cases I know of a son succeeding his father as elder, in ten of them it was said that there was none the less an outstanding quarrel between the son and his dead father, a clear indication of one of the areas of kinship tension). A month or two later Yekule dreamt of his father, and later still Draai's wife was suddenly sick. In both cases it was accepted as self-evident that Ondua's soul was trying to show that these quarrels should be composed. Draai went to an oracle operator, but Yekule did not, although Oguda told me that he should have done. Yekule's quarrel was said to be that he had married his first wife against Ondua's wishes, since the bride-wealth wanted was too high. Oguda had sided with Yekule, saying that it was good that the future mother of a future elder should be a woman of some standing and personal worth. In the rite in which Yekule was involved Oguda therefore also took part, although he had not dreamt of Ondua.

I need not give details of the rites here. In both a diviner (not the same woman in the two cases) contacted the soul with her gourd, and Ondua's voice was heard to speak through her to say that he was troubled because of 'words' that had not 'finished'. The voice did not say that the quarrels were forgiven, but the mere fact of contact with the soul was sufficient. In both cases the diviner then slaughtered a ram (the soul was then with God and so a beast associated with God was used), and its blood was used by her to anoint on the sternum members of the immediate families concerned. She then set up a small shrine, also called *orindi tị zịzu*, on the verandah of Yekule's mother's hut, in his case, and on that of Draai's first wife, in his case. Unsqueezed beer was poured over the stones. She then left. The remainder of the rite was that of 'cleansing the body' from sickness or the threat of sickness. This should be done by the elder of the minimal lineage, who again anoints the members of the compound on the instep and sternum, and then sprinkles sheep's blood on the hut thresholds. He takes sacred grass and places it on the shrine. He then takes the leaves from the shrine, spits upon them, uses the leaves as a brush to anoint the chest and insteps of the members of the compound with his spittle; then he places the leaves on the shrine again, and if on the following morning they are still there, fresh and unsullied by hyena excrement, then it is known that God has shown that the soul has 'agreed' and is at peace.

In Yekule's case, the rite was performed by Oguda. This was because Yekule 'feared' to perform a rite so soon after his father's death. Since in these rites no offering is made at the ghost shrines, it is said that it is not important if the new elder does not himself perform the rites. In the case of Draai's rite, however, there was serious dispute as to who should supervise it. Draai claimed that he should do so, and Oguda claimed that either he or Yekule should, since Ondua had not stated in his last words that Draai should become an independent elder. After much acrimonious discussion it was agreed that Oguda should also perform this rite. This was done, but only after it had been reported by Cakida, the rainmaker, an elder whose lineage is not closely related to Araka, that many omens had been seen near his rain-grove; since he had attended Ondua's last words this was accepted as a sign from Ondua's soul, and Draai was persuaded to relinquish his claim for independence. Omens are signs of God's will, but in this case Cakida said that since the soul was with God, and since as yet no shrine was erected for it, the omens in fact came from Ondua. This is one of the few cases I know in which a rainmaker concerned himself with the internal affairs or another lineage, other than by supervising or attending rites of 'cleansing the territory', to which rainmakers are usually called. But I was told that Cakida was right in so doing, because 'rainmakers know the words of God: that is their work'.

Later Draai himself told me that he had regarded this sickness as a sign that Ondua had intended him to become an independent elder. He said that at his last words Ondua had 'forgotten' to say this, and that to show him by sending sickness was the only way in which he, as a soul, could tell people that this was what he in fact intended. Although Oguda scoffed at this remark, Olimani maintained that 'perhaps' this claim was justified. Clearly this would have strengthened Olimani's own claims. But opinion was against Draai and he was still forced to accept Yekule's ritual authority.

At this rite the new shrine may also be erected. The diviner, she who contacted the soul, asks the soul whether it is willing to drink beer at the new shrine, and so become a ghost. It is said that on this day the 'father' enters the home, whereas until now he has been outside. The dead man is always formally asked, but I know of no case of refusal. His acceptance is a sign of his own new status as a ghost but also of his approval of his successor's new status. The owner of the compound then erects the shrine, and makes a sacrifice to it in the usual way on later occasions, when sickness is believed to come from the ghost in question. In Araka Yekule erected a shrine for Ondua at the same time as the rites I have just described; but Draai did not do so. It was said that if he had done so it would be a sign that he accepted the ritual guardianship of Ondua, and he refused to do this; but it was added that sooner or later he would do so, when he was struck by sickness sent by Ondua.

Case 34

When I finally left Araka, some months after the death of Ondua, Olimani was regarded as the elder of a new minimal lineage, Nyaai. He had already been invited to attend two sacrifices made by men of the lineages Ambidro and Ombavu, the co-ordinate lineages of Araka. He had taken Otoro as his ritual assistant, thus ensuring that for a time at any rate Otoro's aspirations were silenced. He had also made a sacrifice at the external lineage shrine. Okwaya told me that at first he had 'feared' to do this so soon after the death of Ondua, even though Ondua's soul had been contacted and a shrine erected for him by Yekule. He had decided to sacrifice at the lineage shrine as a consequence of his own sickness. The sickness was a general one affecting Nyaai as a single group. Olimani told me himself:

Now the ancestors are angry and we have 'bad luck'. Where are our cattle? Where are our granaries? Long ago we here had many cattle, our fathers sent their cattle here and over there in Nyoro (for grazing, a mile or two away). They had many girls (as lovers). Then their wives harvested much millet and the granaries were full. Our fathers sat there (under the granaries) and their hearts were good. But now we have bad luck, sickness has struck us here. Where are our cattle? Our fields here are small, and we harvest only weeds. Those men of Lari'ba there have destroyed the words of our fathers. Our fathers have not eaten (at the shrines) for a long time, now it is good that we give them food, that they should say 'Truly, our children feed us now, their hearts are good and they follow our words', then their anger will end.

The hostility between the two segments is expressed here, Olimani claiming that Ondua had been responsible for the troubles of Araka. Okwaya told me, later, after this statement of Olimani:

Truly, perhaps Ondua was a witch. Men say that he has walked there (in Lari'ba) as a spectre (I heard no such report in Lari'ba). Now Olimani is 'big', he is to offer food to the ancestors, to show them that his words are good, that truly he is an elder. Now we here his children are glad in our hearts. We here are big now.

He added:

Olimani has feared to give food (at the external lineage shrine) because of the words of Ondua. It is good to fear (or respect) a man who has died. But Olimani's heart is strong. We follow him, and the ancestors are glad that he is now big. Our ancestors and those ancestors of Lari'ba also, they all rejoice in their hearts that we here give them food. Then they will send us many girls. . . . We here will be like Sultans (government chiefs); our words will be strong.

It is interesting that here Okwaya is using the word, 'strong' for Olimani, a term which implies that Olimani is perhaps capable of using witchcraft. It would perhaps not be too much to say that during this period, as segmentation was actually being recognized, that there was a general feeling of euphoria within Nyaai. It could almost be said that after Ondua's death and Olimani's claim to independence he and his dependants were fearful of their new status, and that Olimani's sacrificing at the lineage shrines marked a resurgence of confidence.

Olimani went to consult the rubbing-stick oracle of his friend in Mjrjdrj. He then offered a goat at the external lineage shrine shared by Araka, Ambidro and Ombavu. Lari'ba was represented by Yekule and Oguda (but without Draai, who refused to attend save as an elder in his own right). This was the only occasion at a sacrifice at which I witnessed open argument as to details of genealogy. Whereas before the five lineages Araka, Ambidro, Ombavu, Mitika and Nyaai[1] (the first three being the 'true' lineages of the minor lineage Kimiru), had attended one another's external sacrifices as co-ordinate lineages, their alignment had now altered. There were now six co-ordinate lineages, Lari'ba, Nyaai, Ambidro, Ombavu, Mitika and the other Nyaai. When Olimani made his ritual address, which was extremely short (as Okwaya told me, he 'feared' to say many words when it actually came to the point), he stated that the founder of Nyaai, Licu, was the son of Sambala. This meant that Licu was the brother of Ombasa, the

[1] See Figure 4, and page 141, fn. 1.

founder of Araka, instead of his son, as had been accepted in the past by Ondua. Thus Olimani stated that not only were Lari'ba and Nyaai equal in status, which had of course always been accepted, but that his mystical powers of eldership were of equal antiquity with those of Ondua and his son Yekule. Oguda interrupted to deny this, as he felt 'shame' to hear this statement. Olimani stated that he was right, since it was Licu to whom he was primarily making the oblation, and with him on this occasion in the shrine was Sambala. Sambala is far enough back genealogically for him to be vitally important in this respect. Although the founder of all Maraca is accepted as having been Cereki, Sambala has almost gained the status of the founder of a sub-clan, Sambalaanzi, 'the children of Sambala', are already an exogamous group, and it is clear that Maraca will divide into three separate tribes, Sambala being the founder of one of the three associated sub-clans. He is therefore important as giving mythical validation to the sacrifice, as he is already more than a mere ancestor. Since it is usual for the two incumbents of an external lineage shrine to be father and son (although this is not invariably so), Licu had to be considered as Sambala's son. This would emphasize not only the independence of Nyaai but also its seniority in its own right; in addition Olimani implied that Ondua should have allowed Nyaai its independence before.

In his ritual address Olimani also maintained that the sons of Licu were not Toba, Goloko and Avuye, as 'had usually been accepted, but Toba only. Toba was given as having 'begotten' Cakida, Aliti, Goloko, Avuye and 'perhaps' Pokoni, the ancestor about whom there was always been some uncertainty. 'Begetting', *ti*, may be used to refer both to physical begetting and to succession to authority; by this Olimani had thus placed Otoro and Obitre down a generation, to the level of Edre and Olimani's own son Omba, who will be his successor as elder.

The actual order of performance of the rites I have described in Randra was as follows:

Case		Process	Sacrificer
1	March	Ghostly vengeance	Ondua for self
18	,,	*A'bįva*	Otoro for wife
2	,,	Ghost invocation by Ondua	Oguda for grandson
26	,,	*Lucugo*	Benyu for wife

Case		Process	Sacrificer
3	April	Ghost invocation by Olimani	Obitre for self
28	,,	*Adro-ori*	Okwaya for self
23	May	*Talɨ*	Ondua for self
4	,,	Ghost invocation by Olimani	Otoro for daughter
29	,,	*Oku-ori*	Olimani for self
21	,,	*Anguvua*	Ondua for self
27	June	*Lucugo*	Obitre for wife
5	,,	Ghost invocation by Draai	Draai for son
24	,,	*Talɨ*	Olimani for grandson
6	,,	*Andesia*	Yekule for wife
7	July	Ghost invocation by Olimani	Olimani for son
19	,,	*A'bɨva*	Njima for daughter
8	,,	Ghost invocation by Ondua, Olimani and Oguda	Benyu for wife
9	,,	Ghostly vengeance	Olimani for self
10	August	Ghost invocation by Olimani	Olimani for wife
11	,,	*Andesia*	Benyu for self
12	,,	Ghost invocation by Ondua	Draai for wife
13	,,	Ghost invocation by Ondua	Olimani for self
25	Sept.	*Talɨ*	Draai for son
14	Oct.	*Eralengbo*	Olimani
22	,,	*Anguvua*	Olimani for wife
31	Nov.	*Ajµalɨrɨ*	Ondua
15	Dec.	*Angu edezu*	Ondua for Draai
16	Jan.	Ghost invocation by Olimani	Edre for wife
17	Feb.	External lineage shrine	Ondua
20	,,	*A'bɨva*	Edre for son
32	,,	*Yakani*	Ondua
30	March	*Rogbo*	Oguda for self
33	April	Mortuary rites for Ondua	
34	July of following year	External lineage shrine	Olimani

III. RITUAL AND THE EXERCISE OF AUTHORITY

From these cases it is clear that ghost invocation is usually a response to disputes over authority. These may reflect underlying factors such as shortage of land and increase in population.

Lugbara quarrel intermittently, but on the whole only those disputes which are structurally important lead to the processes of ghost invocation and ghostly vengeance. It is noticeable that where the invoker is senior to the sick person, who is in a relationship of dependence, the reasons given for invocation are usually disobedience to proper authority exercised by the living; whereas when the parties are equal in generation or age-status the reason usually given is impiety and refusal to make sufficiently frequent offerings to the dead; or the sickness may strike a child or wife, as 'representative' for the father or husband, in which case the offence may be expressed as one of disobedience to paternal or marital authority.

The ten cases of ghost invocation from Araka may be classified as follows:

3 were cases of invocation for disobedience of authority within the elementary family (Cases 5, 7, 10).

4 were cases of invocation by the elder, with or without joint invocation by heads of segments who are of his own generation. Of these one, Case 13, was directly against a rival would-be elder, 2 were against wives of heads of segments (Cases 8, 12), and one was against a brother's grandson (Case 2). The wives and grandson were, however, representatives of the heads of their segments, against whom the exercise of elder's authority was really directed.

3 were by Olimani, the would-be elder of a new segment, against the dependants or heads of segments under his authority (Cases 3, 4, 16).

Two points should be made. One is that some of the cases of invocation for disobedience within the elementary family were in fact concerned with the struggles for authority between the elder and his rivals; they became structurally significant as foci for this rivalry. The other is that in almost all the other cases the real structural situation in which they occurred was that of this rivalry. Even though there was a difference in generation between elder and the sick person or the person whom the sick person represented, being heads of segments they are regarded in certain contexts as being of the elder's generation. These are Cases 8 and 16, where Benyu and Edre, although genealogically 'sons' of Ondua and Olimani, are regarded structurally as of their generation since their own fathers are dead and they have replaced them as heads of their own small family segments. So that seven of these ten cases in fact reflect rivalry between men of the same structural generation.

In addition, the cases of ghostly vengeance (Cases 1 and 9) were closely connected with lineage rivalry. The fact that the patients were Ondua and Olimani made it unlikely that ghost invocation would be given as a cause, on account of their 'shame'. And the case of 'cleansing the territory', (Case 15) was also connected with this rivalry.

It must be remembered that this very small sample consists only of those cases of which I have personal experience. In the previous year Olimani had invoked the ghosts against his 'sister's son' Njima, who lives across the stream, and such invocation might be expected. Thus I do not claim that the distribution of relationships in this small sample is that of the total range of cases of ghost invocation throughout Lugbara. There are often cases in which senior men are not concerned, or where the invoker is a woman or a child.

I have good information, mainly from direct observation, about 103 cases, in which the kinship relationships between invoker and invoked are as follows:

Father invokes against son	39, of which 21 were by an elder
Father against son's wife	20, of which 14 were by an elder
Brother against brother	16
Mother's brother against sister's son	9, of which 6 were in the same family cluster
Father against married daughter	5
Brother against brother's wife	4
Father against married daughter's child	4
Mother against son	2
Mother' brother against sister's son's wife	2, both within the same family cluster
Dead brother's son against father's brother	1
Sister's son against mother's brother	1, within the same family cluster

103 cases

I have telescoped classificatory kin. Of the 39 cases of invocation by a father against his son, only 11 were by a man against his own son, the others being against a brother's son (usually a dead brother's son) or other 'son' of the same minimal lineage. Likewise, of the 20 cases of invocation against a son's wife, only 9 were by a man against his own son's wife.

The most frequent cases were between father and son (and especially when the father was an elder), a man and his daughter-in-law (again, the invoker was usually an elder), between brothers, between a man and his sister's son (mostly in the same family cluster), and between a man and his married daughter or her child.

Of the 39 cases between a man and his son, 7 of the 21 invocations by an elder were against a living brother's son and 11 against a dead brother's son; in the latter cases the 'sons' were raised to the generation of their dead fathers. All these 18 cases were structurally directed against brother-rivals. The other 3 cases of invocation by an elder against a son were against his own sons. In the 18 cases by non-elders, 10 were against classificatory sons and 8 against own sons. Cases of invocation by non-elders were more concerned with authority within the domestic family, although it is probable that in some of them wider issues were in fact involved. Of the 20 cases involving invocation by a man against a son's wife, I know that 8 of the 14 involving invocation by an elder and 2 of the 6 involving invocation by a non-elder were in the 'structural' category of expression of dispute with a brother-rival. I think it fair to say that at the least half of these 103 cases were in fact concerned with segmental rivalries.·

In the brief account of the history of Araka minimal lineage at the beginning of this chapter, certain phases in a cycle of development may be distinguished. They can be distinguished in the history of several other lineages also, and I consider that in this respect the history of Araka is typical of that of all Lugbara lineages, although there are obviously differences in emphasis, certain phases being more stressed in some cases, and perhaps even being omitted in others. The phases fall into a pattern of which the salient features are:

1. Distribution of authority and genealogical relationships correspond closely.

2. Conflicts of interest arise within domestic families, mainly as a consequence of the marriages of sons who want livestock and

land. These are resolved by the exercise of authority by the heads of families, who allocate land and livestock, this allocation being accepted without any overt questioning. All segments have equal rights in the land of the whole minimal lineage, which is allocated under the general authority of the lineage elder. The distribution of authority is accepted by all members.

3. Conflicts of authority begin to arise, both between the elder and heads of segments, and between heads of families and their junior brothers and their sons. Typically the factors that cause these conflicts include increase of population, decreasing fertility of land, and changes in the distribution of seniority and juniority resulting from deaths of older men and maturing of young men. Conflicts can no longer so easily be settled within the existing authority-structure. As the authority of senior men is questioned, these have to use the authority of the dead, whose representatives they are, to enforce their own authority and to maintain their status *vis-à-vis* their juniors. At this stage there is also some movement of junior men away from the group to attach themselves elsewhere as tenants and clients (and at any stage there may be an influx of 'sisters' sons' and other tenants, whose presence may exacerbate the shortage of land and alter the balance of authority).

4. Conflicts of authority increase in seriousness and frequency. Conflict is expressed in two ways: in competition for the support of the dead, between the heads of component segments, rather than between senior and junior men only; and by accusations of witchcraft, at first covert and later overt, against the elder and the senior men by those over whom they exercise authority. The elder in particular tries to maintain the authority-structure as it was in phase 1, mainly in ritual terms by obtaining the support of the dead for his actions.

5. Segmentation occurs, typically at the death of the elder. There is then a re-distribution of authority and a re-ordering of genealogies. This last phase may be postponed by the hiving off of segments who move away elsewhere, in order to acquire more land and to escape the authority of the elder.

There are many variations on this development pattern. In a lineage that does not increase in numbers there will still be conflicts of authority as old men die and young men mature, but there may not be segmentation. I know of a few such cases, and it seems that in general the lineage sooner or later dissolves, its segments attaching themselves to other lineages and the rump becoming a remnant lineage. But such lineages are in a minority at the present time. What is important is that offences which involve disobedience to proper genealogically supported authority tend to be considered 'bad deeds' (*yeta onzi*) at phase 2 and as 'sins' (*ezata*) in phase 3 and especially in phase 4.

The ritual history of any lineage may be understood only within this framework of change. I have spoken of the history of Araka largely in terms of competition and ambition, and I now discuss this process of change in the distribution of authority, as it is recognized and validated by the performance of sacrifices to the dead.

Lugbara realize that men are ambitious and want authority. They also realize that it is proper for them to do so, but that some men try to acquire authority which they should not possess and that others abuse it when they have acquired it. We cannot see the structure of any lineage as something static, although usually Lugbara see the total structure of their society as being so. Old men die, and young men grow socially mature; to say that men are ambitious for authority is merely to state these facts in individual, psychological terms. For a man not to feel ambitious in this sense would mark him out as an immature person. Lugbara have no age-set system, but they recognize age-grades, associated with which are certain modes of behaviour. An unmarried man is a youth, after marriage he becomes a 'big youth'. A man who grows old unmarried is an anomaly, and is considered as a witch. I have known only two such men, who were regarded with suspicion and ridicule; even though old they are said to be 'children' and unfit to offer sacrifice to the ancestors; after their death they would, of course, soon be forgotten. Likewise it is assumed that by the time a man becomes middle-aged, with adult children, he will be the head of a distinct segment and will exercise the authority considered proper to such a status. Junior full-brothers, however, cannot do this, but are able to acquire status in other ways, such as becoming oracle operators; today it is my impression that such men have a higher tendency than others to become Christians, and also to stay away for longer periods as labour migrants, even becoming 'lost' by never returning from migration.[1] Later the heads of segments may expect to become elders. Clearly, only a

[1] Out of 67 cases of 'lost' migrants, 32 were junior full-brothers of senior men.

minority can do so unless the lineage increases rapidly in numbers, but the high rate of hiving off of lineage segments to settle elsewhere in almost all parts of Lugbara is related to this factor. It is accepted that men who can see that they may never become elders tend to move and settle with uterine and other kin elsewhere. The rate of attachment of families in this way would seem to be far higher than mere agricultural necessity would dictate, and the fact that segments are typically said to move 'because of quarrelling' supports this hypothesis.

Only people who are in certain genealogical positions are able to increase their status. Status within the lineage and the family cluster is measured mainly by the possession of shrines of various types, as I have mentioned in Chapter II.

Those who already exercise authority, the elder, the heads of larger segments and the heads of families, wish to retain it. It is the duty of the elder to do so, and a weak elder is scorned. The head of a family exercises authority of a different kind from that of the more senior men, and it is said that a man expects his sons to leave him and to become independent domestically, but he compensates for that by at the same time becoming more senior himself and acquiring a measure of lineage authority in other than merely domestic situations.

As I have shown for Araka, Lugbara are themselves quite aware of the underlying tensions involved and also of the underlying motives of men who use ghost invocation as a weapon for the maintenance of their authority or for the acquisition of authority. Yet invocation is conceived in terms of the maintenance of personal authority over a specific individual who has tried to flout it, that is, in terms of personal kinship.

Disputes that are significant for the lineage are in terms of the maintenance of authority between the living and between the living and the dead. Ties of descent are seen to a large extent in the same terms: one obeys one's 'father', who has authority over his 'children'. Ties of lineage change as do those of authority. The former are constructs by which men conceive of relationships that last over time, over generations. The latter are matters of social reality; they change on the ground, in everyday life, and the conception of patterns of lineage organization and kinship change in response.

Certain ties of kinship are mainly domestic in this context.

These include those of husband-wife, father-daughter, father-son while the son is unmarried, senior brother-junior brother while the junior is unmarried, and grandfather-grandson while the latter is unmarried. Also most authority exercised by women is domestic only. The authority of a man over his sister's child is rarely significant in lineage matters, since even if a sister's son living as an attached 'stranger' moves away it does not harm the lineage to any great degree. The structurally more significant relations are those of father-son when the latter is adult and of brother-brother. These contain much tension and ambivalence. They are also the subjects of maxims and proverbs that stress the harmony of interest in them and which inveigh against rivalry or hostility that may nevertheless cynically be admitted to exist.

The relationship of father to son is both an individual one between members of a domestic family and also one between a segment head, a representative of the dead, and a junior in the lineage. That between brothers is both a close tie between equals and also one between an elder and a subordinate (since there can be only one elder in a minimal lineage) or between heads of segments who are vying with one another to become the sole elder. Tension may arise from these conflicts in role. A father should feel affection for his son yet he must sometimes punish him. In his domestic role a father may beat or scold his son, to 'teach' him. In his lineage role a father should invoke the ghosts against him. The former is a private affair in which only the two individuals are concerned. The latter is a lineage matter involving sacrifice to the ghosts and the gathering of lineage kin; everyone over a wide area knows about it and discusses it. For a man to bring this upon his son is not easy. It means perhaps bringing serious sickness upon him. He risks the displeasure of his son and of his wife's kin, who are probably only too ready to seize upon it as a sign of his bad qualities as a husband and father; he risks his son's and affines' accusations of abusing his powers and so being a witch, and also risks the disapproval of other kin and neighbours who may make similar accusations. The changing of the role of domestic father for that of lineage senior is difficult and may lead to serious disruption of the unity of his family. The same applies, though perhaps to lesser extent, to the relationship between a man and a classificatory 'son'; here, although it may be easier for him personally, the risks of accusations of abuse of his power are greater.

And it must be emphasized that if a man does not invoke against his son when he should, he risks losing the support of the dead for his authority as their representative. It is said that a father must sometimes say 'I cannot strike with my hand, the ghosts must strike for me.' In the cases from Araka, there were two invocations of the ghosts by men against their own sons, by Draai (Case 5) and by Olimani (Case 7). In both of them the reasons given were that the sons behaved in a way likely to harm the segment and the lineage by refusing to share their labour earnings: to share wealth among the members of one's lineage is one of the primary obligations of lineage membership. But in both cases there were undertones, in that the invokers were using these offences as pretexts in order to show that they had ghostly support for their pretensions to higher status. During my stay there were plenty of other quarrels between fathers and adult sons, but none of them led to ghost invocation. Both Ondua and Oguda quarrelled with their sons, but settled them 'by striking with their tongues' and bringing shame to bear on them; Ondua in addition enlisted his wife's brother to correct his son's behaviour.

The relationship between brothers should be one of affection, protection and sharing as equals; Lugbara do not distinguish in terminology between elder and younger brothers. Yet within the system of lineage authority a man must exercise authority over his brothers, both real and classificatory. Much of what I have said about the father-son relationship applies also to that between brothers.

Part of the conflict comes from the opposition within the lineage of ties based upon generation and those based upon lineal descent. This opposition is found, of course, in all segmentary lineage systems. Father and son form a single unit *vis-à-vis* members of other descent lines, and the same applies to sets of brothers. The exercise of authority, on the other hand, part of the system of internal administration of any group, is of necessity between persons whose statuses are arranged hierarchically. In the Lugbara family cluster it is exercised between generations, as far as relations between agnates are concerned. Lugbara recognize this in the terminology used between brothers. A man with authority over his brothers (especially classificatory brothers by different fathers) refers to them as 'brothers' (*adrɨezi* or *adrɨpɨ*) in some contexts and as 'sons' (*anzi*) in those of lineage authority. In the telling of genealogies Lugbara use the verb *tị* for to 'beget', the relationship between father and son; it is also used for the relation between brothers where these succeeded one another. In the genealogy of Araka, for example, it is said that the lineage founder, Ombasa, '*tị Oraa pị Licu be*' ('begot Oraa and Licu'). But it may also be said that '*Ombasa tị Oraa; Oraa tị Licu*', since the eldership of the lineage passed from Ombasa to Oraa and then to Licu. What we consider generational differences are not always recognized by Lugbara, as when a man whose father dies may be raised a generation in the sphere of lineage authority to take his father's place; and likewise generational equality may not be recognized either in situations of authority.

Junior kin must accept the authority of their seniors in domestic matters. And they must accept that of the dead. But their position is not so clear in relations and situations that are not domestic only. They must accept the authority of the elder in matters that affect the well-being of the family cluster. But there seems always to be conflict as to the extent of obedience to the authority of other senior men. This is so especially in the case of junior men who are married and attempting to show their ritual independence and to show that they are the heads of small segments that may later develop into large segments and even lineages. The conflict takes two forms: what is the proper sphere of authority of senior men, and what is the identity of the dead who send sickness for offences by the living? The line between matters that are primarily domestic and those that are primarily of importance to the lineage is a fine one. Today older men bemoan the fact that young men go to work as labour migrants, return with money and then refuse to share it among their kin. The young men retort that the older men wish merely to drink it away whereas they wish to use it for taxes and bridewealth. This conflict is hardly a new one, although it takes this new form. As each young man grows adult and becomes a full member of the society the small segment consisting of himself, his wives and children, and perhaps his brothers, becomes in his view a separate entity. But his elders do not usually consider this segment as such to be separate, and his aspirations are seen by them as merely disruptive and directed at weakening their authority. These aspirations and the opposition to them are played out largely in ritual terms. The younger man can acquire status, which is validated in terms of the system itself and cannot be taken away from him, by the possession of junior ghost or ancestral shrines, or both. To do this he must be given sickness by the dead. This sickness must come directly from them, as part of the process of ghostly vengeance. This shows first that he has not been invoked against by his seniors, so is to an extent free of their authority, and also that the dead regard him as the head of a small segment or at least as an adult person in his own right. Almost all the cases of sacrifice at the *andesia* and *a'bjva* shrines made in Araka were by men in this position. There is often opposition from senior holders of authority against this interpretation of the sickness. The oracular interpretation of the situation is, of course, the vital part of the process, and, as in Araka, there is usually considerable competition as to who shall be chosen to consult the oracles. Here however, the authority holders have both the right and the duty to consult them.

This conflict is repeated at higher levels of authority. When a man dies, his son takes over his generation status in the lineage, if he inherits the shrines. The elder brother inherits the father's senior shrines, and the junior can set up only junior shrines. There is usually little conflict between the brothers in their own generation, since the tie between them is very close and only comparatively rarely do they dispute for authority. But in the following generation their sons may dispute, since by then they may all be the heads of segments of some size. Thus in Lari'ba, Abiria is said to have quarrelled with Dria, and in the second generation Draai has quarrelled with Ondua. Status is achieved mainly by showing that such a man is able to invoke the ghosts, against his own dependants, thus demonstrating that he is considered a responsible and mature man by the ghosts, who listen to his invocation. Once it is accepted that a man has authority over a large segment—the acceptance being also shown by his being treated as such in the distribution of sacrificial meat and by his being allowed to make ritual addresses—then he is regarded as equal in generation to the elder in most situations of lineage authority. This was the case in Araka with Olimani, and on some occasions with Draai and Otoro, whose position was not yet firmly accepted. There are lineages in which the elder is much older in years and also senior in generation to the heads of any segment. In this case the situation is rather different, and it may be expected that segmentation will not occur for some time. This state of affairs is, however, usually consistent with recent segmentation: it would be the situation, for example, if Araka were to split into four segments, headed by Yekule, Draai, Olimani and Otoro.

Even though the heads of segments may be regarded as equal in generation to the elder, they are not yet equal in authority. Only the elder is the direct representative of the dead, and only he may sacrifice at the external lineage shrine. But for him to invoke the ghosts against the segment heads directly would bring 'shame' to them and he would be open to charges of witchcraft for abusing his position. A man can invoke the dead against a junior, in terms of kinship, but not against a 'brother', except in only the most serious situations of stress. The history of Araka shows very clearly how Ondua was on several occasions willing to accept Olimani's attempts to show independence by consulting oracles and performing sacrifices on his own, rather than to shame him by bringing the dispute between them into the open. In this situation sickness tends to strike at wives or children of heads of segments, who are thought to represent their husbands or fathers. Some of the Araka cases show this: Case 2, in which Oguda's grandson was sick whereas the offence was committed by Oguda himself; Case 4, in which Otoro's daughter was sick on account of his offences; Case 8 in which Benyu's wife was sick because of Benyu's behaviour; and Case 16, in which Edre's wife was sick on account of her husband's actions. Edre is not of the status of the others, but this principle was still operative, since the invoker was Olimani, not the elder Ondua. In all these cases, however, the true situation was made explicit at the oracular consultations.

As heads of segments grow more senior, and if conditions of population and ecology lead to disputes about the distribution of land and wealth, so does the rate of what are basically disputes between 'brothers' of accepted equal generation increase. The elder may invoke the ghosts against these equals, although it is unusual (Ondua did so against Olimani in Case 13), but he does so more generally against their dependants; he may attempt to control the oracles so that sickness which heads of segments claim to follow from their invocation is in fact shown to have come from him as elder (Cases 12 and 13), thus showing that he has greater ghostly support; he may sacrifice at the external lineage shrine, at which only he may perform rites and whose incumbents send sickness only by ghostly vengeance; this sickness is usually not directed against a specific individual but is a general malaise affecting the whole group, thus showing that the ghosts are worried about the threats to the elder's authority. And he may also ensure that the oracles reveal that on some occasions members of the offending men's segments are sick because of ghostly vengeance sent by their direct lineal ancestors, or because of invocation of these ancestors by the elder. The invocation of collateral ghosts by the elder is an important demonstration that he is supported by the dead.

A man usually invokes the ghosts who are nearest to him—his father, father's brother, or earlier ghosts of the same agnatic descent line. But in his shrines are also the ghosts of collateral lines of agnatic ancestors. A man is less likely to invoke these, it is thought, or rather it is thought they are unlikely to 'hear his words'. An elder is likely to suggest their names to the oracles for several reasons. Perhaps the most usual is merely to supply enough suspects: it is said to be bad to put only one or two names to the oracles, and so other names considered are those ghosts who already have shrines placed for them. They may be angry because of inattention, and, as I have said, Lugbara consider that all shrines should be given offerings regularly lest they become jealous of one another. This is a stock explanation for the occurrence of ghostly vengeance when there seems to be no justifiable reason for anyone to have invoked the ghosts against the sick person. Another reason that he may suggest collateral ghosts, which he would be unlikely to invoke himself, if the patient is of another descent line than his own, is in order to draw attention to impious behaviour on the part of the head of the collateral segment, behaviour which would not justify the elder's invoking his own line of ghosts, either because he might be accused of personal spite or because the segment head is a man of his own age. The ghosts pointed out by the oracles, in this case, are likely to be those of the offender's own descent line. The mystical process involved may be that of ghostly vengeance and not ghost invocation at all, if it is the rival himself who is sick. Only a rash, arrogant or desperate elder would admit to invocation in such a case. If, however, the sick man is a dependant of the rival then the oracles may decree ghost invocation by the elder of his own ghosts. This is tantamount to saying that the rival is not considered senior enough by the ghosts to look after his own dependants and that the elder has done this for him. By producing this verdict from the oracles the elder deals a blow at the segment head concerned, who receives 'shame' from it. The latter cannot openly deny it since the elder would not have put the ghost's name to the oracle without the excuse of some action which may easily be represented as impious or anti-social, since it is so decreed by the oracles.

It is obviously difficult to provide evidence for an elder's motives, since they are largely inexplicit. But Lugbara have often hinted to me that an elder may 'deceive' the ghosts to harm a senior man of his lineage of whom he is jealous because he is trying to break away and to become an elder himself. It is put in terms of 'deceiving' the ghosts since it is axiomatic that on the whole neither elders nor oracles lie deliberately over these matters. For example, in Case 12, Ondua had invoked the ghosts against Draai's wife. The ghost invoked, who 'heard' the thoughts of invocation, was Draai's father Abiria. By this verdict the oracles showed that even Abiria wished to 'show' his own son by listening to the words of the head of the other, main line of descent, that of Moro. On this occasion Draai at first refused to believe the oracle, but when it was confirmed by the second oracle, he had to accept it publicly. I heard later that he was saying that Ondua had 'deceived' the oracles in the matter. It would have been expected that Ondua could convince the ghost of his own father, Dria, and also those of Moro and even Oraa, of the justification of his invocation. But if Abiria also listened to him, this was indeed a sign of his superior authority. There are other examples (Cases 3, 4, 8, 13, and 16).

I have also had many hints that elders may subconsciously make suggestions to the oracles that reflect their knowledge of tensions and dislikes within the lineage. This is also obvious in the way that an elder gives hypothetical examples of the various processes of ghostly sickness. Generally they use the names of members of their own kin-groups as examples, and in every case which I have noted the examples given clearly reflected the tensions and latent quarrels within the group, of which the elder was, of course, aware. In Araka the examples given of people who made discord were almost invariably Draai, Otoro and Jobi. The former two were leaders of factions against established lineage authority, and the latter was a good-for-nothing and insolent youth, a glaring example of filial impiety. The suggestions made to the oracles naturally reflected this knowledge. And, of course, good oracle operators may know of these dislikes, or may find them out during the consultation; in this way public opinion is communicated to the oracles and reflected in their diagnoses.

An elder tries to assert his authority mainly by showing that the ghosts do not accept his rival as being a man of sufficient responsibility. Either he invokes against his rival's dependants or even against the rival himself, an insulting procedure when the rival is of the same generation as himself; or he shows that the ghosts themselves have humbled his rival for his lack of piety, by sending ghostly vengeance. The obverse of this, of course, is that a rival tries to show that the ghosts do accept him as a responsible man who is fit to be an elder. He does this in various ways. First he may consult the oracles himself on behalf of his dependants, so cutting out the existing elder from participation in the process. The oracles may say—at his suggestion—that the would-be elder has himself invoked and that his invocation has been 'heard' and approved by them. There is nothing unusual in this, but if he can show that the sickness and so the occasion for it are both serious, and if he can do this frequently, then it is a sign of considerable authority. Draai had done this, in Case 5, and on earlier occasions as well. Secondly, he will back this up by making his own sacrifices, omitting to call the elder. If he consecrates a beast, promising to sacrifice it if the patient recovers, and if the beast urinates and shows God's approval and then the patient does recover, it is a sign that the ghosts have approved of his pretensions to independent authority. He can thus show that he has the beginnings of ancestral support and approval and must set about winning that of his senior living kin by managing to get them to attend his sacrifices. This is perhaps a more difficult part of the process. Draai made his own sacrifice (Case 5), but he failed to get senior kin to attend (other than Ondua, whom he did not ask and whose attendance did not support him in the way he wanted). A third way is to try to show that any sickness within his own family segment that the elder may claim as the result of his own invocation is in fact due to ancestral vengeance, which is 'little' (that is, not so concerned with structural change and its associated sins), and not the result of invocation. Finally he may accuse the elder who maintains that he has invoked as a response to anti-social behaviour of being a witch and abusing his mystical powers.

A would-be elder therefore tries to invoke ghosts against his dependants frequently. That is to say, he interprets sickness that befalls members of his family segment in this way. If he can consult the oracles he tends to put suggestions to them that will lead to his own invocation being given as the cause. If he cannot consult them since the elder insists on doing so, then he may threaten his dependants that he will invoke the ghosts, and lets this be known publicly. It is then incumbent on the elder to put his name to the oracles. It will be remembered that usually a man does not openly threaten invocation. This is for several reasons: he may be taken for a witch (witches threaten by saying words such as 'you will see me' or 'we shall see these words'); and it is arrogant and ill-tempered to utter threats of this kind, since the ideal of elderly behaviour is to act quietly without losing one's temper. Usually a man does not admit to invoking until after the sickness appears, since until then he has only 'thought' in anger and does not know he has invoked until he is said to have done so by the oracles. It is hardly a sign of a responsible man to go about uttering threats against unruly dependants. We ourselves may think that a reason is that the threat may not be followed by sickness; but since Lugbara believe in the whole process this will not prevent a man from threatening.

As well as a would-be elder invoking, or claiming to invoke, frequently, an elder whose position is threatened is also liable to claim that he has invoked frequently against his dependants. As his authority is taken from him by his rivals, especially when he is either aged or unpopular, he tends to invoke more and more often. Clearly a vicious circle may be set up if he invokes for insufficient reason, and he will further lose popularity and show that he is losing his sense of responsibility. In short, a family cluster that is about to segment may be characterized by a high frequency of claims to ghost invocation, both by its elder and by the heads of its component segments. This is said by its members to show that all is not well with the group and that segmentation should take place to resolve the internal tensions and quarrels. The process reaches its most critical stage when sacrifices are made at fertility and external shrines, which are responses to a realization that orderly relations within the lineage have reached a stage of general disintegration, and when accusations of witchcraft under the guise of invocation start to be made against the elder.

Within the minimal lineage accusations of witchcraft are of two types: a son accuses his father who claims to have invoked the ghosts against him of being a witch; and a senior man claims that the elder, from whose authority he wishes to free himself, is a witch. I have quoted examples of both in Araka. These two types of accusation tend to occur at different stages within the development cycle of any given segment, whether a minimal lineage or a component family segment. Accusations by a son against a father —real or classificatory—occur mainly during the earlier stages; those between equals in generation occur mainly during the later stages. The former occurs when the person against whom the invocation is directed is passing from one age-grade or family status to a higher one. This generalization is supported by quantitative evidence and also by Lugbara statements about witchcraft. I have details of 39 cases of invocation by a father against a son, real or classificatory. Of these 24 were against sons who had two children and so were regarded as the heads of distinct households; 14 of these were said to have asserted that their invokers were using witchcraft against them instead of the accepted method of invocation. None of the remaining 15 sons was said to have made such accusations. Lugbara recognize this situation when they say

A man loves his child; he must teach him good actions. Perhaps he must strike him, perhaps he must ask the ghosts to strike for him, if that child is big. . . . A child does not wish to have shame from being struck by his father. A youth will not have shame, but a man who has a wife and children, who is a 'big youth' . . . will get shame. Will not his wife's brother laugh at him and say 'See, our sister's husband is only a child!'? Then that son will refuse those words of his father, and will close his heart against him. He forgets his father. Perhaps he runs to cry to his mother's brother. . . . Perhaps he thinks in his heart that his father is bad. Then he may refuse his father, and think that his father has forgotten the words of blood (kinship), and think his father to be a witch. Truly he then says nonsense, those words are bad, but we Lugbara are like that, we do not know these things.

Accusations of witchcraft between men of equal generation, 'brothers', tend to occur at later stages in the cycle of development of a lineage, when the heads of large segments wish to become independent. Such accusations are an extreme way of denying the authority of the elder, as I have shown in the case of Olimani.

The accusations are not, however, merely either those between generations or between segments. It is far more common for accusations by a man against another who is in the relationship of 'father' to him to be made by a classificatory son (11 out of the 14 cases just mentioned). In all of these, therefore, accuser and accused were of different segments within the lineage, as well as being of different generations. It would seem that whether or not the accusations are believed by other members of the group depends on these two factors: they tend to be accepted when generation differences are lacking (as with Ondua or Olimani), and to a less extent when genealogical generation is equivalent but authority status is not (as with Ondua and Draai or Otoro); they are not accepted when there is discrepancy in both genealogical generation and authority status, although if the persons concerned belong to widely separated segments there may be a degree of acceptance (for example, we might expect an accusation by, say, Benyu against Olimani to be accepted by some members of Lari'ba).

A point that is of considerable importance, but one which I have not sufficient space to consider fully, is that the proportions of invocation cases to other ritual cases, and also of intra-lineage witchcraft accusations to witchcraft accusations between unrelated neighbours, varies from one area to another. The rate of segmentation varies, as do the average and optimum sizes of minimal lineages. The main factors responsible for variation include population density, carrying capacity of land, and movements that have occurred as a result of European administration. In the long settled north-central areas there is a comparatively low proportion of tenants in any family cluster, whereas there is a much higher one in the south-east, and along the Uganda-Congo boundary. It would seem that in areas with a high proportion of tenants the invocation figures are higher between elders and attached sisters' sons and daughters' husbands than they are elsewhere. It would also seem that in areas such as Adumi and Mbaraka, on the Uganda-Congo boundary, where lineages are very small and remarkably intermingled on the ground, authority is less stable and there is a high degree of breakaway from elder's authority. Here also invocation would seem to be especially frequent, particularly between brothers (a sign of near segmentation). Here also accusations of witchcraft within the lineage are more frequent than elsewhere—in fact, Adumi is notorious as an area of witchcraft and sorcery. I have not the space to discuss these facts at length, but it is clear that since the patterns of invocation and witchcraft accusations are closely connected with patterns of lineage segmentation, differences in settlement and type and speed of lineage segmentation are reflected in differences in the ritual histories of lineages in different areas.

V

THE MORAL COMMUNITY

I. MYTH AND THE FIELD OF SOCIAL RELATIONS

I HAVE described Lugbara society as composed of tribes, clans, sections and lineages. It is more than a mere aggregate of units; it has a structure, consisting of the relations between people who hold statuses in these units. These relations are essentially those of authority. A Lugbara once compared his society to a forest, saying:

There are many trees in that forest there; some are great and some are small. The trees that are big push the smaller ones aside, and the smaller ones use the big ones for support against the wind and against the other big trees. We men here are like that; some are big and others are small, and the small ones lean against the big ones. The big ones are our elders and the rainmakers.

There are no words in Lugbara except those like 'big' and 'small' and 'strong' and 'weak' or expressions like 'a man stands before another' or 'a man follows another' which can be used to express relations of authority. Lugbara conceive these relations in three ways. One is in terms of genealogical experience and myth; another is in terms of a field of social relations centred upon the lineage and family cluster of the actors concerned; and a third is in terms of the action of God and of spirits. These are not three distinct ways of looking at the world; all are related. They enable Lugbara to see their world as something that has an ideal structure but which is also continually changing.

For Lugbara, a man, his family and his lineage are in the centre of a field of social relations, which extends both in space and time. Although this field cannot be delimited too clearly, it consists essentially of relations of authority which are based on kinship and validated by genealogy. At its centre are those relations between a man and the living members of his minimal lineage and the family cluster formed around it. Beyond are less direct relations between him and the living and dead members of his inner lineage, and beyond that are those between him and his more distant living and dead cognatic and affinal kin. This field of relations is, of course, unique for every individual. But the fields for the members of a minimal lineage overlap to a very considerable degree. Lugbara are also aware that they are members of a single social system, which extends in both space and time beyond the field of relations of any single lineage. The relationship between such a field and the total social system is conceived by them in terms of myth. The basic conceptual units of the total social system, as distinct from the basic political, economic, residential or ritual units, are clans. The clans are descended from the first creatures put on earth by God at the beginning of the world. Lugbara say that they are all of 'one blood', which was made by God the creator of men. He created a man, Gborogboro ('the person coming from the sky') and a woman, Meme ('the person who came alone'). Meme bore a boy and a girl. These siblings produced another male and female pair, who did the same in their turn. The names and number of generations of these siblings vary in various versions of the myth. Some myths say that they did not have intercourse in the human manner but that the women became pregnant after goat's blood had been poured over their legs.[1] All versions state that since they were siblings bridewealth was not given at these unions. The creation and subsequent happenings took place at a place called Loloi by Lugbara, to their north in the southern Sudan.

The last pair of siblings produced the two hero-ancestors, Jaki and Dribidu, who came to the present country of the Lugbara and there begot many sons, the founders of the present clans. They were not human as men are now: Dribidu means 'the hairy one', since he was covered with long hair over most of his body. He is also known as 'Banyale ('eater of men'), since he ate his children until he was discovered and driven out of his earlier home on the east bank of the Nile. Dribidu died on Mount Eti, and Jaki on Mount Liru. The heroes came independently, but the myths about them have close similarities. Both could perform many superhuman and magical feats. They are both the subjects of other

---

[1] The point is that the women did not menstruate. Lugbara believe that conception occurs only in the three or four days following menstruation; so that the pouring of goat's blood 'showed' them how to menstruate and like menstruation was followed by conception.

myths which tell how each, accompanied by a sister's son, found a leper woman who gave him fire on which to cook his buffalo meat; of how each cured the woman with medicine of which the secret is now lost, and lay with her and impregnated her, which resulted in fighting with her kin and the subsequent payment of seduction fine and bridewealth. Before this time there had been no fighting between men and there had been no bridewealth (there is an intimate connexion for Lugbara between fighting and bride-wealth, since most fighting was due to quarrels arising from it). The heroes learned the use of fire from the autochthonous people, were the first rainmakers, and gave the secrets of magic to their descendants.

The heroes were not normal human beings, but they mark the appearance of Lugbara society in the form which it has today. They married many women and their sons married wives and begot children in the way that people do now. They transferred bridewealth at marriage and in turn their sons and sons' sons multiplied and became the founders of new lineage segments. Lugbara say that in this way the present-day lineages descended from the founders of the original clans. The ancestors who feature in genealogies, which are concerned with the descendants of the two heroes, are always regarded as having been normal human beings who behaved as men still behave, and men so behave, of course, because the ancestors laid it down that they should. All special rights and mystical powers that are today possessed by certain men or certain lineages—for example, the power to control the rain or to possess certain magical objects—are validated by their having originated at the time of the heroes or of their sons, the clan founders. For Lugbara, the structure of their society today is essentially the same as it was then.

The several accounts of the creation of the pairs of siblings, of the hero-ancestors, and of their descendants, differ in character. I have given them, very briefly, as though they were parts of a single story, in order to show the relationship between them. I have never heard Lugbara doing so: indeed, it is unlikely that they would be told in a single situation. The accounts of the creation and the activities of the sibling-pairs before the heroes may be called mythical. Accounts of the descendants of the heroes are, for Lugbara, genealogical and not mythical. Stories of the hero-ancestors themselves present both mythical and genealogical features; that is to say, they may be placed in either category on different occasions. The heroes, who mark the appearance of Lugbara society, are either at the end of the mythical period or at the beginning of the genealogical period, if we put them on a time-scale. But to do this distorts the significance of these accounts. The difficulty is that our own myths and histories are placed on a time-scale, whereas those of the Lugbara are not.

In our own terms, the significant difference between the periods before and after the heroes is that in the latter the personages were ordinary human beings, who behaved as people behave now, and who were members of clans and so of society, whereas in the former they behaved in a contrary manner and lived in isolation, in a world in which there were no clans. They committed incest—the significance of mythical incest is that ties of siblingship have not yet been recognized, whereas in present-day cases of intra-clan incest they are recognized but ignored; they did not yet pay bridewealth—ties of affinity were not yet recognized; they did not engage in inter-group fighting, which is one of the sanctions for proper affinal behaviour and is the basic political sanction for inter-group relations; they could do marvellous feats which men can no longer perform. The first pair of siblings were called Arube and O'dụ, meaning 'maker of miracles' and 'miraculous omen' respectively; and the other sibling pairs have names associated with magic or the introduction, usually by magical means, of new techniques. They are said to have been born with teeth and, although they are distinct personages in most myths, they are sometimes said to be one person called by different names. Their respective sexes vary. It is their non-human or contra-human characteristics that are important, not details of name or parentage. With the appearance of the heroes and their begetting sons, the clan founders, human beings became social beings Before that time they were not members of a society—there was no society— and they and their world existed in the Sudan, outside present Lugbara territory, every part of which is traditionally associated with a particular clan. Before Dribidu entered Lugbara country he was a cannibal, eating his own children (Lugbara traditionally eat the hearts of dead enemies, but the eating of one's own children repudiates the most fundamental kinship bonds). Once arrived in Lugbara the heroes became more or less social beings, but they always retained some superhuman and magical powers When they first met the leper women they behaved as mythical figures, taking them without bridewealth: the later unions were proper marriages like marriages today. It is at this phase of the heroic period that social settlement began. The superhuman attributes of the pre-heroic figures indicate their asocial nature. Lugbara do not put the pre-heroic and the post-heroic periods on a time scale. The distinction that they make is between the non-existence and the existence of Lugbara society.

A similar use of myth is made in the accounts of the appearance of the Europeans in Lugbaraland. The ancestor of the 'red' people was Angbau, a son of the last of the sibling pairs, so that the red people have a parallel existence to the black people, but one that is outside Lugbara society. Those Europeans who enter it are placed in a different category. Those who first entered Lugbara are called by various names, but they are all given similar attributes. They were cannibals (as all Europeans even today are thought to be, except those well known to Lugbara as individuals), they would disappear underground, and they walked on their heads and could cover vast distances in a day by this means. As soon as they were noticed they began to walk on their legs, and if attacked they would vanish into the ground and come up some distance away; they would then walk away on their heads. I have heard it said that this is still the way in which Europeans behave in their own country 'on the other side of Lake Albert'.

In 1900 the Belgians came. It is said that when they came everyone ran away. The Belgians and their native troops chased the fugitives and found one or two lineage heads and other men hiding in the bush outside the homesteads; these men were made 'chiefs' by the Belgians. Chiefs are known as clients (*atįbo*) of the Europeans. The presence of clients in a settlement is always explained by saying that an ancestor found them without kin or possessions 'hiding in the grass' outside the compounds in no-man's land, outside sub-clan territories, and took them in as 'his people'. The appointment of chiefs is explained in the same way. Other accounts say that since the Europeans came from outside society, as clients come in time of famine, so they were taken in and welcomed by certain elders who acted towards them as 'fathers': their hosts were then made chiefs by the Europeans. It is clear that both versions explain the way in which the Belgians and the new chiefs became part of Lugbara society. It is said that

Mr. A. E. Weatherhead, the first District Commissioner under the Uganda administration after 1914, could walk across the country at fantastic speeds: no sooner was it thought that he was safely away a hundred miles to the north, and people began to plan warfare, than he would suddenly appear in person among them. In addition, he is said to have walked among them without rifles and to have had greatness of personality, courage and sympathy that could have been due only to magic and heroic qualities. 'His words were great', and he impressed them in a way that no other European, before or after him, has ever done.

Since those days Europeans entering Lugbara have had a place in Lugbara society and an expected role to play there. Lugbara can list most of their District Commissioners and missionaries since the days of Weatherhead. Other government officers are rarely remembered, but it is thought that there is some sort of genealogical tie between District Commissioners and between missionaries: it is often surmised that certain Europeans were the sons of earlier figures.

Lugbara myth and genealogy are little related to historical time as we comprehend it. Genealogy is used to explain and to validate social relations which are significant at the present moment. No Lugbara knows much of the genealogies of clans other than his own, since they are for the most part outside his field of everyday direct social intercourse; even within his own sub-clan he will rarely know more than the apical ancestors of major lineages other than his own. Genealogies deal with social beings as members of a given social field, and the ancestors are only significant, and so remembered, in so far as their existence and interrelationships validate the present composition of a group. But these social beings are placed in society, and society itself is given meaning and validity, by myth. Myths, in Lugbara, deal with personages originally not members of society. The mythical themes end by certain personages entering into the society or forming the society and receiving a status in it. As the extent of the society increases and new persons are introduced into it, as the Europeans and their chiefs were, they are given identity and status in this way by means of myth. Mythical figures are outside society and genealogical figures are within it, and there are some personages—the heroes, the Belgians and the first District Commissioner—who belong to both myth and genealogical tradition. The two are thus intimately linked and derive significance and validity from each other. But to set them into a scale of historical time units is misleading, since events are related to each other not by their temporal relationships but by the social relationships of the personages whose activities compose myth and genealogical tradition.

The mythical, asocial phase of any one theme is characterized by the inversion of social behaviour on the part of the personages concerned. The first Europeans were literally inverted; and I use the same term for all the other attributes of mythical figures and events which are the opposite of those that Lugbara values decree as proper for members of society. Together they form a single complex: physical inversion, cannibalism, incest, miracle-working, absence of bridewealth, no fighting, living outside the bounds of society.

The same pattern, with normal members of society at the centre, then a fringe of quasi-members of society who possess some super-human powers, and beyond them the rest of the world peopled with inverted asocial beings, can be seen in Lugbara socio-spatial categories. The relations between people and groups within a social field are validated by genealogical tradition and expressed in inter-lineage relations. Beyond that field other people live—one can see the trees on their ridges and the flame and smoke of their field-burning; one can often hear faintly the drumming from their dances. They may be Lugbara or other peoples, but in the context of social distance that is irrelevant. Social ties cross tribal and national boundaries. What is relevant is that they are beyond the limit of normal social relations, and that they are not therefore part of one's own social field and so not normal social beings. Lugbara give these groups certain attributes, the commonest of which is the possession of magical powers and medicines.

Every family cluster sees itself and its neighbouring lineages as surrounded by a circle of people whose territories are filled with sorcery and magic and who are evilly disposed towards them, even though they live in lineage-groups and are descended from the same hero-ancestors as are their own kin. But this, of course, is relative: when they are compared to groups beyond them, who are even worse, the closer strangers appear almost like one's own kin. Of thoes people beyond the bounds of society people say

How do we know where they come from or what deeds they do? We fear them and we do not know them.

The most distant of these creatures, beyond the magicians and the sorcerers, are creatures hardly human in appearance, who walk on their heads. Such are the Logo, the Mundu, the Lendu and people beyond them. These people love to eat meat that is rotten, and 'bad' meat such as snakes, frogs, hyenas and other night creatures. People such as the Pygmies, the Makaraka, the Mangbetu, the Momvu and the people whom Lugbara know as Niamniam, the Azande, are all cannibals. They walk on their heads, have terrible methods of sorcery, and live, in ways which men cannot understand, in the thick forests beyond the open Lugbara plateau.

These are not mere fairy stories told for amusement. Lugbara apply one conceptual scheme (which we can express only in the separate categories of time and space) to both of two situations: to the mythical and genealogical past and to the contemporary social environment. In mythical and genealogical distance any actual or comparative time-scale is irrelevant. In the myths of origin and that of the coming of the Europeans the same thematic pattern emerges. Similarly any actual or comparative scale of topographical distance is irrelevant to the spatial categories. The same thematic pattern is found in the socio-spatial categories of any group anywhere in Lugbara. It does not matter that for one group the beings with superhuman powers or inverted attributes live ten miles away and for another group they live twenty or fifty miles away. Only the external observer realizes the contradictions in this situation, in which groups only a few miles apart point to one another and make almost identical accusations of sorcery and inhuman attributes and behaviour. In both schemes the essential distinction is between the close people—members of one's own field of social relations, validated by genealogical tradition—and the distant inverted people, who are outside the field of social relations and outside genealogical tradition. It is only the ancestors of sub-clans and lineages within a group's field of social relations who feature in that group's corpus of genealogy. Kin and neighbours and genealogical tradition are different for every group, but the same corpus of myth is valid for all Lugbara. Likewise the inverted beings live far away, outside the Lugbara social system, the limits of which are defined in terms of mythical inversion. The situation may be expressed in a diagram (Figure 9).

There are clearly degrees of inversion, corresponding to degrees of social distance. In general inverted beings are asocial and their behaviour is amoral, outside the system of authority, but the degrees of asociability and amorality vary in different circumstances: the incestuous cannibals are more inverted than are the sorcerers, and are socially far more remote, being in fact beyond contact altogether. The more remote the being, the more its behaviour is conceived as being the utter negation of that to do with kinship: for an ordinary man to eat his own children is for Lugbara beyond comprehension, whereas to ensorcell someone is not.

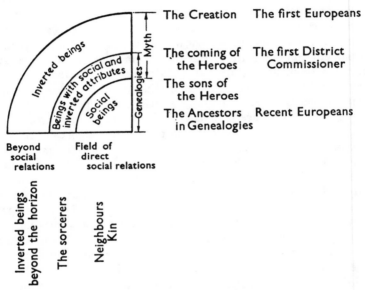

FIGURE 9. Lugbara categories of social space and time.

II. WITCHCRAFT, SORCERY AND DIVINATION

There may also be inverted beings within a field of social relations. These are witches, who have perverted normal relations of kinship and authority. They deny and destroy ties of kinship and neighbourhood and so deny and destroy the ties that are necessary for the existence of any kind of orderly social life. The field of social relations is structured by a network of ties of authority. Lugbara accept that within this field some people will chafe at authority. They do this as they, or those who have authority over them, change status in the generation system. The authority under which they chafe is that exercised by their seniors: they do not try to escape from authority as such, and they accept the ultimate authority of the dead. But there are always some men who cannot accept either authority as such or any restriction on their personal ambitions and desires. These include those who try to destroy the authority of their seniors by making accusations of witchcraft against them, within the family cluster, and also those who attempt to postpone either the legitimate aspirations of their juniors or those of their generational equals. They abuse their powers of authority and representation for their own ends and are accused of being witches.

These accusations within the family cluster are part of a wider complex consisting of accusations between various categories of persons and also of beliefs as to the nature of witches and sorcerers. The usually accepted attributes may not be applied to a particular witch in a man's own lineage. It is merely said that 'perhaps' they have them, since they are witches, 'but how do we know these things? They are the words of witches.' The ideal attributes of witches are significant as showing how Lugbara conceive of witchcraft and its place in the total social system, but they may not be applied to any particular witch known as an individual.

There are several kinds of witch, and several terms used to refer to their activities. A clear-cut classification is not possible but all have inverted characteristics, either physical or moral. The main kinds of witch may have few or many such characteristics, depending on what aspect of the anti-social activity is stressed. Empirically witches as Lugbara describe them do not exist. What do exist are the situations in which Lugbara assume witchcraft to be operating, the beliefs in witches, and the responses that are brought into play as a consequence of events which Lugbara explain in terms of witchcraft. It is only to be expected that Lugbara notions about witches do not form a single consistent pattern. Their ideas must fit changing and different situations and are not part of a single dogma.

A witch is called *oleu*, and sometimes *'ba oleberi*, 'a man with *ole*' (indignation). Witches are always men. The typical situation in which a man feels *ole* is said to be when he passes a homestead and sees the occupants sitting eating, with good millet in its flat basket and with pots of rich and succulent meats and relishes, and he is not called in to share the meal. A man also feels *ole* when he sees another showing off his agility at a dance, being admired by girls and other young men while he stands alone. A man feels *ole* when he sees the wealth of another's home, the fertility of his wives and livestock, while he is poor and his own children and livestock few and ailing. Or a man who wishes to seduce the wives and daughters of other men, may feel *ole* against their guardians who prevent his doing so. Then in his heart he hates the other whom he thinks of as in some way harming him. It is said that a man bewitches another because that is his 'work', or his 'words'; in an analogous way women bear children because that is their 'work'. The initial and the final situations—that of being filled with indignation, envy and hatred by a certain action, and that of the victim falling sick as a result of the witches thoughts—are brought into conjunction by the concept of *ole*. The psychological and other processes that motivate the witch and explain the means by which he responds to the situation and sets his witchcraft into action are not known; situationally they are irrelevant.

A man practises witchcraft when he has *ole* in his heart. He may practise it in several ways; or more correctly, there are several kinds of witch, all motivated by this sentiment. If asked whether one man may practise more than one way of bewitching, Lugbara say, 'How do we know? We are not witches'. Questions of this sort beg the question sociologically, and there is no answer to them in terms of belief and dogma.

The usual example of a witch is the night witch, 'the man who walks at night.' He enters his victim's hut at night 'like a rat', and breaks his bones, which ache the following day. As he comes to the hut he may appear as a moving light, which settles on the top of the hut. All witches can be known at night in that they have a light glowing at their wrists and backs of hands and at their anus. These stigmata are always attributed to witches, including those people commonly suspected of witchcraft. They are axiomatic attributes, and so all suspected witches are said to have them; any particular case in which they are not seen are attributed to their cunning in hiding from other men's sight at night. Night witches are said to be the same as those of the neighbouring Logo and

Keliko, to the west in the Congo, who are said to walk about upside down.

Usually the victim dreams of the witch, in which case his soul is seeing that of the witch; or he may see the witch in the guise of a night animal. Certain animals are associated with witches; they are both omens of witchcraft and may be vehicles for witches, and they are also used as ingredients in sorcery-poisons. They include the jackal, the leopard, the leopard-cat, the bat, the screech monkey, snakes, the owl and several other birds, the water tortoise, if it leaves its riverine home and comes to the compounds, and certain frogs and toads. All these creatures are 'like witches' and are much feared. If a man sees them at night, and especially if in a dream, he is seeing a witch or the soul of a witch. All are night creatures or, like the water-tortoise, out of their normal habitat. Indeed any animal away from its usual home may be suspected of being something to do with witchcraft.

Night witches often defaecate or vomit blood on the victim's hut doorway. In the morning his foot touches it and he falls sick. There may be pieces of stick, or trees of which only witches know the harmful properties, placed by the witch in the blood. The sickness is then even more serious. In eastern Lugbara these blood-witches are said also to stamp on and kick the ghost shrines, to insult the dead.

An evil-eye man is a species of witch. Such a man looks with the evil eye and gives dysentery. He 'walks among people' and feels *ole* in his heart towards those who do not share food and other things with him. An evil-eye man can be told by a squint, or by red eyes, and by a shifty and ill-natured glance.

There are certain physical characteristics whose possessor is likely to be a witch. Besides being red and squinting, a witch's eyes are heavy and sullen and look down at the ground when he is talking. His face is likely to be ugly and his body ill-figured. His skin is said to be 'pale' like the colour of bark or the dung floor of a hut. I have been told that a witch's skin is grey, 'like a photograph'. Often men with some physical disfigurement, such as a missing eye or nose, are thought to be witches.

Some witches bewitch in daylight. These are witchcraft-spitters, who spit on the heads of children, especially those left at home while their parents are working in the fields. Later sores develop on the children's heads. These witches are usually strangers and so unrecognized by the child victim. They are evil mainly because they use spittle, properly used for blessing, to harm innocent children; it is their spitting that is as it were inverted.

A man who sits alone and above all eats alone is always thought to be a witch. Therefore witches often pretend to be chatty and friendly and generous to everyone. Lugbara say that if a man is seen walking about greeting people in their homes then he is likely to be a witch; a witch would rarely sit alone at home all day because then people would think he was brooding over his wrongs and would know him to be a witch, so he simulates friendship. But all men have some hatred towards someone in their hearts, so that an over-friendly person is suspect. 'Why does he walk about all day? Has he no work?' Also, of course, to wander about peoples' homes implies that a man is looking for food and so likely to be filled with *ole*.

A witch hides his words and is always friendly. He laughs and jokes with people. Lo, he is a witch. He comes always to greet people, he is generous, but his heart is evil, he is a witch. He comes every day walking thus and thus and thus, all for no reason. Why? He is a witch.

A man who is especially friendly to someone of his own neighbourhood without any apparent reason is likely to be a witch trying to lull his victim into a false sense of security. The commonest reason given for the appearance of clients, is, as I have said earlier, that they have left their homes elsewhere either from famine or because they have been banished as witches. Indeed, they are usually the first people to be suspected of witchcraft in general, since they are strangers whose past is unknown; also they are in a servile position and usually poor men and so liable to feel *ole* towards those who have taken them in and who have authority over them that is not validated in terms of kinship. In cases where clients quarrel with other people, the taunt of 'witch' is almost invariably levelled at them. In the same way the smiths, who are almost always Ndu who have entered Lugbara individually to practise their craft, which is much feared, are often suspected of witchcraft.

All these witches bewitch people by mystical means. The terms used for the process are several. A witch as well as being *oleu* and *'ba oleberi* is also 'a witchlike person' (*'ba oleuru*), or 'a person who bewitches people' (*ba 'ba ropiri*). To bewitch is *rozu*, *ole rozu* or *rozu olesi*, terms that also mean the process of invoking the ghosts. Witches are distinguished from sorcerers, who are people who use material means (medicines and poisons and other objects) to achieve their ends. They are often called *oleu* although there are specific terms for them. They are motivated by the same sentiment, that of *ole*. I discuss them below.

We may build a stereotype of a witch. He is an ill-tempered, spiteful person who does not behave in a socially approved manner. Evil-eye men are those people whose physical appearance obviously corresponds in some way with the stereotype. Other witches are not so obvious, and are those who use their mystical power to harm others for their own selfish ends. In all the typical situations given for the sentiment of *ole* it is implied that the witch is a man without close kin. Even the man watching others dance is so, since usually a man with brothers and close kin will dance together with them and so not be left out; and a man who is not invited to eat also has no near kin, or he would eat with them, since one of the most important obligations of kinship is to share food.[1] Formerly a persistent witch could be killed by having his limbs cut off. He had repudiated ties of kinship and neighbourhood and could be treated 'like a client: he is not a person, a man of our lineage, but a thing'—a client could be killed by his host, as he was not susceptible to ghostly sickness.

The range of witchcraft cannot be defined very clearly. Lugbara generally agree that a witch may bewitch any people of his own neighbourhood, kin and non-kin. To bewitch his own kin is the worst kind of witchcraft, and is referred to by the phrase *ole jo drịnịrị* (*ole* in the house-roof). Generally a witch cannot bewitch a member of another tribe, 'because you do not know his words; you do not know whether he is a witch or not', and witches cannot harm non-Lugbara or Europeans. 'Strangers' fear and may use sorcery, but not witchcraft.

A witch can bewitch kin and non-kin. Elders are the people most feared in this respect, and a man may be bewitched only by a man older than himself, never a younger person. Witchcraft is

[1] Certain types of personality which we might expect to make a man suspect are not thought of as being associated with witchcraft. A persistent scrounger, for example, may be thought to be a witch, but this is unusual: 'he just begs to beg'. Nor is a greedy man a witch; he is 'just a greedy man'. It is envy and spite that are most suspect. The situations in which these are felt are associated with an implicit lack of close kin in a way that greed is not.

practised between people who are already in some form of social relationship. *Ole*, in both ghost invocation and witchcraft, is aroused by the sight of a person behaving anti-socially.[1] There are no right ways to behave to a stranger or to a person with whom one has ties neither of kinship nor of fairly close neighbourhood, except to spear him if he shows signs of fight—why else does a stranger enter another lineage territory except to make trouble by force? Witchcraft is practised only between men, and on the whole it is only between men that there are orderly social relations that contain a content of expected and socially approved behaviour; those involving women, other than close kin and affines, are generally unformalized. Lugbara say that it is practised especially between elders, whose inter-relationship is especially one of formalized behaviour that is most punctiliously observed, and who cannot exercise lineage authority over one another.[2]

Witches are evil as much because they usurp or abuse the power and authority of elders as because they do actions which are evil in themselves. I was told

A witch is a man. He has a wife and children. He cares for them and loves them and brings them food, and he sacrifices for them to his ghosts.

Authority within the community is in the hands of the elders. A man who is insulted should not take the law into his own hands and bewitch the offender. He should leave his punishment to the offender's own elder or other kin, who can bring sickness upon him in socially approved ways. Witchcraft is an anti-social action either because the motives are selfish and malicious or because the witch ignores the socially approved means of dealing with offenders against kin or community mores. A witch sets himself up above the other members of his community, and tries to do so without the approval of his ancestors, who support him by sending sickness only if he invoke them against an offender. At the same time, a witch is the embodiment of those attributes that are in direct

[1] An exception is the case of daylight witchcraft-spitters. But they should perhaps be counted as sorcerers: see below.

[2] Certainly many of the cases of witchcraft accusations of which I have knowledge were between unrelated elders who were engaged in bridewealth negotiations. On these occasions there is much beer-drinking, the elders having to behave towards one another with considerable politeness and ceremony, taking great care not to spit after drinking or make any other sign that might be taken to show discontent and so a possible intention to bewitch.

contrast to those ideally possessed by elders or senior kin. Senior kinsmen, and *a fortiori* elders, should be 'slow', understanding, gentle, generous, angry only when the interests of their family clusters are concerned and not on account of their own personal pride. A witch behaves in a diametrically opposite manner.

Witchcraft may be distinguished from sorcery, although Lugbara often use the word *oleu* for both. Witches affect their victims by mystical means, but sorcerers use material medicines. There are two main types of sorcerers, the 'people with poison' (*'ba enyanya beri*), and *elojua*. The former are usually women and are said to be traditional; the latter are men and are a recent introduction. Both are spoken of as 'poisoning people'.

'People with poison' are people with bad hearts, filled with malice and spite. They are said to prepare poison, usually from snakes' heads, which they hide under their finger-nails and sprinkle in food or beer; or they place it on the hut floor or threshold or in the thatch. Other poisons used are made from the night animals I have mentioned as being associated with witches. They often use a placenta. An evil woman bears a child and places the placenta in the food of her victim, who may be the child of a co-wife.

I was told that a sorcerer does these things because his or her heart is bad:

His heart is bad to that man, because he has wealth . . . he walks in front of people and can say, 'You are useless, you have no wealth, but I have much wealth'. Then that man's heart grows bad . . . and he thinks 'It is good that I give him . poison, it is good that he should die. . . .'

I was told of a certain woman

Her heart does not stay with others, it is bad. We think she is a sorceress because all people fear her.

Like witches, sorcerers are motivated by envy and are thought to be sorcerers because they are feared; they have certain un-natural and anti-social attributes, physical or psychological.

The ability, and the wish, to poison people by sorcery may be inherited, especially from the mother. A sorceress's mother must be dead before she is feared enough to be thought a sorceress. Accusations of sorcery are made especially between co-wives, who are said always to use placentae as I have described. It is only the senior co-wife who is thought to use sorcery, in order to kill her junior rival.

The other main form of sorcery, that performed by *elojua*, is said to be a recent introduction, brought back from the south of Uganda by returning labour migrants.[1] They buy it, for cash, from other migrants who come from the Congo, especially from those peoples with inverted attributes, the Logo and Keliko. The poison is said to come from a bulb (*ojoo*) found in the Congo. *Elojua* are men. I was told

The words of women are sorcery-poisons from snakes. Women do not wander far away; to wander is the work of *elojua*, they are men only.

These sorcerers may poison their own kin, but they are more usually thought to wander aimlessly, filled with malice. They work especially in markets and at *walangaa* dances, where people from a wide area gather and which are both recent introductions (since about 1930). A sorcerer scatters his poison on the ground, when a victim treads in it and falls down vomiting blood. It is said that today *elojua* even try to poison their own brothers.

Traditionally the use of sorcery is said to have been away on the horizon and never among 'us here'. The horizon is, however, a social as well as a physical one. The use of sorcery by co-wives is significant.[2] It is said

Yes, women use sorcery here in our homes. But they do not ensorcell men, only one another. Women are not 'big'. They are our sisters but they do not know the words of the ancestors. If they had been born men they would know these things but they are women and so 'little'. Does a child understand these matters? Women are like (children), they work in the home but they do not wage feud nor do they know the words of the lineage.

In fact old women, especially the elder sisters of senior men, may play a part in lineage affairs, but generally women have little importance in public affairs. The essential relations are those between men, those of authority; and those between women are structurally unimportant. The other members of a family cluster who are also in some ways outside these relations are clients; but they are men, and are classed by Lugbara as being either witches or potential witches on that account.

[1] The actual word appears to come from the Alur *lojwok*, a magician.

[2] It might be argued that this activity of women should be included as witchcraft, but this runs counter to Lugbara categorization.

Today, however, sorcery is entering into relations between men within this field: the sorcerers are among 'us here'. The appearance of *elojua* is an expression of the fear and resentment of the changes taking place in Lugbara society, changes such as those implied in labour migration, in a cash economy and a market system, and secular *walangaa* dances. Lugbara have no control over these changes, which have no obvious cause other than the Europeans and the many 'strangers' who today wander about the country. *Elojua* is a symbol of all that is unusual and uncanny, and is a response to social change. The fact that it is bought for money marks it as something outside the traditional bonds of kinship and friendship, a thing to be passed between men of different peoples, tribes and sub-clans.

Witches and sorcerers are grouped together, as being evil and anti-social people. There are, however, significant differences between them. Lugbara distinguish different symptoms: witchcraft makes a man's limbs heavy and weak, whereas sorcery makes the whole body ache, and the drinking of water makes the victim fall into a fit or trance. Witches attack neighbours; they may or may not be kin, but they must be members of a small local community. Within this community they are believed to attack those who deserve to be attacked because of their unneighbourly conduct. Witchcraft, though anti-social and if persistent punishable, none the less acts as a sanction for neighbourly behaviour. Sorcerers attack both kin and non-kin and both neighbours and non-neighbours; traditionally they are always 'outside'. And most sorcerers act indiscriminately against people whether they know them or not. Although the motives are often given as the same as for witches, Lugbara conceive of sorcery as being something outside their own social system, although it may today be brought into it by evildoers, who obtain it by the impersonal method of purchase for shillings. These men are abusing their position as members of Lugbara society. They are introducing something alien into Lugbara, a thing that comes from the feared inverted people of the Congo. The man who uses sorcery-poison is worse than a witch: he is a traitor. Men speak of sorcerers, especially of *elojua*, with more horror than they do of witches. After all, anyone can be a witch, and a man almost deserves to be bewitched if he is stupid and mean enough to arouse *ole* in someone else's heart. Witchcraft is associated intimately with the socially approved process of ghost invocation—both are known as *ole rozu*. But sorcery is wholly anti-social and wholly evil. I was told that a sorcerer thinks 'He there has many kin; I am one man, I am without brothers.' This may at first sight seem similar to the fact that witches are also in some way kinless, and may abuse ties of kinship, but a witch is not thought to use this kinlessness as an overt motive. Witches act against people who have offended them by a breach of expected neighbourly behaviour; sorcerers act against people who do not merit their hatred. Sorcery is promiscuous and malicious.

It thus has little function as part of a system of sanctions, as has witchcraft in one of its aspects. Sorcery provides an explanation for certain events which are not directly related to morality, in that the victim has no sense of guilt for a previously committed offence. Traditionally the significance of sorcery seems to have been that it marked, conceptually, the limit of a group's field of social relations, and its significance today is consistent with this. The increase in social mobility, both within and beyond the borders of Lugbara, has introduced new relationships which did not exist before. All these, together with the prohibition of fighting, of killing witches, severely beating one's wife and children, and so on, have led to new stresses and conflicts in the society. Some of these are expressed in terms of sorcery, especially of *elojua*: 'Once there was no *elojua*, then people stayed in their places, they did not wander about because they would have been killed.'

Witches and sorcerers are inverted beings. They are beyond the field of social relations and of ties of kinship, either by definition (sorcerers) or by perversity (the worst type of witches). They present many of the expected features of inversion: they are white or grey in colour, they may have physical blemishes, they are often associated with incest and cannibalism. It is said that Congo witches even walk on their heads. They vomit and defaecate blood, they destroy shrines. Sorcerers may inherit their knowledge by inheritance in the female line. Women are said to be evil:

Women are evil. They do not become ghosts under the compounds. They have no souls. . . . They bring trouble to men, they do not know the words of the ancestors. Women are the things of *Adro* (God in His immanent aspect).

The speaker qualified this by saying that 'perhaps' some women do have souls, as they do in fact have shrines placed for them; but his meaning was clear enough.

Witches and sorcerers are associated with God, and not with the ancestors. They cannot be 'known' by oracles, 'the things of the ancestors, who gave them to us', but only by diviners, who are 'people of God'. Diviners are women,[1] and so considered to stand outside lineage conflicts.

The skill or power (*talĵ*) of divination is inherited in the female line. A diviner is possessed by God when she is an adolescent girl. She wanders about the bush, often naked, for several days. It is said 'she wanders about mad' (*eri acĵacĵ azaza*). Later, when married, she becomes a diviner. A shrine is erected for her, of stones brought from the river where God, who possessed her, is said to live. This shrine is called 'hut of God' (*Adrojo*) and a sheep is killed at its erection by another diviner who sponsors her. A bulb (*ojoo*) with magical and sacred qualities, is placed on the *Adrojo*. Her sponsor contacts God with her divining gourd, and God says that he has possessed her to give her the power of divination. The girl then keeps her shrine for the remainder of her life, even if she does not actually practise as a diviner. It is said:

The sheep is cut at the external lineage shrine by her elder; then the diviner contacts God who says that that girl is his. She now has the power given to her by God, a power that our ancestors do not know. . . . She is taken away from them, her words and theirs are cut at this rite, that of 'turning diviner' (*ojou ojazu*). Now she is a person of God.

The distribution of diviners is not related to that of lineages and sub-clans. They are outside the system of lineage authority, which is exercised by men. They are used to contact witchcraft and sorcery, the recently dead, who are with God in the sky and have not yet assumed the roles of ancestors, and many spirits that have their power direct from God. They are the link between men and God:

It is God the taker of men who takes us in death. So he sends diviners to show us his anger, which he sends by sickness (that is, by spirits which bring sickness). Then he takes men and takes them to him in the

[1] There are a very few male diviners, but they are not well known and are spoken of as being anomalous. They are mainly old men who were adherents of the prophet Rembe, described in a later section.

sky. But we here cry 'where are our father and our father's brothers?' and we send a diviner to ask God for their souls so that we may build them shrines and speak with them.

III. THE POWER OF GOD

The ideological aspects of many of the phenomena that I have discussed in this book may be summarized in a simple dichotomy. This is a dualism made explicitly for the sake of analysis, but it is most certainly implicit in Lugbara thought and symbolism.

Genealogical time and space	Mythical time and space
Lineage and kinship values	Kinlessness and denial of kin obligations
Socially responsible members of society; '*ba* ('people')	Asocial beings; clients, who are *afa* ('things')
Ghostly and ancestral sickness; 'showing' sickness.	Witchcraft and sorcery; killing sickness.
Oracles	Diviners
Men	Women
The compound and homestead	The bushland 'outside'

All the phenomena in the right-hand column are conceived in terms of inversion. And Lugbara express the distinction also in terms of the one category being 'good' (*onyiru*), and the other being 'bad' (*onzi*). These are only the most approximate translations. They may better be understood by words such as 'normal' and 'abnormal', or 'moral' and 'amoral', or 'social' and 'asocial'; at times 'amoral' and 'asocial' may become 'immoral' and 'antisocial' or even 'pre-social'. I have used the word 'inverted' to refer both to physical and moral attributes; the concept 'perverted' could also be used on occasions to refer to the latter.

This duality is far more than a mere analytical or mnemonic device. It is appropriate to the relationship between ideally unchanging and unchangeable authority on the one hand and social change on the other. Lugbara use it to resolve the problem of change, as something that actually occurs, within a system that is ideally changeless. They lack concepts of what we see as historical change and causation; they see what are for us historical events and relations in terms of moral relations, those of sociality and asociality. The authority of living and dead that is part of the ideally unchanging system is thought of as 'good'. Factors that change, destroy or weaken this structure are 'bad', and to represent them Lugbara use the symbol of inversion. They are outside the social order and are seen as being both amoral and asocial.

Lugbara consciously place these examples of inversion in a single framework. I was told of the recently dead:

Those people who have died are 'bad'. They are near to God as were Gborogboro and Meme (the first creatures of God). They are far away, they are like clients.

A man who had died brings trouble to us here. We fear him now. When he was here with us he was a good man, but now he is dead and there are troubles and disputes. Our territory is destroyed and our youths sleep with their sisters, and the words of the ancestors are forgotten. . . . The dead are 'bad'. That is why we ask a diviner to contact their souls; then they come back to us and are 'good' and help us to live in peace. But before they return they are like witches. Who can know their hearts? They are far from us here.

Both clients and witches are associated with incest, cannibalism and other signs of kinlessness. Like the recently dead, they can be brought back into social relationships by various means—a client is given a wife, a witch is 'known' by a diviner who removes his witchcraft.

The distinction between 'good' and 'bad' is a moral one, and Lugbara imply this when they use these terms. It is expressed also by the physical symbols of inversion and 'being outside'. Inverted beings are those who by their nature stand outside Lugbara society —the mythical figures, the beings beyond the horizon, and so on; they may later be incorporated intb Lugbara society and may then lose their inversion. But members of society may deny or foresake their everyday attributes as ordinary members of lineages, as do men who practise witchcraft, and men who are unwashed in order to sacrifice. These are more likely to be said to be 'outside' (*amve*), although if evil they may also have some attributes of inversion. 'Outside' has, for Lugbara, a connotation of physical distinctness that may not at first be obvious to the observer. It is 'outside' the compounds and fields, in and near the streams and bushland, where God in his immanent aspect may actually be seen by those rash enough to go there at dusk. Some men may go there safely: these are the elders who visit the external lineage shrines, set away in the bush. But only elders may do this: they are nearer to God than are other people, and if they are rainmakers they also have powers known to come directly from God. The rites at these shrines are the most important in respect of lineage segmentation —the elders may almost be said to be re-creating lineage structure and so performing what is near to God's work—and the shrines are watched at night by the 'children of God'. It is said:

We do not know what our elders do there. They sit there in the place of God's children and we fear to go near. Those places are 'bad'.

Diviners may also wander about the bushland; they are especially said to be 'people of God'.

Lugbara society is not a closed system, and changes occur in it due not only to recurrent deaths but also to factors that are outside it. Although men cannot prevent death, they can cope with it in terms of their own religious system and their notions about the ideal structure of their society. But change occurs also in other ways. The ideal balance of authority may be changed by ecological factors such as over-population and loss of fertility of land, and by factors such as epidemics of men or livestock. And change may occur as a consequence of the introduction into the system from outside it of new power, which is in conflict with the traditional pattern of authority and which in certain spheres destroys it. Lugbara conceive these changes as being due to the intervention of God. God then re-creates the structure of Lugbara society so that the changes are incorporated into it.

Lugbara see God as being the ultimate source of all power and of the moral order. They conceive him as having two aspects, one transcendent and the other immanent. The transcendent aspect is usually named *Adroa* or *Adronga*, forms which are diminutives of *Adro*, which is used for the immanent aspect. The diminutive is used because God in the sky is more remote, both spatially and in intensity of contact, than God on the earth. Offerings are made to him in his immanent aspect and not to him in his transcendent aspect.

I translate *Adro* and *Adroa* as 'God', although the correspondence of meaning is not exact. *Adro*, the basic form of the term, refers to a personified force, outside the control and beyond the understanding of the living men who are his creatures. There is no way of distinguishing gender in Lugbara. God is referred to as *eri*, which can mean 'he', 'she' or 'it'. He is said not to be a 'person' (*'ba*), but this is because since he created 'persons' he can hardly be one himself:

Adroa made us here on the earth, and he made all the animals. Did he not put Gborogboro and Meme (the first beings) in the world. How then can he be a person? Can you make a person, or can I? No, we do not know what God is like; he is everywhere, in the wind and in the sky. He is far away and we do not sacrifice to him.

However, in his immanent aspect, as I discuss below, he may be said to be conceived in basically anthropomorphic terms. He is, however, omnipotent and has will and understanding, as Lugbara show clearly in any discussion of the way in which he decides that the time has come for a man to be taken away in death. I therefore say 'he' when referring to him, but this is mainly for convenience of discourse. Indeed, unlike our term 'God', *Adro* is used also to refer to a category of objects which are manifestations of divinity and beyond the control and understanding of men. Many apparently miraculous things are called *adro*, such as what I have called the guardian spirit of a man, or even matches; the word is sometimes used for testicles and for the power of procreation.

Lugbara say that both aspects of God are of one God, but that they live in different places. The transcendent aspect is God in the sky (*Adroa 'bua*), and is usually called *'ba o'bapiri*, the creator of men. He created man, woman and cattle at the beginning of the world. Lugbara say that he also created the world itself, and the sun, moon and stars, but this belief is a vague one. It is said 'he made things, as his work'. It is he who is sometimes said to take men away in death, and is then known as God the taker of men (*Adroa 'ba o'dupiri*). But this phrase may be applied to him in his immanent aspect.

God is responsible for all deaths. Death cannot be avoided and it is of no use trying to placate God or to persuade him to spare a man, by prayer or sacrifice. His will is immutable. If a man dies, whether of old age or an accident, it is said 'God hangs or strangles him' (i.e. stops his breath), or 'God takes away breath'. Any sudden and inexplicable death, such as that from a buffalo or spear, or poisoning, is due to God. 'Why else would God have put that man and that buffalo there together?' The agent responsible for such chance is God, not a witch or other human agent as in many other societies. Not that this absolves the sorcerer or other agent from moral responsibility. A man who kills another is killed in vengeance, a suspected sorcerer is given the poison ordeal. Lugbara say that God must have been angry to place the agent and his victim in that particular relationship. Or they may say that a witch brought his victim to God's notice, and so God decided that he should die. There is no moral content in the relationship of man to God, as there is between man and the dead or man and a witch.

It is in his immanent aspect that God comes into direct contact with his creatures during their lifetimes. *Adro* lives on earth, especially in rivers. He is also found in large trees and thickets and on high mountains and rocky places. He is in every stream, but does not permanently occupy the other places where he is sometimes to be found. Lugbara speak of him as one but many. He is invisible to ordinary people, but may become visible to a man who is about to die. Sometimes a sound man sees him and then knows that he will soon die. He is said to be formed like a man, and very tall and white; but his body is cut down the centre and he has only one eye, one ear, one arm and one leg, on which he jumps about. He is very terrible to see. Although invisible to ordinary people, he may be heard crying 'whee whee whee' in grass fires when they burn on a hill or mountain, especially on Mount Eti, Mount Liru or the smaller Mount Aba, in the Congo near Maraca. He is said also to be in whirlwinds and dust-devils. He is not intrinsically evil, but feared and so 'bad'. He is said to eat people if he meets them at night.[1]

Adro has wives and many children, *Adroanzi* ('Adro-children'). Of his wives nothing is known; they seem to be included merely for the sake of logical consistency. His children are many, and live in the streams and large trees and rocks. They are said to be the *adro* (guardian spirits) of the dead. They leave men at death and go into the bush and 'become' the 'children of Adro'. They are little people, male and female, about four foot high, and walk at night:

At night they call with their personal calls (*cere*) they walk with their wives, who call out ululations, and they laugh together. We lie here in

---

[1] *Adro* is used to refer to Europeans because they are white and take people away to prisons; all Europeans are axiomatically eaters of men, as is *Adro*, although a European known personally to Lugbara may not actually practise these habits which define him as a member of a species.

our huts and hear them, and say, 'Who is that calling? Perhaps it is the children of Adro.'

They like to follow human beings at night, but do not harm them unless the humans look back at them, when they kill them. This is done especially by those who live in important rain-groves and act as guardians and follow passers-by home to their compounds to see that they do not enter the groves. It is said 'they guard the territory of the lineage', that is, they have become part of the totality of lineage guardian spirits. In this role they are 'spirits of the grass' (*adro asea*), 'spirits in the water' (*yįį adro*), 'spirits of the rocks' (*ųnį adro*) or 'spirits of the trees' (*patį adro*); they are the genii of the lineage territory and are said to cause various sicknesses. They are thought to be evil omens:

If you see them at night they walk about, and if you see them your brother or sister or your wife or children will die. You will not, you will die another day (of another cause). But some people say that if you see them you will surely die yourself that day. These words are difficult to know.

They, with their father, live near rivers and streams. Children and women who walk near streams at dusk, to draw water, are likely to see or to kick them or tread on their feet (as they may be invisible), and later became sick. *Adro* sends fireflies which place little stones in the offender's chest so that his breathing becomes difficult. The firefly is evil, with an evil soul. It is sent to 'kill people'. The places of stone are removed by a diviner. Offerings of chickens are made to *Adro* for sickness he may bring for a like offence. The chicken is killed by the sick man alone on a rock in the stream, that is, at the place where God in his immanent aspect is likely to be. He cooks and eats part of it there, leaving the remainder for *Adro* and his children.

Adro in these forms of manifestation is common to all Lugbara. In addition, each clan (*sųrų*) has its own spirit called *adro*. The clan is a dispersed group which is not concerned in corporate activity. This spirit is also a manifestation of God's power, and, in many cases, is thought of as having been a distant ancestor. There are myths told about these spirits, of which the best-known is probably that of the clan Aiiku, which tells of lightning entering a granary of an Aiiku man and leaving eggs there, which hatched out and became birds which later flew back to the heavens;

sometimes the lightning is said to have entered the compound in the form of a sheep, a beast associated with God. If there is lightning about, people (of any clan) may say, 'I am a man of Aiiku', so that they may not be struck. The power of God is thus seen as being associated with all Lugbara, irrespective of clan affiliation, but it is also segmented and conceived in the form of spirits which correspond to the main segments of the society, the clans. All clans have myths and spirits of this kind, although they vary greatly in form; there are no rites associated with them.

It is in his evil or immanent aspect that God is connected with diviners. He possesses adolescent girls and drives them into the bush, whence they emerge possessing the power of divination. In this role God may be known as 'God who makes (people) tremble' (*Adro yaya*), and is much feared and thought of as uncanny.

The immanent aspect of God is thus feared and evil. He is an 'inversion' of both God in the sky and of man, being white and cut in half. He lives in rivers and the bush, the waste places between the compounds, which are feared as 'outside' and uninhabited places. These waste places are clearly marked from settlement and fields, which are occupied and used by living men. Although to the casual observer there appears little but compounds and thick cultivation in central Lugbara, this is so only because the ridges between the streams are occupied. But to the walker across the face of the country the patches of bush and long grass are as much a part of the land as the fields, and this impression is the stronger by night when even the fields lying at any distance from the settlements seem cold and inhabited only by the 'children of *Adro*', who are said to leave their patches of bush and come nearer the homesteads when the sun has set.

God the Creator is outside and above any particular field of social relations and any lineage or section. He features in no genealogy and is outside the system of authority. In his immanent aspect he is given characteristics which I call inverted, with which diviners, spirits and other agents and beings are also associated in Lugbara thought. The power of God is outside men and outside society, since it created men. To enter into the system of social relations it must take on various forms or manifestations, which are conceptualized and made comprehensible by use of the idiom of inversion. It may then also be segmented and associated with the basic and permanent units of Lugbara society, the clans. It is clearly impossible and even pointless to conceptualize it when it is not in direct contact with men; it may then remain a mystery, 'in the wind and in the sky' (*oĺja, 'bᵿa*). Inversion, as a concept, represents both being outside human society but also entering it from outside (Heroes, early Europeans) or leaving it to go outside (witches, the recently dead); and it is thus also used for the agents of the power of God.

God is not outside society, but rather above it completely. He features in both the categories of phenomena, the one 'good' and the other 'bad', that were listed on page 250. He is said to be 'behind' all people and all things, as their creator, and so may be in indirect contact with all forms of social action. His presence unites them into a single schema, of which the divisions are complementary and cannot be understood in isolation. But he is explicitly concerned with certain actions and events:

Sacrifices to the dead	Indirect contact, shown by approval at consecration
'Cleansing the body', after death, incest, fraternal quarrel, illegitimate pregnancy	More direct contact, shown by the use of sheep
Offering of sheep to remove meningitis and drought	Direct; 'prayers' are made to him
Death	The soul of the dead person goes to God, and his soul is contacted by a diviner, who has been possessed by God
Divination	The diviner is possessed by God in his immanent aspect
Witchcraft and sorcery	'Known' by diviners and not by oracles; associated with night animals, which are associated with God.

God in his immanent aspect is associated with death (although he is concerned here in both aspects), with witches and sorcerers and with divination. In addition he is concerned in his immanent aspect with rain-groves and with various manifestations of miraculous power that are known as *adro*. It is in his immanent aspect that he is known as 'bad God' (*Adro onzi*); it is in this aspect that he comes into more direct contact with his creatures. In his transcendent aspect he is more remote.

God is distinguished very clearly from the ancestors, as far as sacrifice and offerings are concerned. Offering is made to God to remove meningitis and drought, as I have mentioned. Formerly until the late 1930s, offerings of first fruits were made at shrines known as *kaljan*, which were owned by rainmakers and closely associated with God. And God is associated with rain, by the belief that he gave the power of rain control to rainmakers and that the beings called *adro* protect rain-groves. God is concerned with the well-being of an entire tribe, a unit that is too large to recognize any ritual relationship between itself and any single body of ancestors.

IV. PROPHETS AND THE *YAKAN* CULT

It may be assumed that the most far-reaching and rapid changes that have affected Lugbara society have been those associated with European contact and administration. I have mentioned the myth of the coming of the first District Commissioner. This is a present-day myth. I wish now to describe, very briefly, the first responses of Lugbara to these events, which have by now, fifty years later, passed into mythology.

The whole of the southern Sudan area was subjected to various degrees of Arab influence throughout most of the last century; the ivory and slave traders seem never to have entered Lugbara-land, although they set up a post in Kakwa only a few miles to the north. Junker, Emin Pasha and others described the destruction of the local populations of this region. This, and the rise of the Mahdi in the 1880s had marked repercussions on the life of the numerous small peoples of the area. Many of them had also been threatened by the rise of the Zande and Mangbetu empires. In addition there are records of famines, epidemics, migrations and changes in ecology at the end of the last century. Lugbara were affected, directly or indirectly, by all these events. But they did not meekly accept them. Their response was in the appearance of a cult called *Yakan* or *Dede*, which flourished at various times between about 1890 and 1920.[1]

[1] An account was written by J. H. Driberg: 'Yakan', *Journal of the Royal Anthropological Institute*, 1931. The cult was also known as the Allah Water Cult and was important at the time of the Uganda Mutiny among the 'Nubi' troops.

The cult first appeared, as far as is known, among the Dinka in 1883 at a revolt at Rumbek. It spread to many other peoples of the region, adherents fighting with success against Egyptian troops, the Dervishes and also against the Azande. By 1890 some of the magic water, the drinking of which formed the basis of the cult, was 'bought' by a Kakwa named Rembe. Shortly after, certain Lugbara from eastern Lugbara went to Rembe to 'buy' the water, and dispensed it among the eastern Lugbara, who were able to annihilate two columns of 'Nubi' troops from Emin Pasha's post at Wadelai, on the Albert Nile. Although we know little of this period, which was before the Belgian administration, it seems clear that the water was drunk to give protection against Nubi bullets, and also probably to protect people from cerebro-spinal meningitis, which seems to have appeared in this area about 1895. It was 'sold', for objects of iron, between men of different tribes, and some kind of inter-tribal organization came into existence which enabled Lugbara to form bodies of men able to beat Nubi troops armed with rifles. The main adherents of the cult were known as *opi*, the word today used for government chiefs and traditionally used for rainmakers and 'men whose names are known' (*'ba rukuza*). When the Belgians appeared in 1900 and wished to appoint chiefs, these men came forward and were appointed chiefs, with powers of collecting levies of cattle and grain. They were the possessors and dispensers of the new mystical power that lay in the water, and were considered best fitted to deal with the Europeans on this account.

The cult languished after the setting up of the Belgian administration, and re-appeared in 1914, when the Uganda government took over the eastern and main part of Lugbaraland after several years during which it had been unadministered. This period of the cult was marked by the appearance of Rembe himself, who travelled about Lugbaraland with his assistant. Yondu. The two men dispensed their magic water, and in every tribe set up a pole of wood which they called *dini*, from the Arabic word for 'religion'. At the top of the pole was placed a bough of *inzu* wood, a wood which is today used in certain rites associated with God. Rembe said that these poles were his *a'bi* trees, the burial trees planted on elders' graves. At them he sold the water, and men came to dance, sing the cult songs, and later to drill with 'rifles' made of reeds and of wood. There were gatherings often of many hundred people, a very large number for any Lugbara rite. At them men of all statuses gathered, and girls who slept with them, 'forgetting who were brothers and sisters'. The first followers of Rembe are said to have wandered about the country like 'mad people' (*'ba azaza*). The adherents were grouped into three grades; the first two were the 'chiefs of *Yakan*' (*opi Yakanini*), and members of the top grade were also called 'men whose names are known' (*'ba rukuza*). This ranking was a new principle of organization in Lugbara, and cut across traditional segmentary loyalties. Adherents were promised that the water would preserve them from death; that their ancestors and cattle would come to life again; that they could refuse to pay taxes to the government with impunity, since they could not be harmed by rifles, the bullets of which would turn to water; that they would soon obtain rifles with which to drive out the Europeans, and so should drill now with dummy rifles. Those who refused to drink the water would become termites at death. In 1919 a large meeting was interrupted by police, and a severe fight took place; another occurred a year later, and after that the cult seems to have died down. It continued among the Alur, to the south, and elsewhere in Uganda.

I have been told by men who were adherents at the time that Rembe came to bring them peace, as they had had before the Europeans came to destroy the land, and also that he could cure meningitis, of which there were severe outbreaks between 1912 and 1920; also, at the end of this period, the water was said to cure Spanish influenza. On one occasion a goat and a calf, ornamented with the bracelets of a man who had died of meningitis, were driven into the mountains in the same way as rams are driven to 'pray' God to bring rain. These beasts were known as 'the beasts of *Yakan*'. Water is associated with meningitis since this is a disease of the dry season and stops as soon as the rains come.

The cult was known by the Lugbara as *Yakani* and as *Dede*; Rembe himself called it *Rabbinadede*, a mixture of the Arabic for 'Lord' and the Lugbara *dede*. He possessed a snake oracle, in a pool in north-west Lugbara, near the Kakwa boundary.[1] The snake was called *dede*, and it is said that 'all the words of *Yakani* came from that oracle, from that snake called *dede*.' *Dede* is said, by men who saw it, to have been 'like a python', but of many colours, and also to have been half-snake, half-man or half-fish,

---

[1] Snake oracles are not otherwise known in Lugbara.

half-man. The pool of water was sometimes called *Yakan*. *Dede* is the Lugbara for grandmother, and the Kakwa word is *Yakanye*. It is said that '*dede* protected us from evil things as does a man's grandmother', and 'the water was called *dede* because it was great, like a grandmother.' Dead grandmothers are said to visit their descendants as small green snakes, non-poisonous and harmless, and the same belief occurs among the Kakwa.

The cult had a close association with God. Rembe was a prophet. His oracle, *dede*, although called *andṛi*, the general term for oracles, was rather a medium for prophetic utterances. Men did not go there to put questions to it, but to hear 'the words of Rembe' and 'the words of God'. The power of Rembe and the oracle came from God; Rembe was 'a man of God', and his followers are said to have been 'men of God'. The water, also, which is associated in Lugbara thought with God (who lives in pools and streams in his immanent aspect), was said to give its drinkers eternal life. It is said that they would live with God and the ancestors, but not under the huts as do the ancestors generally, but in the sky with God, as do the souls of the recently dead. If they did not drink they would become termites, which are some-times said to be 'things of God'; termite mounds are used in divination to discover God's will.

The water originated as a response to the appearance of the Mahdi, who claimed to be the Messiah; he was the only non-European to beat the Egyptian government, with its European officers, and his coming must have had an immense impact upon the small tribes of the region. The notion of a Messiah is not part of their cultures, but that of a man who was divinely inspired and possessed by God could be conceived in indigenous pagan terms. Rembe was seen, and still is seen, as such a man. Today accounts of him present him as a mythical figure, with the attributes of miraculous behaviour and other inverted attributes of mythical personages. I was told

Rembe was a little man. But he was like a king (*Mukama*, the Lun-yoro word). . . . When he sat here everyone would gather to hear his words. His words were great and many. He called men and all came to him.

Is Rembe dead? Where is his grave? We have never heard how or where he died. Perhaps he is still alive. If he were locked up he would always escape. . . . We still look for him. Where did he go?

Today possession by God is known by the individual concerned
falling into a fit of trembling. The most frequent occasion is
possession of an adolescent girl by God, a sign that he has
willed her to become a diviner, whose power comes from him.
Not only was Rembe a possessor of oracles, he was also a diviner
with a gourd, and it is said that it was he who first practised this
form of divination in Lugbara. When he divined he trembled,
and today sickness that includes trembling as a symptom is
thought to be connected with the cult of *Yakan*. The adherents
of the cult wandered round the countryside in a state of possession,
just as do adolescent girls today when possessed by God, and the
word *azaza* is used for both states.

The cult of *Yakan* continues today. It is concerned with the
bringing and curing of certain sicknesses of which the main
symptom is trembling or trance-like states, including meningitis.
It is also, to a lesser extent, concerned with the fertility of crops.
Offerings of grain are made at the shrines, after consultation with
a diviner, who also makes the offering. Today *Yakan* is more than
the name of a cult. It is the name of a spirit, force or power that
possesses men. It possessed Rembe and all who drank his water.
It is said that '*Yakan* makes people tremble' and '*Yakan* has
arrived: it wishes to entice people'.[1] If asked what *Yakan* is like
or where it lives, Lugbara say that *Yakan* comes 'in' or 'by' the
wind. *Yakan* has a soul which enters into the soul of its victim:

Yakan strikes a man's heart *ru-ru-ru* and makes it tremble *ya-ya-ya*.
Its soul enters his heart, because of the greed of *Yakan*. It comes to
find food and says 'Long ago you gave me food, when Rembe was here
among people; now you give me none.'

In the old cult a man bought water from Rembe or Yondu,
and so became a 'chief' of the cult. Rembe gave such a man a stick
of *inzu* wood as a sign of status. This was the 'little stick' (*kaljan*).
Its owner was in a close relationship with the power or force,
Yakan, by virtue of having drunk the water. The stick was a sign
that drinking had been done. Its owner could hand on similar
sticks to those to whom he sold water as dispensers, although not
to ordinary adherents. These sticks are still in existence, kept
secretly inside their owners' huts. The sticks, perhaps originally

---

[1] 'Entice' is *o'bu*, to cajole or wheedle, to persuade someone to do something
against his better judgement.

only a sign of mystical status, have by now come to be regarded as a
vehicle for the power called *Yakan*, and also of that called *Kaljan*,
which is 'the same as' *Yakan* and used to ensure future fertility
to crops. *Kaljan* may also bring trembling sickness. Of it it is said:

> *Kaljan* was not a man, but came from nothing, like the wind. It
> came to our ancestors of long ago, to enter their bodies so as to hurt
> them with trembling.

The history of this cult may be summarized. A prophet came
from God as a response to epidemics and external warlike contact.
By his use of magic water the prophet enabled Lugbara to be
cured of sickness and of the evil effects of contact, and to re-
organize themselves to combat the agents of contact. The reorganization was on a wide scale, on a trans-subclan basis, and in it
traditional bases of organization by lineage and generation were
ignored. Since those days the prophet has become a mythical
figure, and the cult today is concerned with sicknesses involving
trembling and trances, states associated with the prophet and his
power of divination, and with God.

There are other spirit shrines. They are all associated with
God, as manifestations of his power: I use the word spirit in this
context only. The most common are those known as *ogbei*, which
'sends' dysentery and similar complaints; *ajualjri*, which sends
sickness to the chest and comes 'in the wind'; *oyakiya*, which
sends earth tremors; *joajoa*, which sends sleeplessness to children;
there are many others, some of which are found in particular parts
of the country only. All of them are said to 'come in the wind' or
'from the sky', from God. They are not connected with lineage
authority and the incidence of sickness from them has no moral
connotation. They are erected and maintained as a sign of contact
with divine power, as a means of dealing with sickness which
would seem to be guiltless. It is possible that some of these spirits
are associated with past cults that have changed their significance,
as in the case of the present day *yakan* and *kaljan*-spirits; but there
is no way of telling their origin. Similar forces are associated with
whirlwinds, dead trees and other phenomena; whirlwinds send
trembling to those who are near them, dead trees may send a
weakness of the back called *girici*. A shrine may or may not be
placed for these spirits. But for all spirits diviners are called to
make contact and often to make the offering, which consists of

grains, beans, milk and sometimes of dried meat, but never of a living animal or blood.

Some of them represent modern external powers. In recent years certain emissaries from a separatist Christian sect in Buganda have appeared, called in Luganda *Abalokole*. For Lugbara *abalokole* is the name now given to a type of possession: 'it is a thing that seizes a man like *Yakan*, so that he falls to the ground and speaks words of *Mungu*'. *Mungu* is the Swahili word for God, used by missionaries in place of the Lugbara *Adroa*. It is said that 'perhaps' *Mungu* is 'like lightning', a sign of divine power and not God himself. I have not seen *abalokole* shrines, but was told that 'perhaps' people would place them. Only a diviner can contact the power of *abalokole*. The diviner's role is to contact divine power and so enable men to control it. The control is made permanent by the erection of a shrine and offering at it. The shrine is a visible symbol of the experience and effect of an extra-social force which has as it were been absorbed into the total social system.

Spirit shrines are thought to have an independent power within them, unlike ghost and ancestral shrines. There are also certain objects, used as protective medicines, which have a different kind of independent power. These are known by various terms in different areas (*adra, jurumbu, 'burunya*) and consist of a fungus found growing on cows' horns which is placed in pots. They are said to send skin complaints and ulcers to thieves who enter the home or fields of their owners. It is said that their power comes from God; the pots are inherited from original ancestors who were given them by God long, long ago.

V. CHANGE AND THE SOCIAL ORDER

I have shown how the cult of the dead operates to resolve conflict, to sustain and to regulate lineage authority and to validate changes in its distribution. The rites of the cult of the dead are performed at points of crisis in the perpetual process of realignment in relations of authority within the lineage. These points occur when there are changes in the internal structure of the lineage as men reach various stages of social maturity, and as resources in land, women and livestock are redistributed to meet changing needs of the lineage members. But Lugbara ideas about their society—or 'society' in general, since they conceive of no other—is of a social order that is unchanging. It is one of a static system of authority relations. Variations from it within the local community are seen as deviant, not as essential phases in a cycle of development. These deviant alignments of *de facto* authority can be made consistent with the idea of an unchanging system in two ways: by their suppression and the maintenance of the *status quo*, or by their acceptance as *de jure* authority. The former is the typical response of the elder, as the holder of lineage authority; he can appeal to the genealogical experience of the lineage to buttress the network of relations that are dependent upon his authority. The latter alternative in fact occurs sooner or later: the lineage undergoes segmentation and genealogical and ritual experience is re-ordered. At ritual, and especially by the making of the ritual address and the order of eating at communion, the experience that is accepted by all members of the lineage, including the dead, is formally stated. This is one way of seeing it; another is to say that lineage experience as such is re-formed. Lugbara do not accept that genealogical experience alters; although they know that people disagree over details of genealogies, it is none the less axiomatic that there *is* a true genealogical experience of a lineage. I do not mean by this that in actual historical fact that is a true genealogy, variants from which are false. I am saying that Lugbara believe that this is so. Ritual addresses are 'true' (*adaru*); this is a basic axiom, supported by every case of sacrifice. By the performance of ghostly sacrifice the living are brought again into a proper relationship with the ancestral, ideal and unchanging order. Accepted experience, as incapsulated in genealogy, is in itself a statement that these two sets of relations, one actual, the other ideal, are consistent and coterminous. A man may state a genealogy but at ritual the statement is accepted by the dead as well as by the living. In fact, it may be said that it is made by the dead and conveyed to the living through oracular verdicts. Just as men are interrelated in space, so they are in time. Their temporal relations alter with the regular and successive changes in their social status. These are affirmed and validated at sacrifice and the reformulation of lineage experience. And the change in spatial relations between lineages and their segments are affirmed at the communion that follows the sacrifice itself. At communion the lineage group is seen as composed of men whose hearts contain no anger: here is represented the ideal of a stable kin-group. It is contrasted to the unstable and intrigue-ridden kin-group of actuality, and communion removes the idea of this unstable group and so removes the instability. Just as sacrifice reformulates temporal experience, so does communion reformulate spatial experience. These essentially moral situations are symbolically enacted in terms of the physical actions of sacrifice and communion.

But Lugbara know well enough that changes do occur, despite the axiomatic changelessness of their society. People die and their authority as living men changes into that of the dead. Although both living and dead are members of lineages, the elaborate *rites de passage* at death make clear the difference between them. Death, particularly that of an elder, leads to a change in the distribution of authority that is of a different order from the smaller shifts of authority that may occur after sacrifices to the dead. The living and the dead, the people of the lineage, maintain the ideal pattern of authority by the rite of sacrifice. Sacrifice renews the social order; it does not change it. Even though in actuality there is discrepancy between ideal and real distribution of authority, there should not be any marked change in the validating genealogical structure of the lineage. By sacrifice lineage members re-form lineage experience, but they do not change it radically. That is done only at death, and many of the rites after the death have as their purpose the acceptance and recognition of changed genealogical structure. Men accept this change but they do not make it. This can be done only by God. Sacrifice cannot be made to God.

We may make a distinction between repetitive and radical changes in a social system, which is that between re-organization and restructuring. It is the distinction between growth by regeneration and a sudden qualitative change in the structure of a social organism. It is one that we can make because we have the concept of a radically changing structure. But Lugbara lack this concept; they see their social system in a different way. For them what we call repetitive change or re-organization involves no alteration in the range and intensity of relations or authority that go to compose the field of social relations of a particular family cluster. What we call radical change or restructuring does involve an alteration in the range and intensity of those relations. This occurs at death—or is very likely to occur—when segmentation takes place. At segmentation of the minimal lineage there is consequent disturbance of former lineage relationships at higher levels and uncertainty as to 'true' ancestrally accepted lineage genealogies and ritual obligations, as I have shown in Case 34 of Araka. Other situations of radical change are more obvious. In all of them Lugbara use the concept of inversion, which is related in Lugbara thought in some way or other, direct or indirect, with God in one of his two aspects, or with a direct manifestation of divine power. The most usual link is through the association of these events with diviners. They include:

1. Changes brought about by increased social mobility as a consequence of European administration and labour migration. This is usually expressed in terms of the appearance of new sorcerers, the *elojua*, who wander about spreading sickness for no apparent reason and who are outside the traditional system of authority. Lugbara also maintain that today there are witches everywhere, bewitching kin as well as non-kin: '*ole* is destroying our land'.

2. Changes brought about by epidemics and cattle diseases, which are seen as sent by God. The effect of these seems to have been so immediate that prophets were recognized as providing a response and a new organization. Men could then at least act in a co-ordinated manner to combat this change, and also to accept it. Prophets came from God, and they also introduced means of divination that are directly associated with God. Rembe used water in his rites, also connected with God.

3. Changes brought about by external political influences. We know very little about pre-European contacts, which must have taken place although Lugbara were not seriously affected by them. The Arab slavers were near Lugbara and it may be assumed that their activities led to some disturbance. Later, Europeans appeared. Their coming is expressed in terms of inversion, and the *Yakan* cult, introduced and controlled by prophets, was also concerned both to resist and later to accept their new power.

4. Traditionally the only people who have entered Lugbara society have been the clients. Although their appearance has presumably never led to changes of the order of those caused by Europeans, this introduction of foreigners into a local field of social relation has been expressed in terms of inversion.

5. And traditionally also the two events that have always occurred recurrently and have been associated with changes in

the order of authority within a local field have also been expressed in these same terms. They are the last phrase in the development of the lineage before actual segmentation, in which the holders of authority, who have to a large extent lost it, are accused of witchcraft; and death itself, in which the soul of the recently dead is said to go to God, outside the sphere of men, to be contacted only by divination.

In all these situations traditional patterns of authority are altered as the field of social relations of groups is widened. Today the formerly almost entirely self-sufficient and independent small local groups have become largely interdependent as a consequence of a widening of the scale of the economic and political systems. The cult of the dead is not a cohesive one in terms of the total society. Relations that are wider in range than traditional ones are therefore seen as being associated with the power of God, a power which is effective over a far wider range than that of any ancestors. Today, then, the manifestations of God's power are said by Lugbara to become more and more frequent. Since they see these changes as being destructive, stress is laid on the obviously evil manifestations, especially on increase in the incidence of witchcraft and sorcery. The obvious agents of change are the Europeans and chiefs. The former are rarely in direct contact with Lugbara, but are in contact through the medium of chiefs. These are often said to be 'bad', and also to be witches and sorcerers ('How else could they have such power and wealth?')

The events that are associated with the introduction of power from outside the social system are later expressed in terms of myth. Myth is timeless, in that a mythical event is outside genealogical history, which is the only context in which Lugbara are able to put historical events. In Lugbara mythical thought what are for us time and space relations are conceived in terms of inversion. The ideal of a timeless and changeless Lugbara social system may by this means be sustained. Lugbara myths do not form a single coherent whole. There are many myths, of the creation, the introduction of European power, the origins of magical objects and medicines, and so on. They cannot be fitted together as genealogies can, since the personages in them are different and distinct.

Once these new powers and forces, which are seen in terms of their introduction by God, are absorbed into the structure of authority of the society, their time-aspect becomes irrelevant and is lost. This is done by myth, and also in terms of the dual aspect of God. God creates in his transcendent aspect. After the creation of these powers and forces, when men are in contact with them, God in his transcendent aspect withdraws from the situation and contact is maintained with him in his immanent aspect. These newly created powers and forces are then controlled by divination. I am here making a distinction which is perhaps more clear-cut than any made by Lugbara, and I do not wish to over-stress it. Lugbara say that Rembe and the *Yakan* cult came from God, and that the souls of recently dead men go to God in the sky. The epidemics that strike indiscriminately in every part of Lugbara come 'in the wind' and from God in his transcendent aspect. But sicknesses that have once been associated with the introduction of new forces which have in time become absorbed into the system of authority are usually said to come from God in his immanent aspect. These include such sicknesses as trembling and possession, and many sicknesses that are not connected with the dead, such as smallpox and dysentery. Manifestations of powers that have been introduced by God are later seen as coming from him in his immanent aspect, and offering can then be made at shrines associated with the specific sicknesses. Diviners are used to state what is the nature of the sickness, but are not necessary at the offering; whereas they are needed for contact with God in his transcendent aspect, as at the rite of 'contacting the soul' of the recently dead.

I have been told that God in his immanent aspect is responsible for evil, for things that are 'bad' (*onzi*). In this aspect also he is the supreme example of inversion. I was told:

Adro is bad. . . . He walks with women in the bush and makes them bad. Then they are diviners. . . . *Adroa* (in his transcendent aspect) is good. He made us all here, and made all the world. We men are good, like our ancestors, yet we have bad hearts and some men are witches and close their hearts to harm other men. It is *Adro* who takes men's hearts and makes them bad.

We come here to a Lugbara concept which is implicit in many of their myths and beliefs. God created the world before society came into being at the time of the hero-ancestors. Men were then asocial and amoral; they were inverted. They committed what would be

called sins if committed by members of society today. But the
significance of their committing incest and cannibalism is that they
did not know the ties of kinship, not that they ignored or abused
them. Similarly a client comes into a lineage territory as a 'thing',
not as a 'person'. He has no kin. A newly born baby is also often
said to be a 'thing'; it is only through socialization that he becomes
a full 'person'. This maturity is measured by his possession of a
soul and of personality (*tali*). Young children and women do not
develop as much soul and personality as men do, except for very
old women, and particularly those who are the elder sisters of
elders. We have here the concept of a 'natural' human being who
is not yet a social person. The concept of inversion relates both to
such a being and to someone who has perverted the power given
to him by his being made into a social person and so reverts to
being a 'natural' person. Such is a witch.

At the beginning of the world men and God were in a direct
relation, and men could move up and down from the sky. Some
say they were linked by a rope, others by a bamboo tower, and I
have once heard it said it was by a tall tree. This bridge between
heaven and earth was broken and men fell down, scattering into
their present distinct groups each with its different language;
before that all men spoke the same language, said either to have
been Lugbara or Kakwa. Since that time all peoples have been
separate, their constituent groups having their own ancestors and
with them forming traditionally and ideally self-contained spheres
of social relations, conceived and structured by agnatic kinship.
This myth validates the entire cosmology of the Lugbara, in that
it explains the separation of men from God, of 'good' from 'evil'
and of the permanent from the changing. Only God can overcome
this separation. The myth distinguishes the small-scale cosmos of
Lugbara thought from the chaos, social and moral, that surrounds
it in space and time; and it also enables both spheres to be seen as
a single whole, the universe.

A LUGBARA BIBLIOGRAPHY

The Lugbara have been a "remote" people in the corners of northwestern Uganda and northeastern Zaire. Relatively few outsiders have observed their culture. Today, after the horrors and disturbances of the Amin and Obote regimes, many of the Lugbara have fled into the Sudan and Zaire, leaving their "traditional" ways of life seriously affected and in some areas destroyed. Given their circumstances, I believe it is worthwhile to include in this reprint a reasonably full bibliography of published writings on the Lugbara. It is incomplete in that I have not included all the many mentions of them in books by early travelers or in more recent works on neighboring peoples (for example, A. W. Southall's *Alur Society*, Cambridge University Press, 1956). Neither have I included all the many brief and superficial references to the Lugbara in the Comboni Mission Society (Verona Fathers) journal *Nigrizia*, in recent publications by Verona Fathers, or in other Lugbara-language publications.

Avua, L.
1968   "Drought-making among the Lugbara." *Uganda Journal* 32: 29–38.

Barr, L. I.
1965   *A Course in Lugbara*. Nairobi: East Africa Literature Bureau.

Collins, R. O.
1960   "Ivory Poaching in the Lado Enclave." *Uganda Journal* 24: 217–28.
1962   "Sudan-Uganda Boundary Rectification and the Sudanese Occupation of the Madial, 1914." *Uganda Journal* 26: 140–53.

Crazzolara, J. P.
1960   *The Lwoo*, vol. 3. *A Study of the Logbara (Ma'di) Language: Grammar and Vocabulary*. London: Oxford University Press for International African Institute.

Dalfovo, A. T.
1982   "Logbara Personal Names and Their Relation to Religion." *Anthropos* 77: 113–33.
1983   "Logbara Riddles." *Anthropos* 78: 811–30.

Dean, V. L.
1984   "Changes in Crop Mixtures and Their Relationship to Gender Role Change among the Lugbara." Cambridge: Harvard/MIT Women and International Development Group Working Paper No. 2. Spring.
1985   "Social Change and Lugbara Subsistence Agriculture in West Nile District." In P. Wiebe and C. C. Dodge, eds., *Crisis in Uganda*. New York: Pergamon Press.
forthcoming
        "Lugbara Illness, Beliefs and Social Change." *Africa*.

Driberg, J. H.
   1931   "Yakan." *Journal of the Royal Anthropological Institute* 61: 413–20.

Evans-Pritchard, E. E.
   1929   "Some Collective Expressions of Obscenity in Africa." *Journal of the Royal Anthropological Institute* 59: 311–32.

Felkin, R. W.
   1888   *Emin Pasha in Central Africa.* London.

Hutereau, A.
   1922   *Histoire des Peuplades de l'Uele et de l'Ubangi.* Brussels.

Junker, W.
   1890–92 *Travels in Africa.* 3 vols. London.

King, A.
   1970   "The Yakan Cult and Lugbara Response to Colonial Rule." *Azania* 5: 1–24.

Lanning, E. C.
   1954   "Fademulla Murjan of Aringa." *Uganda Journal* 18.

Lotar, R. P. L.
   1944   *La Grande Chronique de 'Uele.* Brussels.

MacConnel, R. E.
   1925   "Notes on the Lugwari Tribe of Central Africa." *Journal of the Royal Anthropological Institute* 55: 439–67.

Middleton, J.
   1952   *Labour Migration among the Lugbara.* London: Colonial Social Science Research Council.
   1954   "Some Social Aspects of Lugbara Myth." *Africa* 24(3): 189–99.
          With D. J. Greenland. "Land and Population in West Nile District, Uganda." *Geographical Journal* 120(4): 446–57.
   1955   "Myth, History and Mourning Taboos in Lugbara." *Uganda Journal* 19(2): 194–203.
          "The Concept of 'Bewitching' in Lugbara." *Africa* 25(3): 252–60.
   1956   "The Roles of Chiefs and Headmen in Lugbara." *Journal of African Administration* 8(1): 32–38.
   1958   "Social Change in Northern Uganda." *Contemporary Review* 1112: 92–96.
          "The Political System of the Lugbara of the Nile-Congo Divide." In J. Middleton and D. Tait, eds., *Tribes without Rulers.* London: Routledge and Kegan Paul. Pp. 203–29.
   1960   "Social Change among the Lugbara of Uganda." *Civilisations* 10(4): 446–56.
          "The Lugbara." In A. I. Richards, ed., *East African Chiefs.* London: Faber and Faber. Pp. 326–43.
   1961   "The Social Significance of Lugbara Personal Names." *Uganda Journal* 25 (1): 34–42.
   1962   "Trade and Markets among the Lugbara of Uganda." In P. Bohannan and G. Dalton, eds., *Markets in Africa.* Evanston: Northwestern University Press. Pp. 561–78.

1963   "Witchcraft and Sorcery in Lugbara." In J. Middleton and E. H. Winter, eds., *Witchcraft and Sorcery in East Africa*. London: Routledge and Kegan Paul. Pp. 256–75.

"The Yakan or Allah Water Cult among the Lugbara." *Journal of the Royal Anthropological Institute* 93(1):80–108.

1964   "Three Lugbara Myths." In W. Whiteley, ed., *A Selection of African Prose*. Oxford: Clarendon Press. Pp. 128–34.

1966   "The Resolution of Conflict among the Lugbara of Uganda." In M. Swartz, V. W. Turner, and A. Tuden, eds., *Political Anthropology*. Chicago: Aldine. Pp. 141–54.

1968   "Conflict and Cultural Variation in Lugbaraland." In M. Swartz, ed., *Local-level Politics*. Chicago: Aldine. Pp. 151–62.

"Some Categories of Dual Classification among the Lugbara of Uganda." *History of Religions* 7(3): 187–208.

1969   "Spirit Possession among the Lugbara." In J. H. M. Beattie and J. Middleton, eds., *Spirit Mediumship and Society in Africa*. London: Routledge and Kegan Paul. Pp. 220–31.

"Labour Migration and Associations in Africa: Two Case Studies." *Civilisations* 19(1): 42–49.

"Oracles and Divination among the Lugbara." In M. M. Douglas and P. Kaberry, eds., *Man in Africa*. London: Tavistock Press. Pp. 261–78.

1970   "Political Incorporation among the Lugbara of Uganda." In R. Cohen and J. Middleton, eds., *From Tribe to Nation in Africa*. Scranton: Intext. Pp. 55–70.

The Study of the Lugbara: Expectation and Paradox in Anthropological Research. New York: Holt, Rinehart and Winston.

1971   "Prophets and Rainmakers: The Agents of Social Change among the Lugbara." In T. Beidelman, ed., *The Translation of Culture*. London: Tavistock Press. Pp. 179–201.

"Some Effects of Colonial Rule among the Lugbara of Uganda." In V. W. Turner, ed., *Profiles of Change*, vol. 3. Cambridge: Cambridge University Press. Pp. 6–48.

1972   "The Lugbara of Uganda and Family Planning." In A. Molnos, ed., *Cultural Source Materials for Population Planning in East Africa*, vols. 2 and 3. Nairobi: East African Publishing House. Pp. 249–57, 289–98.

1973   "The Concept of the Person among the Lugbara of Uganda." In G. Dieterlen, ed., *La Notion de la Personne en Afrique Noire*. Paris: Centre National de la Recherche Scientifique. Pp. 491–506.

"Secrecy in Lugbara Religion." *History of Religions* 12 (4): 299–316.

1974   *Les Lugbara de l'Ouganda: Religion et Société*. Paris: Ecole Pratique des Hautes Etudes.

1977   "Ritual and Ambiguity in Lugbara Society." In S. F. Moore and B. Myerhoff, eds., *Secular Ritual*. Assen and Amsterdam: Van Gorcum. Pp. 73–90.

1978   "The Rainmaker among the Lugbara of Uganda." In M. Cartry, ed., *Systèmes de Signes*. Paris: Hermann. Pp. 377–88.

1979   "Rites of Sacrifice among the Lugbara." In L. de Heusch, ed., *Systèmes de Pensée en Afrique Noire: Le Sacrifice*, vol. 3. Ivry: Ecole Pratique des Hautes Etudes/CNRS. Pp. 175–92.

1982   "Lugbara Death." In M. Bloch and J. Parry, eds., *Death and the Regeneration of Life*. Cambridge: Cambridge University Press. Pp. 134–54.

1983 (1965)
         The Lugbara of Uganda. New York: Holt, Rinehart and Winston, 1965. Reprint. Prospect Heights, Ill.: Waveland Press.

1985   "The Dance among the Lugbara of Uganda." In P. Spencer, ed., *Society and the Dance*. Cambridge: Cambridge University Press. Pp. 165–82.

1987 (1960)
         Lugbara Religion: Ritual and Authority among an East African People. London: Oxford University Press for International African Institute, 1960. Reprint. Washington, D.C.: Smithsonian Institution Press.

forthcoming
         "Lugbara Religion." In *Encyclopaedia of Religions*. New York: Free Press.

Nalder, L. F.
1937   *A Tribal Survey of Mongalla Province*. Oxford: Clarendon Press.

Posnett, R. N.
1951   "Some Notes on West Nile Hills and History." *Uganda Journal* 15: 165–78.

Ramponi, E.
1937   "Religion and Divination of the Logbara Tribe of North Uganda." *Anthropos* 32: 571–94, 849–74.

1942   "Nume e re della caccia." *Nigrizia* 3: 37–40.
         "Il ballo della morte." *Nigrizia* 2: 37–40.

Schweitzer, G.
1898   *Emin Pasha: His Life and Works*. London.

Sembiante, F. M.
1943   "I Logwara—studio etnologico." *Nigrizia* 10: 77–78.

Shiroya, O. J. E.
1972   "The Lugbara: Migration and Early Settlement." *Uganda Journal* 36: 23–34.

Stigand, C. H.
1923   *Equatoria: The Lado Enclave*. London.

Stuhlmann, F.
1919–23 *Die Tagebücher von Dr. Emin Pascha*. Hamburg.

Tucker, A. N.
1940   *The Eastern Sudanic Languages*. Oxford: Clarendon Press.

Van der Looy, J.
1938   "De Logwara en hun taal." *Niew Afrika* 8: 366–68.

Verstraete, J.
1935   "Loies et deuils chez les Logwara." *Grands Lacs* 7: 287–90.

INDEX

Abalokole, 264

Address, ritual, 88, 93f, 103, 123, 144f, 167, 181, 265; — and *rites de passage*, 107f; examples of —, 142ff, 176f, 184f.

Adro (guardian spirit), 31, 194, 253ff; *see* God, children of; spirit.

Adultery, 19, 21

Affinity, 9, 21, 42, 60, 170ff

Age status, *see* Generation

Agnation, 5, 7, 18

Agriculture, 4ff

Allah Water Cult, *see* Yakan

Alur, 1, 246n, 260

Ambition, and authority, 16f, 150f, 165, 216f, 220f

Ancestors, concept of, 25ff, 32ff, 52ff, 195, 202, 232; personality of —, 71; *see* Sacrifice, Shrines; —, childless, 33. 52ff; —, founding, 68, 232; —, hero, 7, 27, 100, 102, 106, 231ff

Ancestral vengeance, 54f, 225

Ancestresses, 8, 14, 52

Animals, and dead, 29, 36; — and lineage, 98ff; — and God, 88, 257; — and purification, 101ff, 108ff, 105f; — and night, 29, 241, 257; — and sacrifice, 35f, 87ff, 95f, 97ff, 107; — and sorcery, 241; — and souls, 97; *see* Hyena, Sheep

Anointing, 36, 88, 103ff, 107, 110, 114, 116, 145, 167, 177, 181, 206

Arabs, 2f, 258, 267

Assistant, ritual, 68, 127, 150f

Attached kin, 8, 119, 215ff

Atonement, 100

Authority, and ambition, 16f, 150f, 165, 216f, 220f; — and change, 250ff, 264ff, 268; conflict in —, 16ff, 214ff; — and death, 204; — of elder, 10ff, 14ff, 40ff, 136, 149, 151ff, 157, 192ff, 200f, 204, 211ff, 220, 222ff; — and genealogy, 186; ideal distribution of —, 14f; — in lineage, 9ff, 14f, 18ff, 156f, 186, 192ff, 198, 204, 211ff, 214, 217; — and oracles, 221, 224ff; parental —, 212; ritual —, 13f, 17; — and sacrifice, 123f;

sanctions for —, 23f; — and shrines, 13; — and sorcery, 246f; tribal —, 7; — and witchcraft, 238ff.

Awj, concept of, 88, 117; — *'buru*, 117ff, 122ff, 145f; —*amwe*, 117, 125ff.

Azande, 3, 237, 258f.

'Bad luck' (*drjlonzi*), 36, 57f.

'Bale', 1

'Beer, use of, 88, 96f, 111, 121, 206

Begetting', (*tj*), concept of, 33n, 210, 220

Belgian Congo, 1, 79, 241, 246, 257

Blessing, 36, 88, 103f, 106f, 115f, 145, 181

Blood, concept of, 9, 40, 60, 231; ritual use of —, 96, 109f, 114

Breath, concept of, 29, 105; 'blowing —', 103, 105f, 110, 176

Bridewealth, 42, 98, 220, 231ff

Brothers and invocation, 214ff, 218ff, 222ff; quarrelling between —, 109f, 115, 148, 165, 175, 190, 215ff, 219, 222ff, 257; status of junior —, 136ff, 219ff; — and witchcraft, 227f

'Bull of fornication', 110, 112f, 116, 126

Burial, 29, 95, 97, 194, 200f; — trees, 29, 66f, 106, 185, 200, 259

Cannibalism, 231, 233f, 237f, 248, 251, 270

Cere call, 199

Change, social, and authority, 250ff, 264ff; — and myth, 268f; — and sacrifice, 265f; — and society, 26, 124, 264ff, 268; — and sorcery, 247

Chiefs, 14, 18, 98, 183, 234, 257, 268

Christian missions, 3, 26, 35, 235, 264

Clan, 1, 7f; founding of —, 231f; — spirits, 255f

'Cleansing the body', *see* Purification

'Cleansing the territory', *see* Purification

Clients, 8f, 119, 234, 242f, 246, 250, 267; kinlessness of —, 10, 27, 31, 111, 251, 270

Commensality, 19, 86, 88, 118f, 124ff

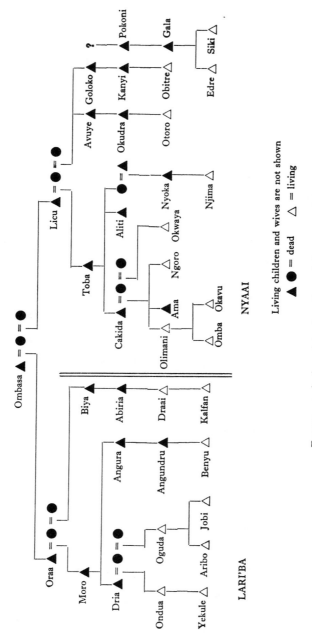

FIGURE 10. Araka minimal section—skeleton genealogy